NIGHT WITCHES

T0192896

BRUCE MYLES

Night Witches

**The Amazing Story of Russia's
Women Pilots in World War II**

ACADEMY
CHICAGO

© 1981 by Presidio Press
All rights reserved

Published in 1990 by
Academy Chicago Publishers
An imprint of Chicago Review Press Incorporated
814 North Franklin Street
Chicago, Illinois 60610
ISBN 978-0-89733-288-0

Cover art: Albert Richardson

Printed and bound in the United States of America

Library of Congress Cataloging-in-Publication Data

Myles, Bruce, 1942–
        Night witches / Bruce Myles.
        p.   cm.
        Reprint. Originally published: Novato, CA: Presidio, c1981.
        ISBN 0-89733-288-1 (pbk.)
        1. World War, 1939–1945—Aerial operations, Russian. 2.
World War, 1939–1945—Participation, Female. 3. Women air
pilots—Soviet Union—History. 4. Air pilots, Military—Soviet
Union—History.
        I. Title.
        D792.S65M94   1988
        940.54'4947—dc19   88-10463
                                                                CIP

Contents

Author's Note

I stumbled on the idea for this book quite by accident. While doing research on the air war on the Eastern Front, one of my first pieces of background reading was the official history of the Soviet Air Force in World War II. There, tucked away and dismissed in a few paragraphs was the revelation that the Red Air Force, for the first time in recent history, had used women in combat. Not merely one or two, but entire air regiments. It was clear, even from the brief references, that these young women had fought in the fiercest air battles and had received their country's highest decorations for bravery. Here, I realized, was a unique story – an exciting, true-life adventure which had somehow been ignored by the military historians. As my research progressed, I felt that a book based on these experiences could become one of the great untold sagas of the war – and a startling example of equality of the sexes preceding the equal rights amendment by forty years.

Investigating further, I found references to the women fliers in esoteric, limited circulation reference books written by Luftwaffe field commanders on the Russian Front. The Soviet Embassy in London and the *Novosti Press* in Moscow, through veterans' association, tracked down for me from twenty to thirty survivors. I made a series of trips to the Soviet Union and taped, mainly through an interpreter, many hours of interviews with these women, both in groups and singly, making cross-references between accounts to satisfy myself of their authenticity. I also had access to their regimental history books, and books that some of the women themselves had written but which had never been published outside their own country.

The more I talked to these women, the more human interest and drama I uncovered. As a reporter of twenty years' wide experience, I knew I had never been involved in such an exciting story. Every word was true, yet it seemed the very stuff of romantic thrillers. I had done enough flying to understand and appreciate the courage and spirit of these young women, scarcely beyond their teens, fighting the invader in the skies over their homeland. Their story demanded to be told and became this book, *Night Witches*.

Bruce Myles
December 1980

1

Operation Barbarossa, 1941

It was 9.30 on the evening of Saturday, 21 June, 1941. Nadia Popova cupped the little tortoiseshell mirror in the palm of her hand and tilted it slightly to the left and then upward a little. The light was not bright where she sat, so she could admire herself from time to time with all the unself-conscious approval of any pretty seventeen-year-old. The jazz band on stage was playing an American song, 'Down Mexico Way'. Nadia sang along in English with the words of the title, which was more than most people in Donetsk could do.

The dance floor was a swirl of colour and movement. Girls in short-sleeved cotton dresses giggled as they teetered around the floor on their unaccustomed high heels. Red-faced partners in shirt sleeves held them clumsily at arm's length. Several called out to Nadia as they swept past. The doors of the wooden building were open. It had been a very hot day, and the sound of the music rose and fell as it carried through the heavy warmth of the late evening. Now and then, the disembodied notes of a tune would eddy briefly as far as the cornfields which stretched beyond the town into the gathering darkness.

It was after midnight when the dance broke up. Nadia planted a brief kiss on the damp forehead of one of the boys who had walked home with her and said goodnight. Then she slipped off her shoes and splayed her toes as the short, damp grass of the garden brushed deliciously against her bare feet. She leaned against a cherry tree and closed her eyes. No school tomorrow, so it was a long lie in bed, then down to the flying club after lunch.

It was growing cold. She pulled her shawl around her

shoulders and walked into the house. Her mind kept coming back to the only serious moment of the evening, when one of the boys had talked about the possibility of war with Germany. She had said quite firmly that it was impossible – there was a non-aggression pact, was there not? War was unthinkable. She was young, pretty, and popular. She had her flying, her family, and her friends. It must never end. She got out of bed, pulled a shawl around her shoulders and silently stole outside again. In the east, the sky was definitely becoming light.

At noon the next day, Nadia was ironing a dress for that evening's dance. Frequently she would stop and place the iron on the hearth to reheat. Her mother sang softy to herself as she stood in the kitchen, cutting up chicken. Leonid, her brother, had gone off to visit his fiancée. Nadia's father switched on the radio, which sat on the lace-covered table near the open window. It took some time to warm up, then came the familiar tones of the Radio Moscow announcer Yuri Livitan: 'There will now be a broadcast by Foreign Minister Comrade Molotov. This is an important announcement.'

Nadia Popova told me, 'I told my mother to come quickly to hear the announcement. I felt a weakness in my stomach and a throbbing in my temples. I feared that he would say the words I was dreading. But of course he did.'

Molotov spoke. 'At four o'clock this morning, without declaration of war and without any claims being made on the Soviet Union, German troops attacked our frontier in many places and bombed from the air Zhitomir, Kiev, Sebastopol, and Kaunus. This unheard of attack on our country is an unparalleled act of perfidy in the history of civilized nations.' Her father stood up and put his arm around her mother. They looked at each other in silence.

A wisp of blue smoke rose from the table where the iron was smouldering through the blue cotton dress. Nadia was running. She felt the wind in her face. She was running towards the airfield.

At 3.15 A.M. on 22 June, 1941, as Nadia Popova lay awake in her room, the artillery barrage opened up all along the front from the Baltic to the Black Sea. German bombers swept low over Soviet frontier airfields and destroyed squadron after squadron of closely parked fighters and bombers as their crews lay in their billets. Operation Barbarossa, Hitler's attack on the Soviet Union, had begun.

Adolf Hitler planned to crush the Soviet Union in a lightning ten-week summer campaign. Panic, confusion, and ignorance reigned on the Soviet side of the frontier. The air strikes had given the Germans almost complete air superiority, and Soviet ground units were paralysed through lack of communication. In Moscow, the Politburo clung to the hope that they might persuade Hitler to call off his attack; they ordered their troops to keep out of Germany and instructed Soviet aircraft not to penetrate enemy territory any deeper than ninety miles.

On 14 June, just eight days before the attack, a broadcast from the Kremlin had described the rumours of a German attack on the Soviet Union as 'an obvious absurdity'. But on the same day, Hitler had travelled from his retreat at Berchtesgaden in the Bavarian Alps to the Reichschancellery in Berlin for an all-day meeting with the commanders in chief and top field generals of the three armed services. It was to be his final war conference for Operation Barbarossa.

One of the most serious blows to the Russians was the destruction of enormous numbers of aircraft on the ground – some of them the latest Soviet fighter designs which had not even had their camouflage paint applied. The official Soviet *History of the War* grimly recounts the crass planning that made the German pre-emptive strikes so successful. The fast new aircraft needed longer runways, so

11

a network of new airfields was built in the frontier zones in the summer of 1941. The *History* says:

As a result our fighter aircraft were concentrated, on 22 June, on a very limited number of airfields, which prevented their proper camouflage, manoeuvrability and dispersal. Also, some of the new airfields had been built much too close to the frontier, which made them specially vulnerable in the event of a surprise attack. The absence of a proper network of airfields on 22 June and the overcrowding of a small number of the older airfields – the location of which was perfectly well known to the enemy – account for the very grave losses our air force suffered during the very first days of the war.

Although there had been over five hundred violations of Soviet airspace by German photo-reconnaissance aircraft in the months leading up to Barbarossa, frontier troops had been given orders not to shoot them down for fear of offending Hitler.

Even those Soviet pilots who did manage to take off that day were, in the main, woefully inexperienced. In the Baltic military district, the young pilots had only fifteen hours' flying experience; around Kiev, some had as little as four hours. They were literally raw beginners and easy prey for the experienced German aircrews.

The military was almost totally unprepared for the ferocity of the blitzkrieg that fell upon them. But the civilian population too had been lulled, as the *History* again points out:

On the eve of the war, great harm was done by suggesting that any enemy attacking the Soviet Union would be easily defeated. There were popular films such as *If War Comes Tomorrow* and the like which kept rubbing in the idea . . . Even some Army papers followed a similar line. Many writers and propagandists put across the pernicious idea that any fascist or imperialist state that attacked us would collapse at the very first shots, since the workers would rebel against their government.

So as spring turned to summer in Eastern Europe in 1941, the population of the Soviet Union pushed to the backs of their minds any fears they might have had about German military intentions towards them. Only days before the attack, convoys of freight trains clanked west to the Reich, bearing Soviet grain for Germany's foodstores, petroleum for her tanks and aircraft, and vital ores for the heartland of her war machine in the Ruhr.

By comparison, the Germans had been preparing, fairly openly, for a possible attack on the Soviet Union up to a year before plans for Operation Barbarossa were finally adopted. Roads and railways leading towards the Soviet border had been built; and across Poland, they had built a total of around three hundred landing strips and airfields for their fighters and bombers. It was from these Polish bases that many of the first strikes against the Soviet airfields were flown.

Those first few days of the onslaught saw many comparatively inexperienced German pilots turn into fighter aces as they shot down unescorted Soviet bombers or outwitted and outmanoeuvred Soviet fighter pilots in desperate air combat. The losses in men and equipment were enormous, but this sacrifice by the Red Air Force bought time for entire aircraft factories in the path of the advancing Germans to be dismantled and shipped east beyond the Ural mountains and out of the range of German bombers.

As November 1941 approached, German armies were only twenty miles from the gates of Moscow. Leningrad was surrounded and besieged. The invaders had taken over three million prisoners. Much of the Red Air Force was now destroyed. Despite its vast reserves of manpower, the air force needed time to train from scratch suitable recruits who had no flying experience.

In the swell of national anger that followed the first shock of the invasion, the patriotic fervour of the idealistic young had brought them in droves to the recruiting offices. Among them, clutching their pilot's licences and logbooks (the official records of their flying careers to date), were many teenage girls who did have flying experience – girls like Nadia Popova. They had joined the Osoaviakhim, the paramilitary flying clubs where, from the age of seventeen, they learned free of charge to fly first gliders, then powered aircraft.

Harassed officials rejected the young women without exception. The response to one young woman, who was later to become a Hero of the Soviet Union, was fairly typical: 'Things may be bad but we're not so desperate that we're going to put little girls like you up in the skies. Go home and help your mother.'

As the full gravity of the situation became clear, however, this position was reversed. A call went out on Radio Moscow from the country's most famous woman aviator, Marina Raskova, for volunteers for women's air regiments. The announcement said that the women selected would have to understand that they would be front-line combat pilots just like the men. Those who wished to volunteer were to write to Marina Raskova without delay.

The response was overwhelming. Every day's postal deliveries brought sackfuls of applications to the little office where the Hero of the Soviet Union and her small staff sat late into the night sifting and deciding on the approximately two thousand who would be summoned for interviews. There were to be three air regiments, each with three squadrons of ten aircraft. And all the mechanics, armament fitters, and the personnel would be women, too. In all there would be around four hundred women in each regiment.

As the winter of 1941 continued into the dark days of early 1942 and the Soviet counter-offensive around Moscow started, young women from the unoccupied territories of the Soviet Union – from as far away as Central Asia – arrived in the capital. Many had never before travelled

14

beyond their hometowns. Few had ever used the subway with its dazzling marble interiors and strange moving staircases which deposited most of them at Prospekt Marx Station, a few minutes' walk from their meeting with the legendary Marina. Sometimes singly, sometimes in groups of three of four – having met on their marathon train journeys – they made for the peeling, dark cream-coloured building overlooking Pushkin Square.

The streets of Moscow were pitch-black – or so it seemed to Larissa Rasanova. The blackout was so efficient that the only lights she had seen were the glowing ends of some soldiers' cigarettes at a sandbagged anti-aircraft gun emplacement near the station. She knew she was still on Gorky Street because she had just checked her bearings with a policemen huddled in a doorway. Turn right two hundred yards further up the street, he had said, and that street leads you into Pushkin Square.

With her battered leather suitcase in one hand, she inched along until she touched the wall of a building and then walked on more confidently, keeping contact with the wall. The suitcase was heavy, but that was hardly surprising. The telegram summoning her for an interview with Marina Raskova, had said tersely: 'Bring suitable clothing. If selected for training you will not be returning home.' Her mother had come into her bedroom that morning and found her sitting on her suitcase trying vainly to close it. She had been crying quietly in the kitchen – Larissa had heard her – but now she burst out laughing and energetically discarded half the suitcase's contents. She shook her head as she removed several summer dresses and light shoes; it was October and you could almost smell the snow in the air. Thrusting her hand into a chest under the window, she pulled out several heavy woollen vests, scarves, fur gloves, and a voluminous overcoat.

Larissa had pleaded and her mother had relented and

allowed her to select one pretty dress to pack in her case. Larissa told me, 'Mama saw that I'd tucked one of my favourite dolls from childhood into a corner of the case. She turned to me and said, "Darling, you can't take that with you to the war – you're eighteen years old now." Then the tears ran down her cheeks.'

There was no guarantee, of course, that Marina Raskova would select her for the women's air regiments. But Larissa, like most of the applicants, was brimming with self-confidence. She could be awkward and shy, particularly in the presence of an attractive man, and she still blushed and giggled at inappropriate moments; but none of this detracted from the professional skills she displayed at her local flying club. On the day she received the telegram summons, she had just completed her first stint as a flying instructor.

The train journey to Moscow had concentrated her mind on the prospects ahead. The entire length of the train had been strafed the day before by German fighters and most of the windows were shattered. When the train braked suddenly, a large piece of glass toppled from its frame on to the floor, scattering slivers over her boots. The train was full of soldiers; two sat on either side of her. They were unshaven, they smelled in a way that made her gag slightly, and one had brushed against her with his arm every time he leaned across to his friend for a light. Oil glistened round the bolts of the rifles they held on the floor between their knees. The only soldiers she had ever seen before were in official parades, with knife-edged creases in their trousers, beautifully pressed coats, and highly polished boots. Seeing them like this had disturbed her in a way she could not explain to herself. She had pulled up the collar of her coat, folded her arms in front of her, and closed her eyes.

There had not been many people around on Gorky Street. As Larissa turned into Pushkin Square, though, she found herself in a large crowd of excited young men and women. She pushed her way through the throng and entered 2 Pushkin Square. Her bulky suitcase was becoming a distinct liability. It banged firmly into the person in front of her. The young woman, Nadia Popova, swung round. Her face was flushed bright with excitement and her teeth were very white when she smiled.

'Can you read the notice board?' asked Larissa.

'Yes,' said Nadia, 'and it seems I've come to the wrong place. Marina Raskova's doing her interviews at the Zhukovsky Academy building this evening.'

Larissa cried, 'You're going to see Marina Raskova? So am I. Let's go together.'

They introduced themselves and pushed their way through the other young people jostling and lining up to see army and navy recruiting officers. It was about three kilometres to the Zhukovsky Academy building and it was already half past seven, so they decided to take the subway. They picked their way through the darkened streets, telling each other about their flying backgrounds.

At the subway station, they paid their five kopecks at the barrier and stepped gingerly on to the escalator which rumbled gently under their feet on its steep descent. On the platform hundreds of people lay on makeshift beds, some singly, some in family groups. The lights shone brightly in contrast to the gloom outside, and a rush of warm air preceded the train that would take them through Belorusskaya Station to their destination, Dynamo Station. As they emerged once more into the darkness and got directions to the Zhukovsky Academy building, the girls reminded each other of the flying exploits of the women they would meet in just a few minutes.

Marina Raskova had inspired thousands of schoolgirls, factory workers, and students to win their wings at local flying clubs. She had become the idol of an entire generation in September 1938 when she and two other women fliers made aviation history. In the twin-engined

17

aircraft nicknamed Rodina (homeland), Marina and her friends, Valentina Grizudobova and Polina Osipenko, had set a world record for a nonstop direct flight by women. It had been an epic journey of 6,000 kilometres from Moscow to Komsomolsk-on-Amur.

The entire nation had gathered around their radio sets as Radio Moscow broadcast hourly bulletins on the progress of the 'Winged Sisters', as one commentator called them. Just under an hour's flying time from their desination, the Rodina had run into a severe snowstorm. Heavy ice coated the wings and Valentina Grizudobova, who was at the controls, was fighting a losing battle to maintain height. As they sank lower towards the forest, the girls tried to lighten the aircraft by hurling out every movable object they could find. Still it dropped through the blinding flurries of snow towards the trees.

Then suddenly the snow was swirling inside the plane itself – Marina was standing beside the open door in the floor of the cockpit, pulling her parachute harness tight around her. She had been navigating, so she knew their approximate position. She scrawled a cross on the map and noted the aircraft's compass heading. Wrapping her arms around herself, she crouched at the opening and then threw herself into the darkness.

Valentina landed the Rodina in a clearing near the tiny forest village of Kerbi. It was ten days before a hunter found Marina in the harsh, desolate forest. She was exhausted, her water canteen was empty, and her rations were gone. The 'Winged Sisters' made a triumphant entry into Moscow at the head of a cavalcade, with tens of thousands cheering them through the streets. All were made Heroes of the Soviet Union, but it was Marina Raskova's astonishing bravery that had captured the affection of the public.

This was the woman they were to meet. Nadia really did feel as if butterflies were tumbling and whirling in her stomach, their wings fluttering here and there on nerve endings so sensitive she felt her body quiver. She squeezed Larissa's arm. An armed soldier inside the entrance checked their papers, looked at the telegrams, and directed them to a second-floor office.

The office door was open. A woman aged about thirty sat alone at a large desk strewn with bundles of papers and letters. She was writing with a school pen which she frequently dipped into a little porcelain jar filled with ink. She wore a major's tunic with the medal of the Hero of the Soviet Union pinned to the left breast. Her thick, dark hair was parted severely in the middle and tied into a bun at the back of her neck.

Larissa knocked almost inaudibly at the door. From the bowed head at the desk came a strong, clear command: 'Come in.' The two women walked in awkwardly and stood, hands clasped in front of them, a few feet from the desk. Larissa's suitcase lay at her feet, and Nadia's belongings were in a large bag on her back. Marina Raskova looked up at them. Larissa told me, 'She had the biggest, clearest blue eyes. I know if I had been a man I would have fallen in love with her straight away. It was a bit like a schoolgirl crush on a gym mistress.'

In fact, they were the first applicants Marina Raskova had interviewed, and it became obvious that the great flier herself was nervous about the whole business. She is remembered as an essentially shy person, and the sight of these two young women, open-mouthed in their hero worship, could not have made things easier. She studied their flying logbooks and asked them questions about their flying backgrounds for about ten minutes. Then she said to Larissa, 'Aren't you frightened to go to the front? Don't you know that these bad men on the other side will be shooting at you?'

'Not if I shoot them first, Major Raskova,' said Larissa.

Marina Raskova emphasized the point: 'The girls I do choose must understand beyond any doubt whatsoever that they will be fighting against men, and they must themselves fight like men. If you're chosen you may not be killed – you may be burned so your own mother would not recognize you. You may be blinded. You may lose a hand, a leg. You will lose your friends. You may be captured by the Germans. Do you really want to go through with this?'

Nadia told me, 'We listened to what Marina Raskova had to say. Of course we knew that what she was spelling out to us in such detail was possible. But we just could not believe it could ever happen to us. Which was just as well.'

Marina Raskova leaned back in her seat and looked impassively at the young women for a few moments. Then she smiled broadly and said, 'You are my first recruits. Report here tomorrow for further orders. Good luck, comrades.' She shook their hands and saluted. Nadia and Larissa responded with a most unmilitary flap of the arm. They were back in the street before they said a word to each other. Then they shrieked with pleasure and threw their arms around each other.

As they made their way back to the houses where they were to lodge for the night, another eighteen-year-old in a different part of Moscow lay in her room fighting back tears of frustration. Galina Junkovskaya was an engineering student at the Moscow Aviation Institute, a qualified pilot, and a member of the Central Aviation Club. She was also a trained parachute instructor with more than twenty jumps to her credit, and that was the cause of her frustration that night. She had written immediately after Marina Raskova's broadcast, offering herself for the women's air regiments. But her parachuting skills made them place a proviso on her acceptance: she would have to train fifty soldiers to jump before she could join the other women who would be selected for training. She was only a little more than halfway through her quota now.

She had a particularly poignant reason for wanting to hit back at the invaders. She had left her family behind in the west of the Soviet Union when she won a place at the Aviation Institute, and the area had been overrun by the German invaders in early July. Since then, she had found it difficult to think of anything but fighting. She had no idea whether her parents were alive or dead.

As Galina ticked off her diminishing quota of paratroopers, a twenty-year-old mother in the sanctuary of the Ural mountains, far to the east, had been suffering the same frustrations. Months before, Katerina Fedotova had been evacuated to the Urals because her skills as an aircraft assembly worker were required in the factories that had been dismantled in the path of the invaders and shipped to the east. There had been no one on the station platform to wave goodbye to Katerina and her two-year-old daughter as the train steamed out of Moscow. Somewhere to the west of the capital city, her husband Yuri was fighting with the army.

Katerina's father and mother had died when she was very young, and she had come to Moscow to train as a factory worker. She had fallen in love with flying. She told me, 'The first time I went up in an aircraft with an instructor I felt this sense of elation quite unlike anything else I'd ever experienced. Flying became an obsession.'

She learned quickly and flew every day, both before and after her factory shifts. Soon she was acting as an unpaid instructor at the flying club attached to the factory. From the day of Hitler's invasion, Katerina had pestered to be allowed to use her flying skills against the enemy. She even wrote to the Defence Minister. 'I became such a thorn in their side that they let me leave my factory job and become a full-time instructor, training military pilots. But I was still a civilian. They wouldn't let me fight.'

The evacuation to the Urals brought an end to her flying duties. Then, on the assembly line that October, she heard Marina Raskova's call to young women aviators to join her regiments. She applied, and Raskova accepted her for training. The day before she left, as little Margarita played around her feet, a telegram arrived with the words every wife dreaded: 'We regret to inform you that your husband . . .' Yuri was dead. The little girl looked up at her mother's face as it contorted in grief. Margarita looked so much like him that it was unbearable.

Katerina made up her mind that Margarita would be safe with her grandparents in the Urals. They loved her and would explain when she was older why her mother had gone away and left her. So Katerina Fedotova held her baby in her arms and then went off to war. She would not see her again for almost four years.

The date set for the new recruits to start their training was 15 October. The training base was to be a small town called Engels, on the River Volga, a few hundred miles north of Stalingrad. Meanwhile, more and more women were interviewed, selected, or rejected. Of course, not all of them would be pilots or navigators; less glamorous but equally important were the jobs of maintaining, refuelling, and rearming the aircraft, and maintaining and repairing radios and other communication equipment. That did not prevent many woman – particularly those who had a little experience on aircraft – from feeling somehow cheated. But as the war progressed, some of them would be given their chance, too, to fly in combat.

In the days leading up to their departure from Moscow, many of the women who were unfamiliar with their capital city witnessed some extraordinary sights as they walked around it and explored. Aside from being the political and cultural centre of the Soviet Union, Moscow was an important military target for German bombers if for no other reason than the railway network that fanned out in vital links to the hard-pressed Red Army. The women noticed some of the elaborate efforts being made to disguise Moscow's central area. In Red Square, they saw artists painting the walls of the Kremlin to make them resemble the fronts of houses. Wooden boards obscured the famous golden domes of the cathedrals within the Kremlin walls; and in Red Square itself, Lenin's tomb was encased in sandbags. The surfaces of several main streets had been painted to look like rooftops, and huge gangs of civilians were erecting dummy factories made of canvas and wood.

It all seemed faintly ludicrous since camouflage was pointless at night and German crews had no difficulty navigating in daylight with the help of Moscow's river bends and the distinctive street layout. Raids by the overextended German bomber fleets were in any case sporadic and were not having any significant effect.

On 13 October, the recruits were instructed to report to the Zhukovsky Academy to pick up their air force uniforms. Larissa Rasanova told me, 'Like all young girls we were pretty fashion conscious, even though there was a war on. Most of us had slim waists and, though we didn't expect uniforms tailored for us by a Paris couturier, we hoped that they had made some little concessions to the fact that we were all a different shape from most soldiers.' It was a thought of quite charming naïveté. In a large room, piled on the floor in separate bundles, were heaps of enormous boots, rough woollen vests, and long johns. In other piles were tunics, trousers, and coats. Larissa walked past the sergeant who had brought them to the storeroom and picked up two boots at random. They were gigantic. She told me, 'I asked him where our uniforms were. He just grinned and swept his arm around the room. We didn't know whether to laugh or cry.'

Several dozen women crowded into the room and, pushing the sergeant out, they began trying on the uniforms. Nadia Popova told me, 'The sounds of hysterical laughter must have been heard all over the building.' Woollen vests dangled down below the knee, trousers hitched up almost to the chin, and greatcoats spilled on to

23

the floor like grotesque bridal trains. And then there were the boots. Someone found a bundle of old copies of *Pravda* and *Izvestia* in a corner, and they stuffed sheet after sheet into the toes.

Lily Litvak was particularly entertaining in this store-room charade. She was blonde, grey-eyed, and coquettish, but what made her a particular object of mirth was her size. She was just over five feet tall, with a stunningly well-proportioned figure, and she stood there enveloped in a tunic that almost touched the floor and boots that would not have looked out of place on one of the clowns at the Moscow State Circus.

Larissa said, 'Some of the girls were very good with scissors, needle, and thread, and we managed to get some semblance of fit out of the uniforms over the next few days. But we must have looked like nothing on earth standing at the station waiting for that train to Engels. We could hardly walk with these boots – we hobbled. Some of the trousers had been shortened simply by cutting some length off the leg, so that they divided just above the knee, and most of the coats were still trailing on the ground at that time. God knows what the Germans would have thought.'

The woman who had been hamming it up for the benefit of the others the day before had spent most of the night cutting and sewing and ironing her uniform. Lily Litvak's uniform was far from perfect, but it looked the smartest of the group by a long way. She had drawn the belt tight round her tiny waist and she had a flower in her cap. That she could look so stunning under these circumstances did not endear her to all of the other women, but it typified the femininity she was to cling to right through the combat experiences that were to make her a household name.

Larissa Rasanova had been a friend of Lily's since they had both been teenage flying instructors at the same flying club. Larissa said, 'The same sort of attention to detail which Lily gave to her personal appearance, she gave to her

24

flying, and that was what made her a superb pilot.' Lily had tried to join a flying club when she was fifteen, but she had been told she would have to wait like everyone else until she was seventeen. She devoured every book she could find on aviation – aircraft design, aerobatics, meteorology, and navigation. She would continually waylay the chief instructor to impress on him how knowledgeable she was. Eventually the club bent the rules and accepted her for flying training at only sixteen. She had a natural talent and learned extremely fast, flying solo on the PO-2 biplane trainer aircraft after only four hours' instruction.

Lily's father was a railway worker. Her mother worked in a shop. Lily knew they would have been horrified at the prospect of her flying an aeroplane, so she had smuggled the theoretical books into her room at their home near the subway station at Nova Slobodskaya Street. Once she actually started to fly, she told her parents she was attending the school dramatic society in the early evenings. By the time her subterfuge was discovered, it was too late.

Larissa said, 'Lily was one of these people who was good at everything she tried. And she was so popular with the boys. I think every man at the flying club was in love with her. Women being what they are, it didn't go down too well with everyone. But, surprisingly, there wasn't nearly as much jealousy as you might have expected of a girl as talented and good-looking as she was.'

If the brightest and the best are doomed to perish in battle, then the shadow would soon begin to cast itself over Lily Litvak. But not yet. On the train journey east to Engels, the young women relaxed. They laughed and joked and speculated on what the boys would be like tomorrow in Engels.

2

Recruits in Engels, 1941–42

Engels is a small country town north of Stalingrad. It straddles the main railway line that crosses the river Volga a few miles further west on its way to Saratov. The quiet peacetime airfield was still well beyond the range of any German bombers, and as the young women got down from the trucks that had transported them from the station, they tried to absorb their first impressions of a military airfield. Ringing its perimeter were sandbag emplacements with the long ugly snouts of anti-aircraft guns pointing at the sky. Soldiers in steel helmets, with rifles cradled in their arms, checked each recruit's papers as they walked past the main gate. The women looked skyward as they heard the familiar *put-putting* engine sound of the PO-2 biplane trainers, on which most of the pilots among them had first flown solo. Row after row of other PO-2s stood in front of the hangars, and large gangs of civilian labourers were working around the airfield, hastily extending hangars and workshops and building long, low accommodation huts.

There was a slight menace about the whole atmosphere which made some of them uneasy. It was so different from the atmosphere of the flying clubs they had been used to. The only reassuring things were the familiar smells of aviation fuel and oil and stiffening dope recently painted on fuselage fabric. A large man wearing a captain's uniform came out of an office and barked at them to get in line and follow him. They were shown to an old school building on the perimeter, equipped with bunks and single beds. They would eat in the officers' mess, they were told.

So a thousand women – most of them little more than schoolgirls – unpacked their belongings, pinned photo-

26

graphs of their families to the bare walls behind their hard wooden cots, and started to get to know each other. They would be living together over the next four years.

Nadia Popova – the girl who'd danced on the eve of war – had been one of the first to get a new uniform tunic and trousers which fitted reasonably well. On the wall above and to the side of her bed she hung the only pretty clothes she had brought with her from Donetsk. She smoothed down a rough wooden hanger with some sandpaper and carefully hung up a white silk blouse and a long light blue silk scarf. In the pocket of her flying overalls was a little brooch in the shape of a beetle which had been a present from her parents. It was to become a lucky charm for her, and she never flew a single mission without it.

Nadia became firm friends with a woman named Marina Chichnova. Nadia told me, 'The friendship that grew between Marina and me was such a close bond that we were like loving sisters. This happened a great deal in the women's regiments. There was surprisingly little bitchiness of the sort you might expect when a lot of girls are flung together like that. But then I think we were all united in a common purpose and that was probably the reason why.'

The friendship led them to work out individual combat tactics to protect each other. Marina, who was small with very dark hair and dark eyes, had a quick aggressive temper and was one of the few women who smoked. It was a habit she introduced Nadia and other girls to as the war progressed, and they learned the soothing and almost instantaneous effect of nicotine on the brain.

Maj. Marina Raskova and her second-in-command, Maj. Yevdokia Bershanskaya, helped with and supervised the training. Yevdokia Bershanskaya, a woman of thirty-two, was married and had a young son; her husband was an officer serving in the army. She had left a teacher-training college when she was seventeen and, bitten by the flying bug, had trained to be a professional flying instructor. In the two years prior to the German invasion, she had been flying airliners inside the Soviet Union. She told me, 'The girls seemed little more than children in many ways. Training was a very difficult time for all of us. Although most of them were good basic raw material, with a certain standard in their various skills, they had an awful lot to learn. And don't forget many of them had never been away from home in their lives before. Marina and I both realized that they needed a certain motherly kindness just as much as they needed to be pushed along with their training. I didn't think of myself as a mother figure at first – I still thought I was a girl myself – but these teenagers didn't give me much choice.'

The training schedule was intense, involving up to fourteen hours of flying and classwork on exceptional days. The demand for pilots was so great that courses that might have lasted for up to two years in peacetime had to be compressed into six months. The authorities have conceded this meant many crews sent to the front were inadequately trained, but there was no alternative. Pilots and navigators were in the air until nightfall in a process of continuous assessment that would decide at the end of six months exactly who was assigned to which of the three regiments – the 586th Women's Fighter Regiment, the 587th Women's Bomber Regiment, or the 588th Women's Night Bomber Regiment.

Without exception, the women chosen for pilot training were obsessive in their desire to fly fighters. At that stage of their careers, any other sort of aircraft was regarded as unacceptable. No one was more determined to fly fighters than Lily Litvak. Larissa Rasanova told me, 'At our old flying club, Lily was always getting into trouble with the chief instructor for doing aerobatics too near the ground. It wasn't so much showing off as a total exuberance for throwing the aircraft around the sky. I think she was determined to show the instructors at Engels, from the very start, that she was the stuff fighter pilots are made of.'

A squadron of Yak-1 single-seat fighters was stationed at Engels. They would be used to train the cream of the volunteers before they were sent to the front with the women's fighter regiment. The young men who flew these fighters had an attractive swagger about them and wore dashing silk scarves at their throats. The young women looked longingly at both men and aircraft, but at that early stage of their training their only thought at the end of the day was to get to their billets and fall into bed.

As the weeks went by at Engels, the pilots flew increasingly on their own, without instructors in the rear cockpits. They practised bombing from various heights on ranges a few miles from the airfield, pulling a wire inside the cockpit to release the little bombs carried in racks beneath the wings of the PO-2. They practised flying at night – first with an instructor, then solo – learning to navigate with only the most rudimentary of instruments and without any radio communication with the ground.

The River Volga was a marvellously reflective surface at night and served like a navigation beacon when there was the slightest glimmer of moonlight. But as the training advanced the women were forced to fly triangular courses farther and farther afield from their familiar landmarks. Marina Chichnova told me: 'Looking back on it now, it's hard to believe we had the nerve to tackle it, really. There we were, a bunch of mad girls, charging around the sky on pitch-black nights, peering at maps on our knees by the light of the instrument panel, and trying to find our bearings when we couldn't see a thing on the ground.'

The pilots navigated mainly with stopwatches and rather crude manually operated computers strapped to their knees. They had measured on the map the distances between the various turning points on their routes. With careful timings, strict allowance for drift caused by the wind, and a lot of luck, they normally made it back to the airfield. Occasionally a flier would blunder around lost until she ran out of fuel and somehow managed to put her PO-2 down in a field or even on a road. Miraculously, no one was killed during these abortive exercises, due mainly to the ruggedness of the old trainer aircraft and to its extremely low landing speed.

The navigators, too, spent many hours aloft, often at night, learning their skills and attempting to point the instructor in the front cockpit in the correct direction. Later they practised with other recruits in the pilot's seat.

As the weeks went by, Marina Raskova and Yevdokia Bershanskaya formulated and wrote up their assessments of the different volunteers. Which women flew well together as pilot and navigator? Whose brain worked more quickly in navigational exercises? Who reacted most calmly during a crisis in the air?

But what the women wanted to know was 'Who is going on to fighters?' There were some fliers who were clearly front-runners. Galia Boordina, the baby-faced, dark-haired woman from the Baltic port of Riga, had been flying since she was sixteen and everyone who had flown with her said she had the reactions of a cat. Just before she came to Engels she had been at Sverdlovsk giving basic flight instruction to men selected for fighter training. Olga Yemshokova had been an instructor, too, and she was already showing the skills that were to see her become the first Soviet woman to fly a jet aircraft after the war. But the one who soared above the others was Lily Litvak. The PO-2, though very slow (top speed of 100 mph), was fully aerobatic, and Lily did things with the venerable trainer that sorely tried the chauvinistic male instructors.

The pilots were encouraged to practise solo aerobatics in any free-style sequence they could dream up. Tactics of air combat were discussed in the classroom from both an offensive and defensive standpoint, depending on whether the Soviet aircraft under discussion was a bomber or a fighter. Veterans of the Spanish Civil War and the

Soviet–Finnish war would cover the blackboard with intricate scrollwork of different coloured chalk as they explained in detail the deadly games of aerial chess.

The PO-2s had no guns fitted, but the instructors tried to teach the women – first in theory and later airborne – the skills of short sharp bursts of cannon or machine-gun fire from close range and the art of deflection shooting to strike a fast-moving target. This sort of flying was the final part of the continuous assessment, for only superb reactions and a natural instinct for control would see them through these violent manoeuvres and mock dogfights. Frequently these dogfights ended with the pilot spinning out of control temporarily, having pushed the PO-2 beyond its limits.

Lily was third to take off one afternoon to dogfight with the instructor, Lieutenant Dobkin. The preceding flier landed as Lily sat at the end and to the side of the runway. When her friend had cleared the runway, Lily pushed the throttle of the PO-2 wide open, and it trundled across the grass, gathering speed. When the airspeed indicator on the instrument panel reached forty knots, Lily eased back on the control column between her knees and the aircraft climbed steadily to the rendezvous. She was to fly to a position three miles east of the airfield and circle in gentle turns to the right and left at a height of four thousand feet. At the briefing after the midday meal, Dobkin had grinned and told the women, 'I'm the enemy. I'll find you. And you'd better be ready!'

As Lily levelled out at four thousand feet and began circling to the left over the village landmark, she kept glancing over her shoulder at the cloud cover to the north. That was where Dobkin was likely to be lurking. She circled once to the left and then, once more over the village, she pointed the nose of the PO-2 down into a dive. As the speed increased, she pulled the stick back and zoomed upward. The PO-2 stood on its tail and she smoothly co-ordinated stick and rudder to roll the aircraft back into level flight once more, this time pointing in the opposite direction. She circled to the right now, her senses racing, her face flushed in the slipstream. There was no sign of an aircraft from the cloud. She cupped her hand, shielding the low afternoon sun from her eyes, and peered straight back at the glowing orb. From its periphery a dark shape was racing towards her rear.

It was Dobkin, attacking out of the sun. She coolly carried on with her gentle turn and started to count out loud, very slowly: 'One . . . two . . . three . . . four . . . five. Now!' Without turning her head, she pulled the stick back into her stomach, pitching the nose up suddenly. At the same time she kicked hard and stood on the right rudder pedal. The PO-2 climbed and rolled simultaneously, executing a perfect barrel roll. As she hung upside down at the top of her manoeuvre, there, flying straight below her, with a look of fury on his upturned face, was Dobkin, the man who should have been on her tail.

Lily pointed her nose at the lieutenant's aircraft and was tucked in behind him even as he started to try to shake her off. She squinted along the nose of the PO-2, pressing an imaginary gun button on the control column. If only this were a Yak. If only he were a German.

The aircraft were matched exactly in performance and handling characteristics. Only superior skill counted now. Dobkin snapped his aircraft into a roll to the right and Lily, her engine roaring at full power, followed him through, the earth and sky tumbling across the front of her aircraft. She squeezed the imaginary gun button again in another short burst. 'You're dead, Dobkin.'

They had lost height in the roll. Lily's adversary went into a dive, slipping and sliding out of Lily's 'sights' as he gained speed. Was he going down to low level? Suddenly he zoomed and Lily followed him all the way up. He hesitated at the top of the loop, then decided to complete it, rolling to the right again as he came out of his loop.

Whatever he did, as he admitted later, Lily was right there, sitting so close to his tail that he had to wave her back. But Lily sat there until she forced him to make a violent cut-throat motion, conceding complete defeat. Lieutenant Dobkin didn't like it one little bit – his reaction was typical of much of the chauvinism that the women had to struggle against even after they went into combat. For Lily, though, it was an important psychological victory. Not because she had beaten a man, but because she had humbled a skilled adversary.

She broke off and made for the airfield. There were no aircraft flying around the circuit and none waiting to take off on the main runway. For the first time, Lily's colleagues were to see the flamboyant manoeuvre that became her trademark after every 'kill'. She swooped over the hangars, soared up into a victory roll, then snapped into a tight turn, and made a perfect landing.

Along with the flight training and the training of the ground staff, the women had been learning to be soldiers. Every day at six they were roused from their beds and, irrespective of weather, spent up to an hour drilling and marching before breakfast. It may have been a necessary part of military doctrine, but it is questionable whether it had the desired effect. Marina Chichnova told me, 'The girls learned to become real soldiers through the experiences they had in combat. That was the real character builder. I know discipline is important in any military force. But really there was never any serious problem of that sort in the girls' regiments. There was so much mutual respect that people just tended to get on with the job without having to be ordered. Of course you need people in command and we had that. But a group of really motivated females does not, I think, need quite the same sort of rigid discipline that men do.'

Also included in the daily routine was indoctrination by

the political commissar. The Soviet armed services placed great emphasis on the importance of this officer's role. Almost 80 per cent of air force officers were Communist Party members – or in the case of the young women, Komsomol or Young Communist League members. Even though much of the so-called indoctrination must have seemed like preaching to the converted, these commissars also had another role: that of keeping up the morale of the combat personnel.

The political commissar of the women's fighter regiment was Maj. Vera Ivanovna Tikomerova. She told me, 'Of course, my job was to keep the girls aware of Party policy both towards the war and towards the girls' place in society generally. It was the way of life of our country and we were all fighting a war to preserve it from the Germans. But as the conflict went on and the personal pressures on the girls increased to an almost intolerable level, I became like a mother-confessor. I know I saved girls from cracking up altogether.' This was the nearest any of the women came to admitting that anyone did succumb to the strain.

In April, Major Raskova pinned to the notice boards a list of the regiments to which the women had been assigned. There were celebrations, there were congratulations, and there were tears. Of course, they had all known that only a third of the pilots would be assigned to the fighter regiment. Lily Litvak's name was there, to be sure, along with Galia Boordina, Olga Yemshokova, and three dozen other fledgling fighter pilots. Nadia Popova and her friend Marina Chichnova would fly PO-2s, which were being pressed into service as the aircraft for the 588th Night Bomber Regiment. Galina Junkovskaya – who had had to fill her quota of trained parachutists before acceptance – was to be a navigator on the Petylakov PE-2 day bomber regiment, and Katerina Fedotova – who had left her daughter in the Urals – was to be a PE-2 pilot. Larissa Rasanova, who had met up with Nadia Popova on the way to join up in Moscow, was to be a navigator on a PO-2 night bomber.

No one showed her disappointment more than Larissa. She told me frankly, 'I was bitterly disappointed. There I was, a highly experienced pilot before the war even started. An instructor. But the trouble was that I was also an experienced navigator. So I landed what I considered to be the most humble and least glamorous job of the lot – navigating a little PO-2 at night. I, who had taught thirty men to fly before the war. I really felt humiliated. I dropped six separate letters into Marina Raskova's office over the next few days. I didn't have the courage to see her personally. The letters detailed my flying background. They pointed out to her how well I'd done during training and they begged her not to assign me to navigating on night bombers. Marina summoned me eventually. I'd never seen her angry before. She made me stand at attention in front of her desk and then for ten minutes she told me exactly what she thought of me.

'"What do you think we're doing here, Rasanova?" she said. "Do you really think we're playing war games? Our people are dying out there every day by the thousands. We'll be lucky if we survive the winter. And you whine to me because you're not getting exactly what you want. Now get out of my office and never let me hear you speak like that again."

'I managed some sort of salute, about-turned and was at the door when I felt her hand on my shoulder. She told me to sit down, gave me a clean handkerchief from her breast pocket, and called me Larissa. She explained to me that I should look upon it as a compliment. I'd been given that job because the new regiment would need navigators of real experience, especially in the early stages. Maybe it was flattery. Maybe I wasn't as good a pilot as I thought I was. It didn't matter. The great Marina Raskova had said she needed me. And it worked. I walked out of there feeling proud.' Within a few months of arriving at the front line,

Larissa had been promoted to squadron navigator.

The women were soldiers now, but of equal importance to them was their femininity. Galina Junkovskaya told me, 'We knew from the outset that we were to be combat fliers, doing exactly the same type of sorties as male aircrews. We were to have equality in every possible sense, though in reality we had to struggle for that in some cases when we got to the front. But, though we were equal in what we were doing, none of us wanted to act like men or look like men when we left our aircraft. We just had to remind ourselves all the time that we were girls.'

Then came an order from the male commandant of the Engels training base that cast gloom over the women. They were to get their long hair cut – all of them. It was not soldierly to have long hair and they were all soldiers now, not film stars, he said. They could cut their hair themselves or a barber would come around and do it for them, but they were all to get it cut short – no more than two and a half inches all over. Larissa Rasanova told me, 'Most of us had long hair and we were very proud of it. But one girl particularly beautiful hair. It was like a shining corn-coloured mane, thick and lustrous, and it hung almost to her waist. It was the sort of hair that any girl would have envied.'

That night, they grimaced into hand mirrors as scissors wielded by their friends clipped their tresses. Coils covered the floor. Many kept a lock and placed it in an envelope or between the pages of a book. The woman with the corn-coloured hair sat on her bed, running a comb through her hair, first on one side and then the other, tossing her head back when a thick wave fell across one eye. She didn't weep but she looked utterly miserable. Larissa Rasanova said, 'None of us could bring ourselves to even approach her with the scissors, and she certainly wasn't encouraging us. So nothing was done that night. But next morning several other girls and I spoke to Marina Raskova before morning inspection. It was a sort of deputation, really.'

The women argued their case respectfully but with great force. With the exception of this one woman, they said, they had all lopped off their hair as ordered. But her hair was so beautiful that it had now become a symbol of all of their femininity. Would it not be possible to allow one exception? After all, they would all be going to the front soon and they knew that she, Major Raskova, did not perhaps feel so strongly about long hair as the male senior officers.

Marina Raskova's long hair was still tied back from her face severely and pinned in a bun behind her neck. The reference to her attitudes about long hair had clearly not been intended as insubordination, she felt. She summoned the girl, a mechanic, and told her to keep her hair securely pinned up under her uniform beret at all times. Agreeing to ignore a regulation was perhaps a risk for Marina Raskova to take, but night bomber pilot Natalya Meklin told me, 'We did not lose any respect for Marina. We loved her all the more for it. She had so much stature among us, so much natural authority. In any case, to most of us she was still almost godlike. We regarded it as a privilege just to be on the same airfield with her.'

Two days later, a general from one of the Air Armies made a surprise inspection visit to Engels. Flying was suspended for an hour while he walked up and down the ranks of women standing stiffly at attention as they had learned to do during the early morning drill sessions of the preceding months. Here and there, he stopped to chat. He was a squat, red-faced man and he did not look as if he was enjoying this particular duty. With their short hair, the women looked ridiculously young and even tomboyish. He stopped to speak a few words to the woman standing next to the blonde mechanic and as he moved off, he glanced at her.

Something caught his attention. He walked back and, looked her straight in the eye, raised his hand and smoothly whipped off the mechanic's beret. With the beret came the hair clasp. The long hair tumbled down, blowing in the wind and partially obscuring the woman's face. There was a collective gasp from the women on either side and in the ranks behind. What would be his reaction to this clear breach of regulations? The general put his hands on his hips, threw back his head, and gave a great pealing roar of laughter. He waved to Marina Raskova to join him, saying, 'Why haven't all the girls got their hair like this? They all look like boys except this one. A girl without hair is like a horse without a mane. What are you thinking about, letting them crop themselves like that?' Marina Raskova managed a wry smile. The incident was of little comfort to the women whose only relics of their long tresses were pressed between pages of books, but it encouraged them, when they got to the front, to let their hair grow again, regardless of what the rule book said.

Meanwhile it was time for the day bomber and fighter crews to train on the aircraft in which they would go to war. The pilots assigned to the 587th Women's Bomber Regiment would be flying the Petylakov twin-engined PE-2 light bomber; and the 588th Women's Night Bomber Regiment would fly the old PO-2 trainers now being pressed into service as operational front-line aircraft.

The PE-2 carried a crew of three – pilot, navigator, and radio operator/gunner. It had two fixed machine guns firing forward, one swivelling machine gun in an acrylic plastic bubble behind the navigator, and two guns operated by the radio operator in the middle of the fuselage – one in the floor for defence of the underside of the aircraft, and one that fired through a hatch above her head. The pilot sat in an armoured seat in the cockpit with the navigator behind her, also in an armoured seat. The radio operator sat about six feet away in the middle of the fuselage, crouched over her equipment and surrounded by boxes of spare ammunition belts for her guns.

The PE-2 was not an easy aircraft to take off. Some twin-engine aircraft have the propellers contrarotating –

38

that is, spinning towards each other – which cancels out the tendency of the aeroplane to turn in the direction of the propellers; but the PE-2's propellers both turned in the same direction, to the left. With both powerful engines on full power for take-off, the bomber had an alarming tendency to swing left. If not controlled quickly and firmly, the aircraft would swing off the runway.

Katerina Fedotova told me, 'That wasn't the only problem. Fully loaded with fuel and bombs, the PE-2 needed someone with a lot of strength to pull back on the stick at the appropriate moment to get the nose off the ground. Most of us had to get our navigators to stand beside us on take-off to help yank the stick back on a given command. It was a delicate business, though, because if the stick was pulled back too far, the aeroplane would lose flying speed, it would stall, and you'd make a big fire on the runway.'

And there was another problem: 'Most of us were small girls – quite a bit shorter than the men. We needed cushions to pad our seats so that we could see out of the windscreen. And some of the girls with particularly short legs had to have special blocks put on the rubber pedals so that they could reach them with their feet.'

The conversions from the PO-2 trainer to the PE-2 bomber were difficult, especially as there was no trainer version of this aircraft, with dual controls for student and instructor. The pilots did considerable ground work with the instructors and thoroughly familiarized themselves with all the controls and the statistics of landing speeds, take-off speeds, stalling speeds, rate of climb, rate of descent, and engine revolutions for climbing, cruising, and so on. They went through the instructor's check list with him until they knew it by heart.

On their first few flights, the pilots stood in the cockpit beside the instructor as he took off, watching his every move and listening to his careful, detailed running commentary on every single action he was taking. After a couple of flights like this, he would settle the PE-2 at an altitude of, say, five thousand feet, then slide out of the pilot's seat and allow the woman to take control. She would land the aircraft with the instructor standing beside her. It was an act of faith and confidence on the part of the instructors: they were there to give advice, guidance, and moral support, but as the runway rushed up to meet them, there was nothing they could do to prevent any disaster. There were a few very hard landings in these early flights, but nothing worse. And while the pilots mastered their new aircraft, the navigators and radio operators learned to function as part of a tightly knit, three-person crew.

For Lily Litvak and the other fledgling fighter pilots, though, the conversion was even more difficult. The Yak-1 was a strictly single-seat machine, so all the instructors could do was to drum into the pilots the handling characteristics and the limits of power and control. Practice started with taxiing the aircraft until it reached take-off speed. The pilot was instructed to allow the Yak to lift off slightly, then ease back on the power and allow it to settle back on the runway. This exercise was repeated again and again to give the fliers some feel for the aeroplane. Then, one by one, they opened wide the throttle lever. As the speed increased, the tail lifted off the ground and visibility improved dramatically as the long nose of the Yak swung down parallel with the runway racing past underneath. Then the pilot eased back on the stick and the plane was airborne.

Galia Boordina told me, 'We only did a series of circuits and bumps, flying round the airfield boundary, landing and then immediately taking off again, that first day. But we were all trembling with excitement. Imagine it – there we were, young girls, up there throwing these fighters around. The power of the Yak was incredible, compared to what we'd been flying before. Everything seemed to happen so much more quickly. None of us – not even Lily – tried anything too adventurous that day.'

In the succeeding days, as they gained confidence in and familiarity with their aircraft, they practised flying in the pairs formations that were becoming standard procedure in Soviet Air Force fighter units. They were also quickly learning the limits to which they could push their Yaks in aerial combat. Throughout the hours of daylight, the women engaged in dogfights with their instructors and each other, learning from combat veterans the tricks that could save their lives. Of course it was exciting – almost unbearably so. The adrenalin flowed in continuous surges, and their necks ached with the effort of constantly craning over their shoulders to look for adversaries on their tails. And they loved it. But no one was allowed to forget it was a deadly serious game they were playing. During the debriefing sessions after each training flight, the instructors would mercilessly chastise the pilots for mistakes due to stupidity or lack of concentration.

They also practised air-to-air gunnery, firing against a target drogue being towed several hundred yards behind a PO-2. The Yak-1 was armed with two light machine guns, mounted one in each wing, and a heavier cannon in the propeller shaft. The firing button was on the control stick; one flicked off a safety guard before pressing the button, which fired all three weapons simultaneously. Galia Boordina told me, 'This was really what it was all about. There wasn't any point in being a great aerobatic pilot if you couldn't hit your opponent in that split second when you had him at your mercy. Our first attacks on the target drogue were from the beam, at right angles to it, in a shallow dive. It was a lot more difficult than it looked – I missed wildly on my first attempt. But what a feeling. To press the button and feel the aircraft shudder as the shells hammered from the muzzles and the tracers among them snaked brightly towards the target.'

While final training took place, the women anxiously

kept up to date with the progress of the war. Every morning at roll call and inspection, Marina Raskova would read out bulletins on the progress of the fighting. The women whose families were now in German-occupied territories were living under enormous anxiety.

Krasnodar had been overrun by the invaders. The night bomber regiment commander Yevdokia Bershanskaya's little boy was there with his grandparents. She told me, 'The strain was terrible. I knew what I was doing when I left him and went off to war. But I felt I had no choice. It broke my heart to leave him but my duty to my country compelled me. Not a single hour of any day went by that I did not think of him. Was he alive? Had he been hurt? Was someone, even at that moment, being unkind to my baby? I put the thoughts to the back of my mind to concentrate on my tasks, but his face kept drifting through everything else till it looked at me in sharp focus in my mind's eye. It was not an easy time. I had to show leadership to the other girls. I had to show an example.'

Nadia Popova had no idea what had happened to her parents. The Donetsk region too had been overrun. Leonid, her gentle brother, would never marry his fiancée; he had fallen in the first month of the war. Nadia told me, 'I didn't know if mama and papa were alive. We heard the most horrifying stories about what the Germans were doing to civilians in that area. I refused to think of anything like that happening to my loved ones. I closed my eyes and imagined the little house the way it used to be. I imagined myself in bare feet, a little girl running through the cherry trees in the garden with mama sitting in a chair outside the door. We couldn't get any letters or any sort of communication with the occupied territories, of course. And it didn't really help that other girls were in the same position.'

There was to be a big party and dance in the schoolhouse to celebrate the end of training. It was 17 May, 1942. The women pulled their beds back against the walls, and the dance spilled through the various rooms. The impromptu band, composed of women and instructors and other crews from the base, certainly would not have passed an audition for Radio Moscow, but as the evening progressed and the vodka flowed, the combination of accordions, banjos, piano, and drums sounded better and better. The lights had been switched off, and the only illumination came from the guttering flames of candles stuck in bottles on window ledges and tables. There was scarcely room to move in the dance spaces, but the young men were clearly content to sway slowly on the spot with the women who had been so tantalizingly out of reach for the last few months.

Lily Litvak was casting her spell again. From where Marina Raskova and Yevdokia Bershanskaya were sitting, watching their charges with benign but beady eye, it was clear that one lieutenant fighter pilot was quite besotted with her. Lily and the young man sat on a bench on the fringe of the dancers. It had been raining heavily outside and some of the later arrivals were dancing in muddy rubber boots that brushed against the young man's trousers occasionally. He did not notice. He was talking earnestly and his eyes were boring into hers.

Nadia Popova was sitting with another pilot on the chairs behind Lily. She told me, 'I could not help overhearing what they were saying. The boy was one of the instructors in the Yak conversion squadron and he had obviously fallen very heavily for Lily. He was pleading with her not to see any other man, not to write to anyone but him when she left Engels. And she had only just met him, remember. She did look dazzling that night with her big grey eyes and blonde hair, and I could see that she was enjoying the adulation of this attractive boy, but she didn't want to hurt him. She said to him, "Let's get the fighting over first, darling – then maybe we can talk about love, eh?" Then she got up and danced with someone else. But as soon as she'd finished the dance, he dragged her down to the bench

43

beside him again. She had this extraordinary effect on men.'

As the war progressed, many of the women had passionate love affairs, usually with pilots and navigators they met from squadrons who were sharing the same airfield. These romances were often cut short by sudden death of one of the lovers, so the women learned from bitter experience to make no firm commitments to a man, no matter how strongly their hearts might try to dictate any.

At midnight, Marina Raskova got up and clapped her hands and the band stopped playing. 'Time for bed, girls,' she said. 'And boys,' she added, grinning. She switched on the lights and stood there until the last man had walked out into the night. It was not the way that most of them had hoped it would end.

At morning inspection the next day, Marina Raskova announced that the 586th Women's Fighter Regiment was going to the front. There was a moment's pause and then an outburst of wild cheering. Everyone broke ranks and hugged each other. It was the moment they had been waiting for. The regiment's Yaks were being ferried in that day, and the fighter pilots would fly them across the Volga to the military airfield at Saratov where they were to be based. Marina Raskova told the other women that their regiments would be assigned in the near future.

The fighter pilots drew their 7.62 mm automatic pistols from the airfield armoury and secured them in the holsters at their waists. They hugged their friends and walked to the line of Yaks, pulling leather flying helmets over their heads and chattering excitedly. They strapped themselves in, pulled the canopies shut, and took off from Engels in formations of four. The last formation waggled its wings in salute as it swept low over the airfield and headed west for Saratov. They were ordered to test their guns en route, and the short bursts smashed through the new fabric pasted over the gun ports. The women had gone to war.

3

Baptism of Fire – the 586th Fighter Regiment at Saratov

That day the Germans launched their second summer offensive – a drive south to capture the Caucasus and the vital oilfields of Baku. The Soviet's first winter campaign against the invaders had spent itself and, though the Germans had been hit hard, Hitler was confident that his new offensive would finally smash the Russians. They had reached Moscow without taking it, but Leningrad – under siege – was hanging like a ripe plum. Most of the Ukraine had been taken in the lightning summer campaign, and no one believed that the Soviets could sustain the same sort of crushing losses as last year and survive. In the first three weeks of their new offensive, the Germans captured 400,000 prisoners, 1,250 tanks, and over 2,000 guns. It had all the appearances of the beginning of a rout.

The Yaks of the 586th Women's Fighter Regiment peeled off from their formations and landed one by one at Saratov. It was a clear spring day. They had crossed the wide Volga, muddy brown from the recent thaw, and to the west the steppe stretched towards the River Don.

The propellers of the Yaks swung to a halt at the dispersal point and the *pinging* sound of contracting engine metal followed the women as they jumped on to the wing roots and walked towards the commander's office.

Their primary task was to defend Saratov, its railways, and its munitions factories. One squadron of ten aircraft would fly night missions and the second would fly during the day. At any one time, the third squadron would be composed of different women from the regiment undergoing advanced training.

A map on the wall of the commander's office showed the

city of Saratov and its surroundings divided into four sectors. To avoid the dangers of collision, the regiment would put up only four fighters at a time during heavy night raids on the city. As the first four came back for refuelling and rearming, the next four would be taking off. There would be one fighter patrolling each sector of the city at night.

Galia Boordina told me, 'We had done quite a bit of night flying, but of course we had never been in battle before. On moonlit nights when one could see the odd landmark on the ground, it was one thing. But keeping to one sector of a city while searching for an enemy you couldn't see in the dark was quite another.'

The women had a baptism of fire on the second night. Galia, Valeria Khomyakova, and the eight others on night standby sat in the crew room. On the stove a kettle was simmering. The girls were writing letters home, talking to each other. Galia recalled, 'The conversation was strained. Everyone was very nervous, but no one wanted to show it. Girls were laughing a bit too loud when someone made a feeble joke. There was a steady procession to and from the lavatory. Then the phone on the table rang and everyone shut up immediately.'

Olga Yemshokova, the squadron leader, grabbed the phone and repeated into the mouthpiece: 'Twenty plus enemy. Six thousand feet. Heading zero nine zero. Twenty miles from Saratov.' The women had already scrawled the heading on their maps. They heaved their parachutes on to their backs as they ran to the aircraft. Smoky, hooded flares guided the taxiing fighters to the take-off point. Galia was second of the group of four to take off. She told me, 'It was to be the same feeling every time I took off. I felt ashamed of it at first but I came to terms with it eventually. I was retching as I taxied out for take-off. I felt like switching off and getting out. My hands were shaking as I followed Olga's aircraft out to the end of the runway, swinging the nose around to see what was in front. Ground control was talking to us over the radio and when he asked me to respond to the instructions on the height and heading we were to fly, I was sure my voice would give me away. But it was strange – the moment the aircraft left the ground and I raised that undercarriage, all my nerves disappeared.'

There was no moon that night: it was obscured by clouds at ten thousand feet. As the women took off and climbed at thirty-second intervals behind Ogla Yemshokova, they kept their eyes on their instrument panels. In the glow from the instrument panel, only the girls' cheekbones and eyes could be seen above the oxygen masks that clipped on to their flying helmets. There was no horizon visible outside the cockpit. They watched the tiny aircraft symbol on the panel which hovered above a horizontal bar to indicate that the nose of the plane was still pointing up in the climb. Their eyes flicked constantly across the dials – the engine revs, the airspeed indicator, the oil pressure and temperature gauges, the fuel indicators, and the turn-and-slip dial that warned them if they were flying sloppily. Galia told me, 'It demanded terrific concentration. And, though we'd been taught from the start of night flying training that we must believe the instruments every time, it was very easy to disbelieve them. Sometimes you were convinced that you were upside down when the instruments told you you were right side up. It could literally be fatal to trust your own instincts in the dark.'

At seven thousand feet, Galia levelled out. She should now be a thousand feet above the enemy bombers. She knew the speed of her aircraft and she knew how long it would take to fly from one part of her sector to another without straying into another pilot's area. She started her stopwatch and began to patrol above the outskirts of the darkened, sleeping city, rolling the wings into left- and then right-hand turns and peering down for the first sight of the enemy.

The controller's voice crackled in their headphones; ground observation posts confirmed that the enemy bombers were maintaining their heading. 'The problem at that stage of the war,' Galia said, 'was that our radio communication equipment was still pretty crude. Although we could receive messages from ground control, we couldn't transmit anything back. It didn't make our job any easier.'

Galia thought she saw something in the darkness below her wing. She thrust the throttle lever fully forward with her gloved left hand and stood the Yak on its right wingtip in a hard turn. Her right hand pushed the stick over and pulled back at the same time to keep the nose from dropping. As the aircraft screamed round through 360 degrees, she strained her eyes down through the ink, into the centre of the circle she had created. She was right – there was another shape and another. And another. The bombers were sliding past beneath her wingtip, into her sector. In about two minutes they would be over the city, raining down bombs.

Galia told me, 'There wasn't really much to think about. I could see them passing below me to the right and left, these vague shapes. I reckoned I must be right above the middle of them. I flicked the guard off the gun button and pushed the nose straight down. I started firing right away and, keeping the power full on, I just charged straight through the middle of the formation. It was terrifying. I passed very close to one of them as I dived through, then I pulled the stick back and zoomed up above them again, and did the same thing again. I don't think I hit any of them with my cannon and machine-gun fire, but I suspect they thought there was more than one fighter attacking them. The formation broke up and jettisoned their bombs in the field. I still had some ammunition left, but I couldn't find them again. A minute or so after my second attack, there was a series of terrific flashes and explosions on the ground as the jettisoned loads hit the field.'

Galia felt no great sense of elation. The strain of simply

flying the aircraft on instruments and the sheer terror of that headlong dash through the packed formation had left her drained. She was running low on fuel. She set a course for the airfield and, after submitting her written report of the engagement, flopped into bed.

Across the Volga at the Engels training base, the waiting was over for the 587th Women's Bomber Regiment and the 588th Women's Night Bomber Regiment. They too had been assigned their first tasks on different parts of the front. They said goodbye to their friends and flew off in their PE-2s and PO-2s. The mechanics and other ground crew followed in transport aircraft.

As the women flew out, about a thousand young men arrived to start their flying training. Then into this totally male stronghold dropped a ravishingly pretty woman, Valentina Petrochenkova, one of the last recruits to the women's regiments. She was nineteen and a qualified flying instructor. Like Lily Litvak, she had persuaded her local flying club in Moscow to bend the rules and allow her to start training at sixteen. In the middle of her first day as a full-time flying instructor at the club Mariupol, she had heard of the German invasion. The club was moved to an airfield on the Volga near Stalingrad, and it was there she heard about the women's air regiments.

She told me, 'Though Marina Raskova accepted me for training, the military man who was now in charge of the flying club wouldn't let me go. One of my jobs was also to train parachutists. He said that I couldn't go until I'd fulfilled a training quota of sixty men. It was frustrating [as it had been for Galina Junkovskaya] but the commander wouldn't bend an inch. I had to train them to jump from the wing of my aircraft. My sixtieth and last trainee was a young boy. We got up to the correct height over the airfield and he stepped on to the wing. He was supposed to jump off backwards and pull his ripcord. He froze completely –

wouldn't move. I shouted at him, implored him. He knew I needed that sixtieth jump to free me, but the boy was absolutely petrified. I even offered to kiss him. Didn't make a bit of difference. I had to land with him absolutely rigid on the wing.' But back on the ground she did kiss him, they went aloft again, and the next day Valentina was on her way to Engels.

The commander at Engels was not pleased at having a woman suddenly deposited with him. There was a war of survival going on and he was responsible for training several hundred young pilots and navigators. Women like this, he knew from experience, were likely to be a load of trouble. He told her that she could not remain because there was nowhere for her to sleep. The schoolhouse and all the other accommodations had been taken over by the male trainees.

Valentina told me, 'He was a senior officer, but I stuck to my guns. I spent most of a day in his office and told him that I would sleep in the men's dormitories. I didn't mind, I said – though the thought of it made me quite ill. He had to give in, in the end. What he did was to screen off the end of a large hut for me, and I had a bed behind that. You can imagine how I felt that first night walking down that dormitory past all the men's beds and pulling that curtain behind me. But it's true that there's safety in numbers, and the men were probably more embarrassed than I was.

'Once we got over that initial embarrassment, the men were wonderful to me. I can't pretend I didn't enjoy being the centre of attraction – the only woman among all these men. After three months another girl, a radio operator, arrived for training and she shared my quarters behind the screen.'

Valentina progressed easily from the advanced training on the PO-2 biplane into the closed cockpit of the Yak with its three-bladed propeller and its dramatic manoeuvrability. The base commander, a colonel, was a fighter pilot himself and actively instilled the competitive spirit. He had a points system for the best pilot on the course, and Valentina came second. She told me: 'I'm certain I would have won if he hadn't still had this lingering objection to me as a woman.'

Many senior commanders in the Red Air Force were vehemently opposed to the idea of women flying in combat. Despite the desperate situation the country was facing, they felt it was too great a gamble. In battle, after all, a man had to be confident that he could rely on his comrades. Women were a completely unknown quantity in air combat. Many men felt that the middle of a battle for a nation's very survival was not the time to start this sort of experimentation. So it was against this sort of male chauvinism that the untried women of the air regiments went to the front.

Valentina, having received her assignment to the 586th Fighter Regiment, packed her belongings into her kit bag. She had been keeping a collection of clippings from newspapers and magazines about the exploits of fighter pilots already establishing reputations at the front. The photographs showed the fliers the press had chosen to make popular heroes. The unsmiling official poses did not reveal the anguished strain of combat, the tousled hair, the red-rimmed eyes, or even that unself-conscious exultation of the warrior fresh from the kill. Nonetheless they had a haunting poignancy. Valentina knew most of them were dead.

But not Valeria Khomyakova of the 586th. Her clippings took pride of place in a separate sheaf, tied with a blue ribbon. Valentina took a deep breath. This was the sort of woman she was going to have to try to live up to in the weeks ahead: Valeria Khomyakova – the first woman in the world to shoot down an enemy aircraft in combat. Patrolling her sector of Saratov, she had broken up a formation of Junkers 88 bombers and hit one with cannon fire as she scattered them. The flames from his crippled engine had been like a beacon to her as she pursued him, diving through the blackness and hitting him with long bursts until the aircraft erupted in a great orange explosion.

On the day that Valentina Petrochenkova flew off to join the 586th, another woman was navigating her new Yak from Penza, three hundred miles south-east of Moscow. Agneea Polyazeva had been a test pilot since graduating from Moscow's Aviation Institute. She was thirty-two when Hitler invaded and she had been trying to join the women's fighter regiment ever since Marina Raskova's radio appeal. But the authorities considered her work too important to release her for the front. She told me, 'My job was to test-fly new aircraft as they came off the assembly line to make sure everything functioned properly before they were ferried to the front. I also test-flew aircraft that had been to the factory for repair after serious battle damage. I can't properly explain to you the frustration I felt. Every day, I spent hours in the sky flying every type of fighter. I had to throw them all around in all sorts of extreme manoeuvres to make sure they were airworthy. I also had to test-fire their guns against aerial targets sometimes.'

Agneea had several friends who had been able to join the women's air regiments before her. They wrote frequently from the training base at Engels telling her of their experiences. Finally she was accepted. Her training pro- gramme was an abbreviated one, due to her great experi- ence; and, like Valentina, she had an initiation period of several weeks with the experienced women, who passed on the lessons they had learned the hard way – in combat.

By the autumn of 1942, the 586th fighter regiment had moved to an airfield near Voronezh, which was a major junction for road and rail communications and also controlled crossings to the River Don. The regiment's task was to patrol an area with a radius of 100 kilometres between the rivers Don and Vorona, protecting railways,

52

stations, and bridges of strategic importance. The town had become a key point in the Germans' summer offensive in the south and was vital to the success of their campaign; but by the autumn, the Germans had failed to take it.

The survivors of these regiments have told me that they kept up their morale by concentrating their hatred on the invaders and trying to shut from their minds the possibility of defeat. This must have been a very difficult mental state to achieve, though, as the Germans seemed to be everywhere. In the Crimea, Sebastopol had fallen to the enemy and, although their part of the front was holding, it was obvious to the women that the Germans were advancing towards their objectives.

As they patrolled above the areas they protected from enemy air attack, they would watch the progress of the land battles from the enclosed cockpits of their fighters. On the days when they made little contact with the enemy in the air, it was a strangely insulated view of the desperate struggle in which they were all involved. As they wheeled several thousand feet above the patchwork of fields, villages, and country roads, the broad flow of the Volga or the Don, or the numerous smaller rivers running east to west across their area of operations, they saw the flashes of the artillery and the explosions of striking shells and watched the apparently snail-like progress of convoys of trucks and tanks and other armoured vehicles.

Sometimes they were ordered on ground attack strafing missions when the Germans had made a breakthrough in their area. It was a test of low flying and low-level navigation, flying only two or three hundred feet above the ground, following the contours and swiftly reacting to landmarks which would lead them to the enemy. Despite the red stars on their fuselages and wings, there would be the occasional racketing outburst of small-arms fire from their own troops as they swept overhead.

Then the target. The aircraft would be pulled up quickly

to around a thousand feet to identify the enemy formation, then rolled into a steep dive. They could see machine-gun, cannon, and tracer shells striking off tanks and trucks, and stitching up the banks and hedgerows a spurting line of earth and dust where frightened grey-clad figures hurled themselves. They sometimes flew through the smoke and flame of a truck exploded three seconds' flying time ahead. Fingers pressed the firing button, feet kicked at the rudder bar to keep the nose and the guns pointing straight up the convoy. Then empty road and green fields ahead. Pull the nose up and climb to the left, looking back up the convoy. Frequently through the smoke and flames a pilot could see her girlfriend's Yak, at treetop level, flickers of gunfire from the wings and nose. It was exhilarating in a way that only personal experience can properly convey. But the dominating sounds were those of their own guns and the roar of the engine on full power. The sense was still one of being once removed from the killing.

At the time, the women's fighter regiment had not yet lost one of their own in combat. But what was filtering through was the suffering of their loved ones in the occupied territories. Anastasia Kulvitz, a ground radio operator, lived under enormous personal strain. She and the other girls were still training at Engels when the first of the mass evacuations of civilians began from Leningrad across their 'lifeline', the ice road of the frozen Lake Ladoga. Her parents and young sisters were not among those refugees who had escaped; instead, they were trapped in Leningrad. By that time hundreds of thousands of civilians had already died of starvation. Was her family among them? She had no way of finding out. In a city of three million, one million were condemned to die of starvation in the 900-day siege.

Another woman, Masha Batrakova, received some letters from her father in the Ukraine which had been smuggled out through friends in the partisan network. They spoke of rape and other atrocities and of the reprisals against villages where there had been partisan activity. Agneea Polyazeva told me, 'If only the Germans had realized how much that sort of news helped us in our determination to beat them. I used to fly across our sector and look down at the fields and rivers, and I had this overwhelming feeling that this land was ours and these people were violating it, and we must kill them and throw them out.'

The breadbasket of the Soviet Union, the Ukraine, was in enemy hands along with enormous stocks of food. So, although aircrews were given some priority on rations, they frequently had to get by on one meal a day, consisting of soup and black bread. During the day they would nibble at the concentrated dark brown chocolate they carried with them in their aircraft as emergency rations. They were under no illusions – their country was fighting for its very survival, and in Leningrad their people were starving to death in the thousands. It helped them bear the hunger pangs. But when the temperature dropped to thirty and forty degrees below zero and the ice formed a film on hands clasped to blowing lips, then hunger made their demanding job a supreme effort of will. A light head and gnawing stomach pains do not aid co-ordination and concentration.

When the temperatures were that low, the women depended on the large potbellied stove that they moved with them from one airfield to another. They would take turns staying awake so that the stove was kept burning through the night. Whenever possible in warmer weather, the women would change from their uniforms and flying gear into nightgowns; but when the thermometer plummeted, they were glad to huddle under their blankets, fully dressed and, often, wearing their overcoats as well.

The standard air force pilot's uniform of baggy khaki blouse and loose trousers tucked into boots was not the most flattering of outfits. New winter flying boots lined with thick grey fur had just been issued, though, and Lily Litvak spent an evening improvising. Cutting strips of fur from her boot linings and snipping along a paper pattern of her own design, she sewed the fur around the collar of her tunic. It matched the colour of her eyes exactly, and everyone agreed it had quite transformed the uniform. The commander agreed, too; but regulations didn't provide for individual fashion sense, she said, and the whole idea was that they made everyone look the same. Besides, there was to be a visit by a senior officer the next day, and there would be an inspection.

The women already knew of the impending visit. Having formed firm friendships with each other during the training days at Engels, the three different air regiments corresponded with each other through the erratic military postal service or through the help of other pilots visiting their airfields. The night bombers and their little PO-2 biplanes were at the town of Grozny in the North Caucasus. The day bombers were at Kirshatz on the north-west front, still training in their PE-2s; soon they would be going to the Stalingrad front.

Some of these units had recently been inspected, and word had reached the fighter regiment that the officer had been appalled by the poor state of the uniforms. Fighter pilots' uniforms were in poor shape, too, and they saw the visit as an opportunity to do something about it. Galia Boordina told me, 'Normally we'd have done a lot of last minute sewing and general mending. This time we all agreed not to. We pressed our uniforms and cleaned them up, but we left the holes in the sleeves and shoulders, and several girls even made tears worse in their tunics and trousers. Aircrew and ground crews had been wearing these uniforms now for about a year and they were really getting worn out.'

The women were well aware that whatever the opposition was to the principle of women in the front line, the very men who objected most strongly were often those who could not bear to see a woman looking shabby. Within a few days of the inspection a batch of new uniforms arrived. They were the same old design, of course, but they were made of finest English wool.

The women were becoming combat veterans. With each sortie they flew, they developed almost imperceptibly another fine coating of experience. Still, there was always the unexpected – as Olga Yemshokova reminded them all on the day she was flying on a high-level sortie with her wingman and two others. As they passed up through nine thousand feet to level off at their patrol height of ten thousand feet, they switched on the oxygen supply. It gently hissed up the airline into their face masks as they flew in the slightly thinner atmosphere. The patrol was uneventful; no contact was made with any enemy aircraft. Then, fifteen minutes into the sortie, there was drama in Olga Yemshokova's cockpit.

She told me, 'I became conscious of something happening inside the flying boot on my left leg. I thought it was imagination at first and ignored it. But then there was a distinct movement. Whatever it was, it was crawling up my leg. I tugged my trousers out of the boot and a large grey mouse scrambled on to my lap. I screamed out loud.

'I know it sounds crazy – a fighter pilot frightened by a mouse – but I'd always had this fear of mice. And particularly now it was sitting on my lap looking up at me, in that tiny cockpit. I brushed it away with my gloved hand and it moved very slowly – it wasn't breathing oxygen, of course. But the next thing I knew it was crawling up my arm on to my chest. I shrieked aloud again, I could feel my flesh creeping.'

There was only one thing for a resourceful pilot to do. Olga undid the handles above her head and slid the cockpit canopy back on its runners. There was a great roaring and rushing of air; the slipstream slapped against her face, and she had to tuck her maps between her legs. Lily Litvak, who was flying above and to the right, watched in astonishment as Olga thrust her hand into the slipstream and released the tail of the flying mouse, two miles above the Don.

Lily Litvak and her close friend Katya Budanova had been flying with the 586th Fighter Regiment since they went to the front in May. Though the principal role of the women's fighter regiment was to drive off enemy bomber formations before they reached their targets, they also had a number of rather inconclusive skirmishes with the Messerschmitt 109s that sometimes escorted these bombers. Lily and Katya had not shot down any of these fighters, but their flair for individual air combat had been noted by the regimental commander, Maj. Tamara Kazarinova. It was now September 1942. In a few days' time, first Lily and then Katya would be transferred to join the men of the 73rd Fighter Regiment in the furious battles being fought in the skies over the burning city of Stalingrad.

Lily had bubbled over with excitement when she was told that she was about to be transferred. She understood that it would be a different sort of combat – she would be roaming the skies seeking out enemy fighters. It would often be single combat, but she told her friends in the regiment that she was looking forward to it more than anything in her life.

Lily wrote to her mother just before her transfer to Stalingrad:

Dearest Mamenka, I am writing this sitting in the cockpit on readiness. I'm thinking of sitting with you in our dear home. I'm eating my favourite fritters in my dreams. I often dream that I'm with you, going somewhere in a hurry, to the theatre perhaps. We look so well dressed and happy in my dream and you are so young and cheerful. I look so happy, too. May all this come true one day. Please send me a parcel when you have a moment. I need the following things – white helmet from good material, close-woven and easy to wash, if there's such a thing available. Two pairs of warm gloves and socks, toothpaste. Oh, and about ten exercise books with lines. And if you have some silk handkerchiefs, too. You know how nice it is to get things from home. Flying in the fighters with the closed cockpit isn't cold like the old PO-2s. In fact it's quite warm, since you ask. I really feel part of the Yak now – I feel we've grown up together. Plesae remember to send father's photograph next time. Your loving daughter, Lily. PS Please, Mamenka, don't address your letters to pilot Litvak. Just make it L. Litvak. The names of pilots are supposed to be a secret!

These rather breathless letters must have been a deeply moving reminder to the small woman in Nova Slobodskaya Street, Moscow, that her daughter was still very young. Lily packed her belongings into her rucksack. The only eating utensil she would take with her would be the tin mug with her name painted across it in a flourishing script. Along with the socks, gloves, and a silk handkerchief, she packed the white, fine wool helmet that had arrived a few days before. And on top of everything else she placed the pile of exercise books in which she had already begun keeping a diary of her life at the front.

Most of the others were already asleep. A draught caused the candle flame to gutter and smoke. Lily wondered if Stalingrad were quite as hellish as it was rumoured to be.

4

Night Witches – the 588th Regiment on the Southern Front

The PO-2 biplanes of the 588th Night Bomber Regiment droned through the sky towards the southern front. They flew in two loose 'V' formations led by their commander, Yevdokia Bershanskaya. It was a clear day, and from their height of five thousand feet, the women could see the yellow-green landscape of the steppes stretching below them. There was a slight tail wind, but even so their speed over the ground was just over a hundred miles per hour; the landmarks that the navigators in the open rear cockpits checked off on their maps seemed to take an interminable time to slide past under their wings.

Marina Chichnova, tucked in behind Bershanskaya's aircraft, adjusted her flying goggles where they were digging into her high cheekbones. It had been only an hour since they left the training base at Engels and set their course for the south. She recalled Marina Raskova walking up the lines of aircraft, their two-woman crews standing to attention in front of the propellers. She had made a little speech, smiling broadly as she told them that they were no longer students – they were now soldiers. She chatted briefly with each woman, and when she stepped back and returned their salutes she had bade them farewell with the words: 'Happy skies, happy skies.'

They were now less than half an hour's flying time from their operational base. Marina Chichnova's face felt numb in the cold slipstream, despite the bright sunlight. Still, the distinctive *pop-pop-popping* of the five-cylinder engine gave a feeling of familiarity and security. The landscape below looking tranquil. It was hard to believe there was a war going on. Marina turned around to smile at her navigator,

Olga, and said over the intercom, 'Isn't this just marvellous.' Olga smiled her acknowledgement.

At that moment, their little aircraft bucked violently and a wing dropped in the backwash of turbulence from three fighters that were diving through their formation. The sound of fighter engines bellowed in their ears as they swept past, terrifyingly close. Marina Chichnova told me, 'We scattered in all directions. I felt weak with fear. How could we have been so slack? How could we fly along in a trance when we knew that the Germans still had air superiority and that their fighters were roaming all over the area? Instinct and training took over and I put the nose straight down and dived at the earth below, jinking and weaving at the same time to make myself as difficult a target as possible. I shouted to Olga to forget about navigation, to keep her head turned to the rear for the enemy.'

She saw three other PO-2s diving straight down too. Then she was concentrating on her flying. The wind rushed through the struts and wires that braced the frail wings. Marina did not dare look at the air speed indicator, but she was sure she was exceeding the permitted speed in the dive. Would the wings suddenly and without warning peel off and flutter away? At that moment she truly did not care.

The altimeter read one thousand feet, and she hauled back on the stick to recover from the headlong dash towards the ground. The little aeroplane levelled out at around four hundred feet and, with the engine still roaring on full power, Marina eased the stick forward again. Down, down, down. Three hundred feet, two hundred feet. Horses in a field galloped in terror before her as she dropped still lower.

She turned the aircraft to the right to survey the area to her rear. The altimeter read one hundred feet. She tilted the nose gently downward yet again and the biplane slid down to hedge height as she came out of her turn. The long grasses of a meadow were beaten flat under the downwash of the propeller as the little bomber rode the contours of the undulating landscape, hugging the earth and depending on the green-and-brown camouflage of its fuselage to escape the fighters. It was flying that demanded the utmost concentration.

'Where, where?' cried Marina.

'At five o'clock – two of them.'

Marina hauled the PO-2 around to the right, turning towards her attackers. She had a blurred impression of their shapes as the fighters with their massively superior speed overshot the almost stationary biplane. Marina told me, 'It was all happening so quickly that I could not have told you what fighter types they were. I was convinced, though, that it was a matter of life or death. I knew they'd be pulling up from that attack, looking for me and diving down again. We didn't even have a single machine gun at that stage of the war, and it was a terrible naked sort of feeling, waiting to be shot at. I couldn't understand why I hadn't heard any gunfire on that pass or on the one that had broken up our formation. But I didn't ponder too long on that. I had to do something to keep us alive.'

A birch forest loomed ahead. Marina pulled the stick back and climbed around fifty feet. She had already realized a basic fact of survival that was to stand the PO-2 pilots in good stead when they were attacked by enemy fighters: though their aged trainers were slow, they were exceedingly manoeuvrable. The two characteristics combined were to make the PO-2 virtually attack-proof in daytime, provided they were at very low level and – of vital importance – that they saw the enemy before he saw them. Then they could turn the fighter's high speed to their advantage.

Marina quickly saw what she was looking for. A quarter of a mile ahead in the forest was a firebreak. It was just twenty yards or so wide, but that was more than enough for her purposes. She maintained her height and dropped the

PO-2 down neatly into the firebreak, like a coin into a slot. The tops of the mature trees flashed past forty feet above the aeroplane as Marina concentrated all her flying skills on keeping it pointing straight down the middle of the avenue that had become their escape route. Olga's voice was hoarse in the pilot's ear: 'I hope you know what you're doing, Marina.'

'So do I,' came the reply.

Olga looked over her shoulder. Boring down the firebreak behind them came two other PO-2s, the leading aircraft's wings rocking a little in their slipstream. The other aircraft was too close behind them, but the pilot now had little choice but to struggle through; the only way she could increase the distance would have been to reduce power, and that would have meant sinking and then crashing on to the forest floor.

Olga looked at the helmeted head in front of her. The PO-2, being a trainer, had a complete duplicate set of instruments and controls in the rear cockpit where she sat. She carefully rested her feet on the rudder pedals and placed the tips of her fingers on the control column between her legs. For a few seconds she shared the awful responsibility of her friend Marina, the pilot. The rudder pedals were in perpetual movement, a continuous series of tiny corrective movements in conjunction with the stick being twitched back and forward and from side to side as Marina kept the wings level and the nose pointing straight up an imaginary centre line of the firebreak.

Just as gently, fearful of applying the slightest pressure that might upset Marina's corrective measures, Olga lifted her hands and feet away from the controls. She looked up at the narrow causeway of blue where the birches almost seemed to touch. The enemy fighters screamed across the patch of blue at treetop height, searching against the skyline for a glimpse of their quarry. The women flew on for a full minute, then Marina told Olga, 'I've had enough

63

of this. I'm going up again.' They lifted out of the firebreak, above the trees. The sky was clear. They were safe. Olga spotted a landmark and gave Marina a course for base. On the way, as they straggled back into some kind of formation, they counted the other aircraft. They were all accounted for.

Marina Chichnova told me, 'We landed and immediately reported to Bershanskaya. None of us could understand why the enemy fighters had not actually fired their guns at us. If they'd done so on their very first pass, they would have got several of us for sure. Major Bershanskaya had got back several minutes before the rest of us. She looked distinctly uncomfortable, and when I started to make my report to her about the evasion of the enemy, she cut me short. It was hardly surprising in the circumstances.'

The women of the 588th could not have been off to a worse start in their efforts to convince everyone they were equal to the men at the front. The fighters that had dived on them had been Russian planes sent to escort them to their airfield. They had been unable to resist the temptation to give the women a bit of a scare, particularly as the regiment had not even seen them coming. Major Bershanskaya had recognized the fighters, as had several other women, but the majority had panicked and broken formation. By their raw experience, they had given some very convenient ammunition to those who felt the front was no place for women.

The next day the commander of the bomber division to which the regiment was attached arrived and summoned Yevdokia Bershanskaya into an hour-long conference. Yevdokia told me: 'First of all lined up in front of our aircraft, standing stiffly at attention. He inspected the regiment without saying a word. We knew that people were laughing at us over what had happened, and the girls all looked very serious. The divisional commander looked serious, too. He took me aside and told me that he didn't think we were ready for combat yet. I protested, but it was no good. He said we would be introduced into combat gradually if everything went well, but that on our showing so far, things didn't look very promising. I didn't want to tell the girls the truth – their morale had taken a knock anyway. So I told them they'd be kept away from the main action for a week or two, just like any other unit new to the front. But I knew they didn't believe me.'

Marina Chichnova told me, 'We all knew the real reason, and it hurt our pride. After all that intensive training at Engels and all the anticipation, it was a terrible anticlimax. But we tried not to let it show to the men who were sharing our airfield.' For the next two weeks, the women flew day and night training exercises, familiarizing themselves with the terrain and gaining confidence in themselves again. In their moments of spare time they studied aircraft recognition manuals, showing German and Soviet aircraft from different angles and in silhouette. It was not that they had not known their aircraft types before that humiliating experience of the other day; it had simply been a case of straightforward panic obliterating training. They were all determined it would not happen again.

The Luftwaffe were frequently amazed at the relatively rude facilities out of which the Red Air Force operated. From servicing and general maintenance facilities to runways and radio communications, the Germans were generally far more sophisticated technically. But the fact that the Soviets were able to function at this primitive level and yet wage modern war was to prove an increasingly important asset to them as the conflict progressed.

Though the women of the night bomber regiment often lived in underground bunkers, as did their counterparts in the other two women's regiments, their first home on the southern front would merely have confirmed the worst opinions of the German invaders. It was a cowshed. Marina Chichnova told me: 'Some of the girls felt at first that it was just another humiliation being heaped on us, but the truth was that there simply weren't any accommodations for us at the airfield itself, and they did try to keep us segregated from the men as far as living quarters were concerned. It was a large cowshed on a farm close to the airfield. There weren't any cows in it, of course, and most of the traces of the previous occupants had been removed, but the smell was pretty vile. We got cans of disinfectant and lots of hot water and scrubbed and scrubbed until it was fit to sleep in. But we never quite got rid of that smell.' The women's accommodations became the butt of another joke among the flying units in the area: some wag dubbed it 'The Inn of the Flying Cow'.

On 8 June, 1942, the women were given their first combat mission. The target was a local headquarters of a German division near Voroshilovgrad. Only three aircraft were to fly the mission. Yevdokia Bershanskaya herself would fly the lead aircraft; the commander of one of the squadrons, Luba Olkovskaya, and her navigator Vera Tarasova would take off two minutes later, followed by Anya Amosova in the third PO-2. They were the regiment's most experienced crews.

Yevdokia Bershanskaya told me, 'We were all very tense. Not just we six who were flying the mission, but all the other girls too. It was the test we had all been waiting for. Our intelligence told us that this target was only lightly defended by anti-aircraft guns, but we would have to navigate very precisely or we could stray over some heavily defended areas.'

There were four little bomb racks under the lower of the two fabric-and-wood wings. They would be taking off with a maximum load of around eight hundred pounds – tiny by present-day standards and even by the standards of more conventional bombers of the time, but a remarkable load for a little veteran trainer aircraft pressed into service as a bomber.

The aircraft taxied out to the end of the grass runway

and, one after the other, at the agreed time intervals, they trundled down the field. Despite their loads of bombs and fuel tanks, the PO-2s staggered into the air after only five hundred feet of take-off run. The rest of the regiment – pilots, navigators, and ground crew – stood at the end of the runway listening to the popping sound of their friends' aircraft fading into the balmy night.

Guided by her navigator and using her stopwatch and map, Major Bershanskaya approached the target at a height of just over three thousand feet, then cut her engine and glided down through the darkness. The wind rushed through the struts and she concentrated on her instruments, keeping on the compass heading her navigator had given her. The navigator thrust her arm over the edge of the open cockpit and dropped two parachute flares into the slipstream. They ignited and, suspended from their little parachutes, cast a fierce incandescent light over the landscape. They were right over the target.

Yevdokia Bershanskaya told me, 'I felt a fantastic sense of achievement. I could clearly see the buildings and I knew that if I hit the target then Luba, behind me, would be able to aim at my fires that I started. The Germans hadn't heard me coming because of the gliding approach, but now the searchlights came on and the flak started coming up. I realized, as I got more experienced, that this was indeed light opposition, but on that first night it seemed pretty terrifying to me. I didn't want to spoil my aim so I just flew straight on through the explosions until I was right over the target. The aeroplane bucked in the blast from some of the explosions, but we kept on flying. Then I yanked the release wire and dived away from the searchlights and steered for home. I saw flames coming from one of the buildings and thought that Luba would have a beacon to aim for now.'

Back on the airfield, the rest of the regiment was waiting for their friends to return. Marina Chichnova told me, 'We heard the first aircraft coming back. It landed and taxied up to dispersal. Then out of the gloom we saw Yevdokia Bershanskaya's familiar long-legged stride. We rushed up and hugged her. Yes, she said, she'd hit the target; and with the fires that that had started, she was sure the other two would hit it, too. We were all terribly excited. This was really going to show the men what we were made of.'

Anya Amosova and her navigator landed fiteen minutes later. The first twinges of unease spread through the waiting groups. Luba and Vera should have returned before them. But perhaps they had had some difficulty in navigating back. There was no immediate cause for concern, they assured themselves. The women had enough fuel for another hour's flying.

But an hour passed, and the feeling of dread replaced the initial euphoria they had felt when their commander had landed. The warmth of the evening had given way to a damp chill. Still the women huddled together, talking quietly and trying vainly to convince each other that all would be well. After two hours, Yevdokia Bershanskaya gently persuaded them there was little point in waiting there on the airfield. No doubt Luba and Vera had made a forced landing with some mechanical trouble and would be back with them the following day. No one believed her, and she did not believe it herself. From the front line, about twelve miles away, the flashes of a heavy artillery barrage stabbed the night sky in a ripple of violent light. A light summer fog was beginning to roll across the airfield as the women trudged back towards their cowshed.

It was not until after the war that the women discovered exactly how their friends had died, but they had been correct in their fears about navigational error. The lone PO-2 had been bracketed by searchlights, and the heavy flak had downed them behind German lines. In the morning, Russian villagers had found them before the German patrols reached the crashed aircraft. The plane was largely intact, but the women must have been dying even before the crash landing. Still strapped in their cockpits, they had bled to death from the awful gaping wounds caused by the shrapnel that had torn through the thin fabric surrounding their cockpits.

The Germans arrived and had taken their revolvers, their maps, and the few personal papers they had carried with them in their flying suits (though the fliers were ordered when flying over enemy territory not to carry anything that might identify their units). The Germans had dragged the bodies from the cockpits and left them lying there when they drove off again. The villagers bathed the blood from the faces of these two friends and buried them on the edge of their village.

Marina Chichnova told me, 'When you lose two dear friends like that, you wish you hadn't sometimes behaved in such a petty way. Luba was a lieutenant and sometimes she would chide some of the more untidy girls about the state of their beds. Some of the girls thought that she was unnecessarily strict about that, and there was a little resentment. It didn't seem to matter now. The picture I shall always carry in my mind is of Luba milking a cow at the farm to which our cowshed belonged before she flew that last mission and joking about the Flying Cow as she handed the warm milk round to us.'

Their first combat mission and two women had gone. Was it to be like this every time? Morale was in danger of collapsing completely. Major Bershanskaya spoke to divisional headquarters, and they agreed: the entire regiment would fly against the Germans that night.

All twenty aircraft took off and bombed a railway junction and artillery battery. They had been given a very lightly defended target, there were no navigational errors, and all returned safely to base. The crisis of self-confidence was passing, and a few missions later they were in the thick of the air battles on an equal footing with the men.

That summer Marina Chichnova was promoted from

sergeant to second lieutenant. She confided her fears to Major Bershanskaya, who told me, 'Marina was very worried about the promotion. She felt that several of the girls were more experienced and she felt very uneasy about being placed over them. She didn't want to spoil any friendships. And she didn't think she had enough self-confidence to do the job. But I knew she was a natural leader and I told her that a bit of self-doubt was no bad thing.'

Nadia Popova, one of Marina's closest friends, summed up the problems of resolving very close personal friendships with the inevitable promotion of some women over others: 'The biggest problem for most of us was to remember to call our friends of senior rank by their title and not their Christian names if male officers were around. I don't think any of us would have wished to embarrass our friends of senior rank by ever being awkward when they wanted us to do something. But that sort of situation hardly ever arose. We were all so committed to what we were doing that there wasn't any need for anyone to pull rank. When you have a group of young people as dedicated as we were, then these things tend to resolve themselves. If any one girl had become difficult we'd all have jumped on her.'

Marina Chichnova's promotion coincided with one of the regular examinations of the pilots' basic skills by one of the regiment's most experienced older pilots. Having this monitor in the rear seat acting as both navigator and examiner put considerable pressure on the young pilots, but they had little choice in the matter. Still, she was a friendly woman, and her experience might be very useful on night combat missions.

Marina's target was a railway station. She followed her navigator's calm, clear instructions to the target, making a course correction every now and then in response to the orders carefully enunciated in her headphones. Then the flares were released over the target. Searchlights immediately bathed them in a glare that blinded the pilot, and the fiercest flak Marina had yet experienced exploded all around the aircraft.

She told me, 'I was completely disorientated. I couldn't see a thing. I heard pieces of shrapnel richocheting off the engine, and the explosions around the aircraft were so loud I thought they would burst my eardrums. I yanked the bomb release and dived and turned to the right. We were still in the beams of several searchlights, but as the aircraft turned in the dive my eyes where shielded for a moment and I managed to look at my instruments, and she shouted instructions to me on which way to turn until finally we twisted out of the lights. But the aircraft had been badly damaged. The engine was running rough, and I could hear the loose pieces of fabric flapping in the slipstream where the flak had pierced it. I cringed every time a piece of shrapnel whizzed off the engine for fear that it would strike the fuel tank above my head.'

They navigated back to the airfield, and Marina flew around it in a wide sweep at a height of five hundred feet until she picked up the line of landing lights angled to be invisible to enemy intruders approaching at normal bombing heights. The older woman in the rear waited until the fixed undercarriage of the PO-2 had thumped down on the grass and Marina had pulled the throttle lever back before she said with mock gravity, 'I think your flying is up to standard, Lieutenant Chichnova.'

The thrust of the German summer offensive of 1942 was gathering momentum. Extracts from the regimental log of the night bomber regiment show the extent of their role as the Soviet forces were pushed back.

11 July – Railway station destroyed and fuel tankers blown up in a great explosion after four attacks.

25 July – Helped destroy crossing of the River Don.

26 July – Flew 47 sorties, destroyed motorized unit and personnel trying to cross Don.

27 July – Entire regiment again flew, destroyed Don crossing and caught German troops attempting to cross in boats and rafts.

As summer drew into autumn, the women were sometimes flying up to ten sorties a night each. Frequently their targets were less than ten miles away; between sorties, pilots and navigators would often remain in the cockpits, their helmets in their laps, their heads lolling back with tiredness. It was like a shuttle service – back and forth from early evening to the first light of dawn, hitting at the same targets all night long. The nights were frequently very warm, and when they returned from a night's sortie the women often would wrap themselves in blankets and fall into an exhausted sleep under the wings of their aircraft.

It was no less exhausting for the ground crews who slaved for hours on end, refuelling and hanging bombs from the racks beneath the wings. During the daytime, these ground units would often drive to some convenient field close to the front line – the PO-2 could operate from the roughest strips – and they would stock these sites with fuel and bombs. At nightfall the aircrews would fly in and await orders; from these sites, their flight time to the target was often very brief.

Hooded flares guided the little bombers down the strip; in the woods and hedgerows occasionally could be seen the glow from a cigarette of one of the soldiers guarding the strip. Sometimes the women would be wakened from their naps in the cockpits by the clattering outburst of small-arms fire from quite close by as their forces engaged an enemy patrol. Aircraft continued to take off and land, but the muzzle flashes from the ground did nothing to aid the concentration of the young women attempting to land, always tired and sometimes wounded.

With their distinctive *popping* engine sound, the PO-2s came to be dreaded by every German soldier who served on the south-eastern front. Particularly at times when the Germans were advancing – and on some days in the summer of 1942 the infantry was required to cover thirty miles on foot – their rest at night was vitally important. The PO-2s denied it to them. Subjected as they were to almost uninterrupted combat, the Germans found the psychological impact of the night-long harassment almost too much to endure. They have since disputed the effects of the PO-2 night bombing in terms of physical damage, but they found the effect on morale devastating. Troops nicknamed the aircraft the 'sewing machine' and the 'duty sergeant', and the pilots were dubbed 'the night witches'. Troops already exhausted after a day's march were obliged to hack deep trenches for shelter and take great care with any lights that might help guide the little bombers on to their position.

The Germans found, though, that the fliers' tactics played into the hands of their anti-aircraft defences. The sound of the engine could be heard a long way off, even though the pilots switched off to glide into the attack. The flames from the engine exhausts were also clearly visible from a long distance. And, most dangerously for the PO-2 pilots, they all tended to follow the same flight path, one after the other. This gave the searchlight and anti-aircraft batteries an opportunity to set up co-ordinated attacks. During the day the German flak batteries would be moved to potential target areas and installed in ferocious depth, to lie in wait for the night raiders.

With a reckless disregard for their own skins, the women devised a counter to this tactic. Nadia Popova explained, 'We started to fly in pairs. I flew an attack on a river crossing with my friend Marina Chichnova. I was to draw the enemy fire and Marina was to make the first attack.' They flew up the line of the river at three thousand feet. The half moon sparkled faintly on the river surface as the clouds parted. Nadia left her engine on full power and pushed the nose of the aircraft down into a dive. The bridge was just visible, a vague outline against the river surface. Marina's attack would begin when the guns opened up on her friend. She cut her engine and went into a slow descending curve across the riverbank.

Marina told me, 'It wasn't a nice feeling knowing that your friend was inviting the enemy to shoot her down. They must have heard her very clearly, and I could see the flames from her exhaust pipes as she dived away from me. But it was a full thirty seconds before the firing started.'

Nadia said, 'Wide, solid looking beams of light were cutting through the sky from several directions, trying to trap me in one great pool of light. One of them swept right across the nose of my aircraft, but before he could track back I had gone into a hard diving turn and they lost me. The anti-aircraft fire was intense. I could hear pieces of shrapnel tearing through the wings. Then I saw the flares dropping from Marina's aircraft, and a few seconds later her bombs exploded near the bridge. I climbed away from the river and then glided down to attack the bridge while Marina, her engine switched on, drew the enemy fire. It was only the exceptional agility of our aircraft that kept us alive using that technique. But it worked.'

Of course it did not work all the time. Pilot Nina Raspova's aircraft took some severe hits from enemy ground fire while acting as decoy several nights later. Both pilot and navigator had been badly cut by red-hot shrapnel splinters and were losing blood. Shrapnel had also pierced the gas tank – without exploding it, amazingly – and the engine was spluttering and dying from the interrupted flow of fuel from the gravity tank. Nina was losing height and preparing to ditch the crippled aircraft in the middle of the river when the engine sputtered into life again briefly and limped to the opposite bank before coming to a grinding halt on its smashed undercarriage.

Nina was fairly certain that she had landed near a Russian bridgehead, but there was intense probing activity from German patrols across the river. As the engine had come to life over the opposite bank, she had heard the enemy shouting a few feet below them. The guttural German accents floated up quite clearly through the creaking sound from the splintered and weakened wing spars of the PO-2. There had been a brief burst of automatic fire, then silence.

The women felt weak from loss of blood. An agonizing pain was beginning to throb through Nina's thigh and her torn overalls felt sticky and wet. The stench of gasoline was overwhelming; it was dripping steadily from the shattered fuel tank. The women unfastened their harnesses, gathered their maps, and struggled clear of the cockpits. One of the wings of their PO-2 had crumpled on impact halfway along its length. The fuselage was peppered with gaping holes. It would never fly again.

A flare went up from the German side of the river and heavy firing started immediately, first from the enemy and then from their own lines, four hundred yards behind them. They hobbled a few yards from the downed aircraft and flung themselves into a slight hollow in the damp ground. Nina turned her head to the left and looked through splayed fingers towards the German side of the river. Several machine guns were firing, and there was an almost continuous rattle of dozens of light automatic weapons and rifles. The flashes could be seen clearly even in the bright glare of the flare. The heavy machine guns were firing in sustained bursts of up to ten seconds. It was almost hypnotic to listen to the rattle and watch the lines of tracer bullets lancing through the air, sometimes crisscrossing tracers from the Russian fire.

Hadn't their own troops seen them? They did not dare signal. Every few seconds a burst of high velocity bullets would drum through the earth near them with a vicious dull *thwacking* sound. The German fire was ripping through the remains of the PO-2 fabric. The women had got out just in time. There was a sudden violent explosion as the aircraft's remaining fuel ignited. Earth and small pieces of fuselage rained down on top of them. Whether the Germans then assumed they had finished off the 'night witches', the women would never know; but just as suddenly as it had started, the firing from the German line stopped. The PO-2 had burned itself out. There was a sound of running feet from their right, and someone with a strong Ukrainian accent challenged them to identify themselves. They were safe.

While the 588th Night Bomber Regiment was fighting in combat in their PO-2s, the 'plywood-and-string' trainer was being used elsewhere in clandestine operations. By day and by night, pilots of special air regiments like the Long Range Air Regiment flew highly dangerous and daring missions to supply the partisan units who were operating in the German rear in the vast forests and in areas like the Pripet marshes. One of the outstanding pilots of this regiment was the legendary Valentina Grizudobova, one of the heroines of the epic prewar flight with Marina Raskova.

The PO-2 was ideally suited for this sort of mission. It could land and take off in very short distances and on rough unprepared strips, and in winter it could land on skis. The PO-2s were even fitted with ingenious plywood tubes on the wings which could be used to transport key personnel and even evacuate the wounded.

Pilots like Valentina Grizudobova kept the partisans supplied with rations, weapons, ammunition, and medical supplies. It was one of the biggest success stories of the Russian Air Force. The partisans, who were almost wholly dependent on the PO-2s for orders and information as well as vital supplies, were a major problem to the Germans. They achieved big successes in destroying airfields, bridges, and convoys; they tied up large forces in attempted countermeasures; and they killed large numbers of German troops.

The pilots on the partisan PO-2s found night navigation behind enemy lines extremely difficult, but they were helped by prearranged light signals along the route across the dense forests. The landing areas, hacked out of the forests, were identified by lanterns or straw fires, lit in a prearranged code sequence arranged by radio. The Germans made desperate efforts to capture the PO-2s by luring them to false airfields after discovering the codes; in one night, six aircraft in one squadron were trapped this way. The Germans flew reconnaissance missions over the vast areas infested by the partisans, seeking their airdrop and landing fields. Eventually they even formed a special wing of one hundred antipartisan aircraft. But their efforts were largely unsuccessful, and the PO-2s continued on their vital missions.

When thick snow made night landing impossible, Valentina Grizudobova used to specialize in delivering her supplies come what may. She would fly very slowly over the drop site and, often without parachutes attached, the supplies would be dropped in their containers from just a few feet. What must have tested the nerve of her strongest passengers was when she flew low and slow over the snowdrifts and instructed them to slide themselves out of their plywood tubes, without parachutes, into the drifts. She would reassure her human cargoes that no one had suffered worse than a shaking – yet. It was literally cold comfort.

The PO-2s were also used as courier aircraft for important personnel at the front who needed to get from one point to another quickly. Marina Chichnova landed a daytime assignment like that. She strapped into the rear cockpit a distinctly nervous looking army colonel. She was simply told to deliver him to a village near the front. He was in full combat gear, with a revolver at his waist and a submachine gun on his lap. As she started up the motor and taxied out to the runway, he pulled tight the chinstrap of his infantryman's steel helmet and pulled it low over his forehead. He also had a map case, and Marina assumed he was going to take command of a unit near the village – perhaps, she thought, he was relieving someone else or was taking over from someone who had been killed in action. But he was not in a talkative mood.

It was only twenty minutes' flying time to the village, and it was not a difficult navigational problem. What was going to be tricky was finding somewhere to land, as there was no recognized airstrip near the settlement. Marina circled the village, checking the wind direction and looking for a suitable field. Because of the intense enemy fighter activity, she had flown to the village at a height of only three hundred feet; the dirty grey-green camouflage made the PO-2 very difficult to spot from above on such an overcast day.

The village was badly damaged from heavy shelling. In the ruins of the buildings on the main street she saw the upturned faces of a large number of Russian soldiers – waiting, she assumed, for their new commanding officer to descend upon them. She craned her neck back in a routine sweep of the sky around her. A Messerschmitt 109 was bearing down on her, and she saw the winking flames along its wing edge as the guns began to fire. She kicked hard on the rudder pedal with her left foot and at the same time banged the stick across to the right. The PO-2 sideslipped sharply, skidding down and away, and the German bullets ripped noisily though the fabric of her right upper wing.

She was down to a hundred feet. She straightened the wings and quickly took her bearings. Straight ahead and half a mile away, the 109 was standing on its tail, zooming straight up in a high-speed climb. It would be curving back towards her in a moment, she knew. She must escape. She was flying diagonally across the village towards the main street. She dropped lower and slid the aircraft neatly over the rim of a ruined building. She was now flying straight down the main street, her wheels almost brushing the surface. The colonel had looked nervous before they took off; she wondered for an instant how he was looking at the moment. A hundred yards ahead, at the centre of the village, the road split into a T junction. The walls of the adjacent buildings were still intact.

At rooftop height the Messerschmitt pilot was screeching towards her. He was holding his fire for when she pulled up the nose of her aircraft to clear the line of buildings ahead. But she didn't. As she reached the T junction, she pulled the nose up and at the same time tipped the little aircraft on to its wingtip – executing a smart right turn.

She was now completely masked by the line of buildings, and the German screamed harmlessly overhead. She straightened out of the turn, eased back on the throttle, and put the aircraft down on the road. It trundled to a halt within fifty yards and the Colonel, without waiting for instructions, leapt ashen-faced from the rear cockpit.

Marina had been too busy out-thinking her enemy to feel frightened. Now she suddenly realized that if the German made an attack at right angles to his last one, he would have her, sitting defenceless on the ground. Take-off now could be suicidal. She left the engine ticking over and ran from the aircraft into an empty house. She told me, 'I really thought I was going to lose my aeroplane. I heard the sound of a fighter engine again and I cringed, waiting for the sound of the German bullets ripping through my little plane. But the gunfire when it came was from two Yaks. They swept across the village very low, in furious pursuit of the German.' There was no sign of the colonel. Marina got into the aircraft, let her heartbeat return to normal, and took off down the street.

The women of the 588th Night Bomber Regiment were now in the North Caucasus, helping to stop the German thrust south towards the Caspian and the vital Russian oilfields around Baku. The nights at the 'Inn of the Flying Cow' were behind them, and for some time they were to be billeted with local families. Apart from those homes with old grandparents, most of the households had no men; the husbands, fathers, and older brothers were all at the front. Returning from their night missions, the fliers would either march or be driven in a truck to their various temporary homes to sleep. After what they had put up with in the preceding months, these simple peasant homes seemed like the promised land.

Nadia Popova told me, 'Several of us shared a room, and often we had to sleep on mattresses on the floor. But the families kept the rooms spotlessly clean. They were desperately poor, and of course food was in short supply. We gave them things like chocolate, and they treated us like their own daughters. They treated us with love and we loved them in return.

'The girls found it very moving. Every day when they woke up, there would be the fragrance of freshly picked flowers standing in a stone jar on the table beside the window. They were simple homes, without electricity, running water, or inside sanitation. Many had tin roofs, not tiles, and a number still had the traditional hard earthen floor of the peasant family.

'The mothers could never quite come to terms with the fact that these young women – most of them scarcely older than their own daughters – were really fighting in the savage war that seemed to be rolling inexorably towards them. When the girls washed their hair, the mothers would comb it and brush it for them, and the girls would talk to them about their hopes and fears as they would have done with their own mothers in another time and another place.'

Men's air regiments were frequently based on the same airfield and, although they needed no encouragement, it did give the women an added incentive to look as feminine as possible. They would smear their lips with the lightest touch of lipstick before they arrived at the airfield. It was strictly against regulations, of course, but Major Bershanskaya and the other senior officers ordered them to wipe it off only if there was to be an inspection by a male officer.

Under their leather flying helmets, they wore close-fitting white silk helmets. In their billets in the evenings, the women would dye the silk in a blaze of different colours, using herbs and berries collected by the families they lived with. Often the young daughters of the house would steal into the fliers' rooms and sit on the ends of their beds and mattresses to listen with wide eyes as the pilots and navigators told them of their experiences. They told them only of the excitement and the exultation of flight, of warm night skies and balmy slipstreams, and the thrill and satisfaction of their responsive flying machines. They told the children nothing of the fear which made them vomit or the pain of the wounds which made them scream out loud.

Nadia Popova was reported missing on 2 August, 1942. Her friends saw her PO-2 spiral down in flames during a bombing strike near the town of Maykop in the North Caucasus. After several anxious days, her friends resigned themselves to the fact that the vivacious Nadia and her navigator were both dead.

What had happened, Nadia told me, was 'the thing every crew dreaded – the fuel tank set on fire by flak. We were under a thousand feet when it happened, bombing from low level, and I managed to land, more by luck than good judgement, in a large field. The whole upper wing was alight. But at least we were on our side of the lines.' They walked until daylight and then joined a main road. Normally just wide enough for two cars to pass in opposite directions, the road was choked with people and vehicles, soldiers and civilians, women, children, and farm animals. Nadia had flown over such scenes before but she had never been part of one.

A column of T34 tanks was clanking up the road towards

the front, raising an enormous cloud of dust. Nadia thought to herself that they would make a very obvious target to any aerial reconnaissance. Without slackening speed, the leading tank jerked sideways, thumping one set of tracks in the shallow ditch, and swept on at around twenty miles per hour. Sitting on the sides and rear of the tanks were infantrymen with steel helmets, bayonets fixed to their rifles, and blankets tied diagonally across their shoulders. To the side of the tank column and stretched out behind apparently endlessly came more troops.

In the opposite direction streamed the refugees: pathetic family groups clutching cardboard suitcases and mothers with crying babies in their arms, stumbling through the dust and heat and the choking blue exhaust fumes of the tank engines. Some pushed handcarts filled with tables, chairs, and bundles of clothes – all that could be snatched from abandoned homes before the arrival of the dreaded German invaders. The roadside was littered with possessions dropped by the countless refugees who had fled before them – letters, children's books, ornaments, and treasured family photographs, the smiling faces trampled underfoot and shredded in the armoured tracks of a weapon of war.

It was a shocking experience for Nadia, and it seemed to her quite literally hellish. She told me, 'I had been fighting this war for several months now, but stumbling down that road, carried along by these frightened people, I realized for the first time what it was really all about. At least I had a chance to hit back at the Germans. What could these women and children and old men do?'

Then the Stukas came. Nadia had heard stories of the sound of these German dive bombers; now she was to experience it herself. She looked up and saw the gull-wing shapes of the German aircraft roll on their backs one by one from their formation and plummet straight down in a vertical dive, pointing at the tank column. The sound was dreadful. As the bombers' speed increased, the slipstream howled through the 'screamers' attached to the under-carriage legs. The howling grew to a crescendo. It was terrifying. Then the bombs fell from the bellies of the aircraft as they followed each other down the dive.

Nadia flung herself into a field. She lay several yards from the roadside, her face pressed into the long grass, her hands covering her ears. This was what the weary German troops went through night after night from her and her friends.

Each aircraft seemed to drop two bombs. The explosions seemed enormous. She heard screams from the road and somewhere a child was wailing. The howling of the aircraft reached an almost unbearable pitch, then died away as another Stuka pulled up from his dive. After three or four seconds, his two bombs struck. The troops on the roadside were blazing away with everything they had, but it had no effect on the raiders.

It was all over in five minutes. Nadia picked herself up and walked through the long grass to the road. The two leading tanks were burning furiously, and troops were dragging a body from the turret of the first one. Ammuni-tion was exploding in the tanks, and Nadia ducked instinctively as she wandered, dazed, down the road. She stepped around the bodies of several soldiers. One had lost his head, and the blood was still seeping from the shattered neck and welling over his tunic on to the dust of the road.

The bombs that killed these men had missed the tanks and blown enormous craters in the road and in the fields opposite. Above the sound of the exploding ammunition and the harsh shouting of orders, she heard again the wailing of a child. A boy of about seven years was tugging and pulling at a woman lying face down in the ditch. Her legs were sprawled apart like a broken doll; and as the child kneeled, pulling at the light cotton dress, an old man – his grandfather, Nadia thought – gently picked him up and turned him away from the figure on the ground. Nadia looked around her, still dazed. There was a haze of dust. She had lost contact with her navigator sometime in the last few minutes. It was to be two weeks before they met again.

Farther down the road a young nurse was bandaging the wounded. Nadia knelt beside her to help, holding the roughened, dirty hand of a middle-aged soldier as the nurse applied a tourniquet to his leg. It was very hot and Nadia rolled up the sleeves of her flying overalls. The nurse was interested to learn that Nadia was a pilot who had been shot down. She led her to a shattered tree stump where a young man was sitting, eating some black bread.

He had dark hair and blue eyes, and when he stood up to shake hands with her he was slightly taller. His name, he said, was Simon Harlamov, and he was a fighter pilot. A cotton bandage obscured the middle portion of his face and was heavily padded around the nose. 'I only ask you one thing,' he said to Nadia. 'Try not to make me laugh. It makes my face hurt.' Nadia decided not to embarrass him by asking what his injury was. She had learned it was best to leave it to the injured person to talk about it if he wished. She could only see his forehead, eyes, and mouth, but she decided he had a very attractive voice.

She told me, 'Although I hadn't even seen his face, I was very attracted to him from that first moment. I wouldn't have believed it possible, but there it was, happening to me.' For days they were both swept along in the retreat from the advancing Germans. Communications were chaotic; Nadia and her navigator tried constantly to contact their regiment, but it was impossible. Besides, there was no possibility of getting transport at that stage to join them. Nadia wanted to get back in the air again and she knew her friends would be desperately worried, but there was no way to let them know she was still alive.

At night the soldiers, women, and children were all crowded into any shelter they could find. It was not a time for being alone. People slept in barns, schoolhouses, and even under trucks. Nadia and Simon had each been given a blanket by the soldiers, and at night they would lie close to each other in the darkness while Nadia entertained him by singing in a whispered voice every verse of every song she could remember.

The bond between the two young pilots grew closer as the days went by, but both were becoming increasingly anxious about reporting back to their units. Finally, after two weeks, the retreat halted; at the local headquarters they each made contact with their regiments, and Nadia met up again with her navigator. It was to be the parting of the ways. Neither Nadia nor Simon knew if they would see each other again. Nadia squeezed Simon's hand and leaned over, carefully tilting her head to avoid brushing against his bandaged face, and kissed him on the chin. Then she and her navigator hitched a ride to the new airfield to which their regiment had pulled back during the retreat.

Nadia told me, 'We had promised to write to each other. He had told me how much he liked me. But letters could take such a long time. I still didn't know what he looked like, and as the truck jolted along the road to our airfield I realized that he had still not told me what his injury was. I felt quite weak in my stomach as the thought occurred to me for the first time – perhaps he had been embarrassed to talk about his injury because he had lost his nose completely in the crash. If he were horribly disfigured like that, would it make any difference to the way I felt about him? I told myself it wouldn't matter, but how could I know until I was faced with it?'

A few days later, returning from a sortie just before dawn, Nadia landed at a diversionary airfield to refuel her aircraft. The sky was lightening in the east, and she was anxious to make her way back to her base before enemy air activity made the flight unnecessarily hazardous. She jumped from the cockpit to stretch her legs, then stood leaning against the fuselage chattering to her navigator, who was checking her map for navigational landmarks on the flight back. A mechanic ran up to her and told her that another pilot wanted to have a word with her. Nadia followed the man towards a group of fighter aircraft parked a few hundred yards away. She had taken off her flying helmet and ran her fingers through her thick hair and moistened her lips in anticipation of meeting this unknown man. She wondered if the goggles had left their usual curving marks across her upper cheeks. The dark-haired pilot standing at the tail of one of the Yaks turned around as she approached.

He smiled broadly as he stepped towards her. 'Don't you recognize me, Nadia? It's me, Simon.'

Nadia told me, 'As soon as he spoke I knew it was Simon, but I had never seen his face before. I thought how handsome he looked. But more important – he had a nose. He had a nose! I ran to him and threw my arms around his neck and kissed him gently, right on the end of it. I was so happy.'

A red scar, still very livid, ran all the way across the bridge of Simon's nose. It was obviously still a little tender where the stitches had been, for he picked her up and playfully held her away at arm's length. Then he put his arm around her shoulder and they walked down the airfield together. Yes, he told her, he had been a little embarrassed about his injury. The German who had shot him down had fired a burst of machine-gun fire through his cockpit and a bullet had smashed through his nose, leaving it hanging by a thread of skin. He had lost consciousness but regained it just in time to make a belly landing in a field. A doctor at the field hospital had managed to sew the nose back on, but it really had hurt even to smile for the first few days.

It was now broad daylight – time to be flying back to her base. Nadia felt sure she loved him and found an apple she had stuffed into her overalls before take-off the previous night. She rubbed it on her sleeve until it shone and gave it to him.

'Take care, darling Simon,' she said. She pecked him gently once more on his beautiful nose and walked to her aircraft.

They did not meet again for several months. Nadia's aircraft had been damaged during a raid, and the repairs could not be carried out at her airfield. She flew to the main workshops at Baku, well behind the front, where specialist repair teams would make it airworthy once more. As she was walking towards the hangars, she saw a group of men approaching from the opposite direction. The one in front was tall, with dark hair, and he was wearing a leather coat peppered with holes and tears. It was Simon. They ran and embraced each other tightly. He told her how he had missed her, and she asked what had happened to him. He said he had been shot down again the day after she had given him the apple. The aircraft caught fire and his coat had been burned and torn as he struggled to throw himself from the fighter. As he floated down in his parachute, German ground troops had fired at him from their lines; their bullets had whirred close to him, but he had not been hit. His leg, however, had been burned severely as he escaped from the aircraft.

Nadia told me, 'I felt a wave of love for him as I thought of the pain he had been suffering. But what he told me next made me want to cry with frustration.' For Simon had been taken for treatment to a hospital at the very airfield where she and her regiment were based at that time. Day after day Simon had read in the newspapers of the combat exploits of the women's regiments. Some of the women, including Nadia, were becoming household names. He would lie in his bed and listen to the little PO-2s taking off on their missions at night, but it never occurred to him that it was Nadia's regiment. He thought about her a great deal and reread a few letters she had managed to send him since their first meeting. And all the time he lay there, she was only a few minutes' walk away from his bedside. Life could be so unfair.

Nadia had to wait at Baku for two days to pick up a

replacement aircraft. Simon and his group were the nucleus of a new regiment and they, too, were picking up new aircraft. He and Nadia went to a dance. Nadia had not brought her pretty blouse with her, of course, but she had washed her hair and borrowed an iron to press her uniform. Girls in pretty dresses danced with the uniformed young men. Nadia looked at them and felt neither envy nor bitterness at their carefree enjoyment; to them, the reality of the war must have seemed a long way away (though the Germans were eventually to get within fifty miles of Baku). Watching them took her mind back to that night before the outbreak of war when she had whirled around the dance floor. It seemed a long time ago. She hoped that she was basically still the same person, but she knew that the war had already changed her in many ways. Her skin was fresh and unlined and bore remarkably little sign of the pressure of daily air combat. In her mental attitudes, though, she recognized a toughness that had never been there before. She had always been determined, but now she knew that her experiences under fire had given her a ruthless single-mindedness. She hoped it would not affect her personal relationships.

What she came to realize was that most of her friends and colleagues were undergoing the same rapid maturing and toughening process. In direct proportion to the mental toughening grew a bond of loyalty so intense it could never be shared or even properly understood by those who had not served with these elite units. The bond of love and friendship seemed almost to have been planned to compensate for the hard protective layers which nature had obliged them to grow for their own preservation.

After Baku, Nadia and Simon saw little of each other until near the end of the war. They made no pledges of marriage – no one did in these circumstances. But it was understood, implicitly, that if they both came through, they would be together. Through letters and newspaper stories they followed each other's lives and prayed they would survive.

5

The Free Hunters at
Stalingrad, September 1942

Stalingrad is an enormous city stretching for thirty miles along the banks of the Volga. On 23 August, 1942, the Germans had broken through to the river on a five-mile front north of Stalingrad. On the same day 600 aircraft attacked the city, killing 40,000 civilians. As the German bombers turned for home, the entire city was enveloped in flames and a great pall of smoke floated over the Volga. Retreating Russian troops made their way through thousands of refugees, many of them wounded, streaming from the stricken city. Peasants with their livestock and agricultural implements fought with residents of the city for places on the ferries across the Volga.

Gen. Vasili I. Chuikov, who commanded the Sixty-Second Army throughout the Stalingrad siege, wrote:

From a distance we could see that the pier was crowded with people. As we drew closer, many wounded were being carried out of trenches, bomb craters and shelters. There were also many people with bundles and suitcases, who had been hiding from German bombs and shells. When they saw the ferry arriving they rushed to the pier with the one desire of getting away to the other side of the river from their wrecked homes, away from a city that had become a hell. Their eyes were grim and there were trickles of tears running through the dust and soot on their grimy faces. The children suffering from thirst and hunger were not crying, but simply whining and stretching out their little arms to the waters of the Volga.* And continuously the Stukas and the Messerschmitts bombed and machine-gunned them.

---

*V. I. Chuikov, *The Beginning of the Road*. London: MacGibbon & Kee, 1963.

This was the hell of Stalingrad. It seemed to the demoralized civilians and the beleaguered troops that the Germans were invincible. Gen. Friedrich Paulus's Sixth Army and the Fourth Panzer Army had encircled the Soviet Sixty-Second Army between the two arms of their pincers. It seemed to many Russians that the invaders were poised for another victory of encirclement that would gain for them the vital Volga crossings and open the way for the drive to the oilfields of the south.

The fact was that Paulus and his troops were marching towards disaster, and Stalingrad as such need never have been taken. Aerial bombardment and artillery barrage could have achieved the objectives of denying the Russians both the city's manufacturing capacity and the Volga as a major oil supply route.

At that stage, however, the picture looked grim for the Russians, and even their official writings concede that morale among the defenders was very low. The enemy had complete air superiority, and their fighters and bombers – flying up to three thousand sorties a day – appeared to be suspended over the city from dawn to dusk and then on through the night. The scenes of disorder and panic were becoming reminiscent of the initial routs of the blitzkrieg of the previous summer. The evacuation of the city's 600,000 residents continued, as did the round-the-clock aerial bombardment of enemy positions. In its way, this bombing was to prove more effective in providing ready-made defences than anything the Soviet army could have erected, And while the Germans advanced into the city, the air force raced against time to build new air bases on the far side of the River Volga. Thousands of civilians helped the construction battalions, and fifty new airfields were hurriedly laid down, their command posts and sleeping quarters housed in underground bunkers protected by earth and sandbags.

*   *   *

From a thousand feet up, it was just possible to see the dark, narrow strip of the runway of one of these new airfields in the fading afternoon light. The strong gusting wind caused the Yak fighter to crab sideways awkwardly on its descent and blew a cloud of grey smoke from the burning city across the runway. The pilot eased back the throttle lever, reducing engine power, until the Yak was about ten feet above the runway. As the fighter approached the point of stall, the throttle was closed abruptly. With a final kick on the left rudder pedal to straighten the nose, the Yak thumped on to the runway, became airborne for a second, and thumped down again.

The Yak's long nose swung left and right and left again as the pilot's eyes strained in the growing darkness for the smoky oil flare that marked the narrow taxiway leading to the aircraft dispersal area. A flight of four that had landed immediately before trundled through the ruts of the taxiway. Belches of flame leapt from the four exhaust pipes on either side of the engine cowlings as they gunned their motors to take them over the rough patches.

The Yak pilot was marshalled into a space in the middle of a line of about twenty other Yaks. On either side, mechanics swarmed over the fighters. The fabric on several fuselages was torn into gaping holes, and the wingtip of the aircraft to the right had disappeared. Armament fitters in bulky kapok jackets moved clumsily under the weight of drums of cannon shells and machine-gun bullets as they rearmed the guns. A mechanic, cursing softly, peeled mittens from his fingers to poke a wrench into a recess of an engine.

The pilot climbed on to the wing and dropped lightly to the ground. After sitting for over an hour in that cramped cockpit, it was difficult to walk the two hundred yards to the squat curving roof of the underground operations centre. The pilot turned at the top of the flight of steps leading underground and listened for a moment to the distant but incessant hammer and clattering of small-arms fire and the awful contrarhythms of the big guns firing, exploding, exploding, and firing. The wind from the south-west carried with it minute particles of debris, burned black. It was part of the funeral pyre of Stalingrad. The pilot walked slowly down the steps, paused at the heavy metal door, and then pushed it open.

There were about twenty young men in the large underground room. Several shaded electric bulbs cast pools of light over map tables. A gust of cold air came through the open doorway and someone shouted irritably to close it. As the door slammed shut, the light over the table nearest the door swung gently in the draught, casting a pendulum of light over the faces of the pilots debriefing after their last sortie. For a few seconds the rhythmic strokes of light and shade etched more deeply the lines of strain already spidering around the young eyes. The newcomer's lips opened to speak and a hand fumbled inside the bulky sheepskin flying jacket as if to produce orders or transfer papers. But the pilot conducting the debriefing stood up, his face half in darkness as he steadied the swinging lampshade, and signalled the newcomer to sit down. He turned his back and, barely halting his flow, carried on questioning the young pilots on their missions.

An old potbellied stove stood in the centre of the bunker. Pushing the lid aside, the pilot stuffed in several long birch logs from the pile that lay drying around its base. The logs sizzled into flame and circulation returned to the pilot's cramped, cold limbs. Fragments of conversation drifted over to the stove: 'I know I'm his wingman, but how could I have followed him through that turn with half my ailerons shot away? . . . Yes, they were from Richtofen's group . . . I saw him going down, but didn't see his parachute open . . .'

The pilot, still muffled in flying gear, pulled a chair across to the stove and started to peel off the outer layers. First the heavy sheepskin flying boots, then the fur socks worn over two pairs of woollen socks. Listening to bits of earnest conversation and voices raised in excitement as the men relived the battle fought less than an hour before in the skies over Stalingrad, the stranger sat on the chair, recently thawed fingers fumbling occasionally with the overalls' zips and fasteners. In a couple of minutes these, too, lay over the back of the chair, and the pilot slipped the flying boots back on. Then the sheepskin jacket and finally the flying helmet were tugged off and joined the pile.

Quite suddenly the pilot was aware that the only sound in the bunker was the crack and sizzle of the stove and, buffeting at the door, the howl of the wind. All conversation had ceased. The eyes of every man in the room were turned towards the stove.

The standard issue tunic only seemed to accentuate the tiny blonde woman's full breasts. The pistol in its holster leaned into her slender waist as she stood up and pulled her tunic straight. She had grey eyes that crinkled slightly as she grinned. 'Hello. I'm Lieutenant Lily Litvak. I'm your new pilot.'

Ina Pasportnikova, who was soon to become Lily's personal mechanic, told me: 'Lily's effect on the men when she arrived at that base was quite stunning. She had a really beautiful figure. But admiring a beautiful girl was one thing, and wanting to fly with her was quite another. Lily and Katya Budanova were in for a terrible time before they were allowed to do the job they'd come to do.'

Ina and Lily had met and become friends during the initial selection interviews at the Zhukovsky Academy in Moscow. Ina had been training as an engineer at the prestigious Aviation Institute in Moscow before the German invasion, and her flying experience was extensive. She had qualified as a pilot on the PO-2 through a sports flying club, and she had trained as a parachutist, too. For a woman with her obvious aptitudes, her assignment in the women's fighter regiment came as a crushing disappointment: she was to be a mechanic. Marina Raskova herself explained that it was no reflection on her other abilities – on the contrary. Her engineering skills were in short supply, and in the circumstances she would be doing a lot more good maintaining the aircraft for other women to fly.

Ina told me, 'When you can fly an aircraft as well as any other girl and you're told that you'll spend your war on the ground watching others do the fighting, it's hard to bear. But because I was a flier, too, Lily and Katya were able to discuss their problems with me and I know I was a help to them when the going was tough.'

Katya Budanova flew in the next morning at first light. She and Lily were ordered to report to the commander of the regiment, Col. Nikolai Baranov. Lily, Katya, and Ina had been given quarters well away from the men, in a house on the edge of the new airfield; now they walked across the airfield together. Lily's Yak, with its distinctive number three painted on the side of the fuselage, was parked next to the fighter that Katya had just flown in. Both were being refuelled, and machine-gun and cannon ammunition was being loaded. The aircraft were about 150 feet apart, parked in a three-sided shelter made of earthwork and wood. These were to protect the aircraft from indirect hits from enemy fragmentation bombs. The wide separation between planes was to minimize the chances of one explosion igniting the aircraft on either side.

Katya was talking excitedly about her cross-country flight. She had flown a curving flight path east before heading back on a south-westerly heading, to keep as far away as possible from enemy ground fire. But as she had approached the burning city, the air had been full of aircraft: black German Stukas pulling up from their vertical dives, dozens of Junkers 88s droning in crisscross patterns across the city, and everywhere the savage *danse macabre* of aerial dogfighting.

The sound of gunfire was clearly audible even at the

airfield. Ina told me, 'It's a sound you can never forget. At first you thought of it only in terms of noise. Then as it went on and on and on, you began to think of our people in the rubble of the city – they were being killed and maimed by the guns that made that noise. After that you never thought of it as simply noise, ever again.'

Stalingrad had been visible earlier that morning, but now the new fires started by the Germans' incendiary bombs were sending up great black columns over a mile high. They expanded outward and drifted into each other, and the city disappeared behind a curtain of smoke and flame. Ina reported to the officer in charge of engineering maintenance, and Lily and Katya continued towards the commander's bunker.

Katya Budanova was twenty years old. Her hair was still clipped short, and from a distance she looked like a young boy. She had an openness of facial expression which displayed her vulnerability, and Ina Pasportnikova remembers her as a woman who could be easily hurt. She had lots of self-confidence, though. The cockpit of a fighter was no place for a shrinking violet, and Katya had proved cool in combat during operations from Saratov and the surrounding region.

They were now at the top of the steps leading to the bunker. The door opened and a group of pilots ran up the steps. Lily recognized Alexi Salomaten, the man who had been conducting the debriefing the previous evening when she had made her entrance to the bunker. He was around medium height with broad shoulders and fair curly hair, and his squarish face still retained some of its deep tan from the summer campaign. Colonel Baranov had his arm on Salomaten's shoulder as they ran up the steps, clutching their maps and parachute packs. They were laughing at some joke. Lily and Katya snapped to attention, and Lily opened her mouth to speak. But Baranov ignored them and strode past, talking quickly to Salomaten.

Ina told me, 'Baranov obviously must have seen them and he knew who they were. He told one of his officers to tell them to report to him that morning. Alexei Salomaten grinned at Lily as he went past, and one of the other pilots asked Lily and Katya if they were the ferry pilots who'd brought the two new aircraft in.' That was crushing enough for women who had been flying in combat for about five months, but there was worse to come.

Lily and Katya followed the pilots to the dispersal area where their aircraft were lined up, fuelled, and armed for the day's first sortie. The two women watched the men pull on their parachutes, wriggling their shoulders through the webbing harness and pulling the straps through their legs to fasten in a central buckle. They pulled on their flying helmets and clambered into the cockpits. The women could not believe their eyes. A man was climbing into Katya's aircraft and another pilot was slinging his leg over the edge of Lily's number three. Baranov was already in his aircraft and his head was down, studying his instrument panel as he started up the engine.

Ina continued, 'They thought at first that it must be a misunderstanding. They knew Baranov was a busy man with enormous responsibilities and more to think about than just them. They were sure they could easily sort it out when he had finished his sorties for the day. They did not know as they stood and watched the Yaks take off that in Baranov they had an apparently implacable opponent of women combat pilots.' They were right in their estimation of Baranov as a man under enormous strain. It was the middle of September and the Germans were only two miles from the centre of Stalingrad. Only supreme optimists could honestly have seen any light at all at the end of the tunnel of despair – and Baranov was above all a realist.

A professional pilot, he had been an officer in the Red Air Force at the time of the German invasion in June 1941. He was one of the few pilots in his squadron in the western region who had been able to get his biplane fighter off the ground before the Heinkels and Junkers had annihilated the closely parked rows of aircraft. In the succeeding days, he had weathered the storm of German air supremacy in his hopelessly outmatched fighter as the remnants of the Red Air Force retreated in confusion towards the east.

He had lost many friends and good pilots then and in the awful succeeding months. Those who knew him said that he felt very deeply about each loss. He had lost a high number in the past few weeks. Some had been with the regiment for such a short time that he could not even remember their names. And to replace these boys they were sending him girls.

He had looked at the flight records of Litvak and Budanova. He had to admit they looked good on paper, and Litvak in particular had been commended for her air-to-air gunnery. But in the air, particularly flying in pairs, a man had to be able to depend on his wingman completely – that was the whole essence of the new tactics being worked up by the free hunters. He was not prepared to risk any of his men to some slip of a girl sitting above his wing and supposed to be protecting him from the might of the Luftwaffe. He knew the women's regiments had been doing a good job protecting the bridges and railway junctions around Saratov. That was one thing. But this was Stalingrad. It was the fiercest air battle he had been involved in so far, and he wanted a chance to build up at least the core of a good unit.

The fighter pilots who had just taken off and wheeled towards the Volga were 'free hunters', part of an elite group of fliers recently organized by the Red Air Force. Their role was to fly in pairs in groups of up to eight, seeking out enemy targets of opportunity (as opposed to being scrambled to intercept known enemy formations). The Soviet Air Force was now actively encouraging decisive independent action by their pilots, particularly against German bombers, and the operations of the free hunters were the epitome of this new attiude.

The Germans were becoming uncomfortably aware of this new organized aggression from their adversaries in the air over Stalingrad. How different it was from the assessments they had made of their enemy's capabilities in 1941. The initial hammering blows against the Red Air Force on the ground had been devastating, of course; but senior officers of the Luftwaffe like Generalmajor Klaus Uebe had thought that, even allowing for the pre-emptive strikes by the Germans, the Russian pilots were vastly inferior due to a lack of feeling for aviation, mental inertia, and inadequate training. Inadequate training, Uebe thought, also caused the generally evident and exaggerated caution that often bordered on cowardice. 'In spite of their numerical superiority,' he said, 'the Soviet Air Forces were not a dangerous opponent.'

Colonel H. H. von Beust, commander of a Luftwaffe bomber group, considered the average Russian aviator 'an opponent completely incapable of independent air attack operations and representing only a small threat in defensive action. The impression was often received that Soviet pilots were fatalistic, fighting without any hope of success or confidence in their own abilities and driven only by their own fanaticism or by fear of their commissars.'*

But the free hunters, led by combat veterans like Baranov, were forcing a reappraisal of the worth of the Russian pilots. They were the cream which Lily and Katya had been sent to join. Adapting techniques they had learned in daily combat, they were evolving their own tactics.

When attacked by German fighters, the Soviet fighters had always immediately formed a defensive circle. The

*W. Schwabedissen, *The Russian Air Force in the Eyes of German Commanders*. New York: Arno Press, 1968.

Germans found it relatively easy to separate individual planes from the circling unit and destroy them. Baranov, Salomaten, and the other free hunters abandoned the defensive circle technique. Instead, they based their tactics on the principle of attack and cover – two aircraft, leader and wingman, alternately attacking and then defending each other's rear. And they took advantage of the better manoeuvrability of their fighters to counteract the superior speed and rate of climb of the German Focke Wulfe 190s and Messerschmitt 109s.

As the Soviet pilots exploited their newfound aggression and self-confidence over Stalingrad, they were helped by a reorganized radio network on the ground. It consisted of radio stations at the airfields of the divisions and regiments and, along the front line, target control stations that had direct communication with pilots in the air. Thus the free hunters could be warned of approaching swarms of enemy fighters or bombers and notified of tempting targets elsewhere in the many square miles of airspace above the city.

After being airborne on their first sortie for half an hour, the Yaks returned, sweeping very low across the airfield. They were coming back to refuel and rearm, a process that would take about twenty minutes. They flew downwind to just beyond the airfield perimeter and then curved left and left again, heading into the wind to land. Watching at dispersal, Lily and Katya counted seven aircraft. One had been lost in combat somewhere above the cauldron of Stalingrad. Katya's Yak landed safely, and Lily saw with relief that her 'Troika' – number three – was down safely too.

It was not the time to approach the commander. He and the other pilots jumped to the ground and pulled off their flying helmets. Captain Salomaten's fair hair was damp and curling across his forehead. Lily watched him rub his sleeve across his eyes. The six other pilots crowded around

Baranov as he spread a map on the wing of his aircraft.

Lily and Katya were helping pull the trolleys bearing ammunition to the aircraft. They came within a few feet of the pilots as Baranov's aircraft was rearmed and heard them discussing the missing pilot, whose aircraft had exploded while attacking a Junkers 88. They were intent on tactics, and Baranov was instructing someone to assign another pilot to make up the pair that had been split by the recent death. Alexei Salomaten looked up from the map, caught Lily's eye, and winked. Ina said, 'It was fairly obvious from their first meeting that the attraction was mutual. It was almost inevitable, looking back.'

The free hunters flew three more sorties that day. They climbed from their Yaks in the late afternoon, pale, strained, and a little unsteady on their feet after so many hours in the cockpit They had shot down a total of six German aircraft, for the loss of one of their own. Lily noted that 'Troika' was apparently undamaged, but several of the other Yaks, including Katya's, had holes in fuselage and wing and tail surfaces.

Baranov strode towards the command bunker where the debriefing would take place and where tactics would be discussed in light of their most recent combat. Lily and Katya fell into step beside him and Lily saluted him. 'Sir, I should like to discuss my flying duties for tomorrow with you, if you can spare the time.'

He looked at her briefly and then looked away. His reply was curt and quite unequivocal: 'I will not have girls flying with me. No arguments about it. You'll be transferred out of here within two days.'

Ina recounted, 'Lily and Katya could think of nothing to say. In fact it seemed there was nothing to say. Although it didn't surprise me as much as it surprised them. While I'd been working on the aircraft between sorties that afternoon, some of the men mechanics told me that my friends didn't have a chance of becoming free hunters – not with

Baranov's group, anyway. We hadn't realized it, but apparently there had been two other girls sent to his group some weeks before and, despite their official transfers to his command, he had managed to fob them off with a regiment in another air division. It was plain that that was what he was planning to do with Lily and Katya, too.'

Ina was finding that she too would have to fight hard to retain her self-respect against an onslaught of male chauvinism. On the following morning, the Yaks were being prepared for their first sortie as the sun began to edge up over the eastern edge of the steppe. Ina was working on Lily's Yak, with the engine cowling swung up and her hand in a recess of the motor, making an adjustment to the fuel supply. She had a cotton rag tied like a headband across her forehead to prevent the sweat from running into her eyes. These September days did not yet carry any hint of the fearful winter to come, and it was hot work in the confines of the protective pen.

A young lieutenant approached and asked which aircraft was number three. Ina, a sergeant, saluted him, her oily right hand brushing against the cotton band, and told him that she was working on it. Ina told me, 'I asked him if he was to be flying that aircraft, but he didn't answer me. He just gave me a look that was angry and contemptuous at the same time, and strode off towards the command bunker.'

He was back within five minutes with the chief mechanic of the regiment. Ina saluted him and said, 'This aircraft is ready for flight, sir.'

She told me, 'The chief mechanic went red in the face. He was clearly embarrassed. I asked him very respectfully if there was something wrong with my work. He said there was nothing wrong with my work as far as he could see. He had been watching me yesterday, he said. However, this pilot did not want to fly this aircraft because it had been prepared by a woman.'

The pilot demanded, 'How long have you been a mechanic?'

'Ten months.'

'But what if the engine should stop?'

'Why should it?'

The pilot was adamant. He told the chief mechanic he would not fly that aircraft and he stomped off towards the command bunker once more.

Ina told me, 'I was so angry – I really understood what Lily and Katya were feeling now. I forgot all the discipline I'd been taught and I spat on the ground in the direction of the pilot's back. I told the chief mechanic that the pilot was more of a woman than I. He was a decent sort. He pretended he hadn't seen what I'd done and said. I could see that he sympathized more with me than with the pilot. But now we were all intrigued to see what the commander would do about the pilot's refusal to fly in Troika.'

The Yaks were hauled out of their three-sided shelters for engine starting as the pilots approached. Alexei Salomaten detached himself from the group and walked briskly towards Ina. She told me, 'He asked if it was Troika – as if he didn't know what it was. He kicked the undercarriage wheel, gave me a grin and said, 'What's all this I hear about you frightening my pilots, then?" He asked Ina to help him on with his parachute, then climbed in. On a later sortie that day, the pilot who had refused Troika went down in flames beyond the west bank of the river.

Not that it was any consolation to Lily and Katya. Ina told me, 'Lily was a woman, but she was also so much a little child. I caught her at one stage that afternoon with a little rose in her fingers, pulling the petals off one by one and muttering as she did so, "Yes, he'll let me go; no, he won't; yes, he'll let me . . ." Lily wasn't a conceited or an arrogant girl, but she was well aware of the effect she had on men and she was accustomed to getting her own way with them fairly easily. She still believed that if she could get a chance to work her charm on Baranov, then she would be able to swing everything her way.'

The colonel was tired when he landed after his last sortie. He was only about thirty, but he looked older at that moment. He had taken several hits on the front end of the aircraft and, though it had still been flyable, the engine had been losing power all the way home. A fairly bad oil leak had sprayed the thick black fluid over much of the windscreen. Shell fragments had pierced part of the windscreen, and Baranov's face was streaked with oil, too. It was clearly not a good moment to approach a man whose mind was already apparently firmly made up.

Katya was very upset about their rejection, although Ina had tried hard to convince them both that a return to the women's air regiment was hardly the end of the world. Lily told Katya it would be best if she went to Baranov alone. After a suitable length of time, she set off across the airfield.

Baranov was seated at his table at the end of the command centre when Lily entered the bunker. His mood seemed to have improved. He was laughing loudly and he and another officer were slamming two empty vodka glasses on the tabletop. His face was still streaked with oil and his thick dark hair fell across his forehead. As Lily approached, she could see the imprint of his oily fingers on the bottle and on the glass in front of him. He still wore his flying jacket, but he had unburdened himself of his automatic pistol, which lay in its holster on the maps in front of him. He looked up at her approach and his smile froze.

Lily told Ina later that Baranov lit a cigarette, leaned back in his chair, and said, 'What do you want, Litvak? I've told you my decision. There's nothing more to discuss.'

'Please, Colonel,' she said, 'please let us fly. We couldn't have been sent here if we hadn't been good.' Baranov wiped a film of oil from his eyelid and did a head-shaking double take. He stared in disbelief at Lily's uniform cap. There was quite definitely a small yellow rose in the band.

'There aren't even enough planes for the men to fly,' he replied. 'You know perfectly well that I've had to give your aircraft to a male pilot. And I make no apology for that.'

Lily said, 'Sir, I don't think you're being fair. Katya Budanova and I came here to fight.'

Alexei Salomaten had come into the bunker. He sat down on a chair next to his friend Baranov, just as the colonel was winding up the conversation. 'So, Lieutenant Litvak, tomorrow my adjutant tells divisional headquarters that I want you transferred back to your regiment.'

Lily felt she now had very little to lose. 'We want to fly with you, and I'm sitting here until you tell me we can.' And she added somewhat incongruously, 'You know, I was born on aviation day, 18 August.'

Alexei Salomaten clearly felt that it was time to intervene. He had been Baranov's friend since flying school days and, though at twenty-two he was several years younger than his commander, they were very close. Salomaten never exploited the friendship, but it was said in the regiment that Baranov would have done anything the younger man asked.

The young pilot looked at Lily and then back at Baranov and said, 'Well, have you decided what you're going to do about the girls, Kolya?' Baranov said that he had and that they were not staying with the regiment. Salomaten winked over his friend's shoulder at Lily. 'But surely, Kolya, you understand – she's a pilot. She must be given the chance to fly with us,' he said, clapping his friend on the shoulder.

Baranov sat silent for a few seconds and then stood up. 'Okay, Alexei. Tomorrow morning, Lieutenant Litvak flies as your wingman. But, by God, she'd better be good. And don't forget it's your responsibility.' Which of course it

104

wasn't. Baranov was the commander, it was his responsibility, and he knew it.

Lily's eyes were bright with excitement She had won. But she had not finished yet. She took a deep breath, 'What about Lieutenant Budanova, sir?'

Baranov looked for a moment as if he would explode, then Salomaten broke the tension by laughing loudly. The colonel managed a grin himself. 'I'll let her fly on my wing tomorrow sometime – if we can find any Germans to fight.' It gave Baranov no joy, but he did not think it likely that the two girlfriends could survive the sort of air combat he had been experiencing for the last few days.

Alexei Salomaten was a successful fighter pilot with a number of 'kills' to his credit, and all the ground crew knew that he was to be flying with Lily for the first time that morning. He came to the flight line to check his aircraft and talk to his mechanic before briefing Lily and the other two free hunters who were to fly with them on that mission. Salomaten was cheerful but brisk, as he always was before a sortie. It was the time to concentrate his mind and psych himself up for the flight ahead. There was a lot to think about.

He had already been briefed on the disposition of enemy forces in his area. The Soviet counteroffensive had not yet begun, and enemy air activity was still intense. Their mission that morning would be to roam the airspace, seeking and destroying enemy fighters, bombers, and air transports. If no contact was made with enemy aircraft on that sortie, his flight would be free to hit 'targets of opportunity' that presented themselves on the ground. He had marked on his map the locations of known concentrations of German troop reserves and supplies. The Ilyushin-2 Shturmovik ground attack aircraft would already be pounding at these, but the free hunters would add their firepower before returning to refuel. The flight leader had also noted the radio code words for that day. A complete wave band was allocated to the area he would be flying, and he had noted the frequency to be used and the call signals. To make life as difficult as possible for enemy radio intercept stations on the ground, the frequency, codes, and call signals were very likely to be different on the second sortie of the day.

Ina Pasportnikova recalled, 'It was a beautiful September day – perfect flying weather. There was hardly a cloud in the sky, and if you turned away from the smoke of the city and the sound of the guns, you could almost have imagined yourself back at the sports flying club. How I longed to get airborne myself.

'I had taken extra special care of Troika that morning. I spent a long time polishing her windscreen to give her the best possible visibility. I sat in the cockpit, pulled the canopy shut, and wiped it clean as well.'

Lily walked towards her aircraft. Alexei Salomaten walked beside her, and the two men who were flying as the other pair were slightly behind. Lily looked very serious. She said nothing to Salomaten and when Ina smiled at her, her response was tense and unnatural.

Salomaten stood beside the wing of Lily's Yak as Ina helped her wriggle into the parachute harness. He smiled at her in a reassuring way and said, 'I know it seems a silly thing to say at a time like this, but don't worry. And remember – just do everything I do. Follow my every single move. Forget about protecting me – just stick to my tail like glue no matter what I do.'

Lily muttered her agreement and bit hard on her lower lip. Sitting in the cockpit, she pulled the shoulder straps of the safety harness into position and clicked both straps into the round metal clasp that secured them to the lap straps at the top of her legs. She wriggled into a more comfortable position against the familiar bulk of the parachute which curved from her hips up to her shoulder blades. After a final adjustment to her safety harness, she reached back over her head and pulled the cockpit hood shut with a dull clunk. She locked it with the securing handles and started her pre-take-off checks.

She looked over her shoulder as she pushed the stick between her legs back and forth. Beneath the tail, the elevator that raised and lowered the Yak in flight obediently swung above and then below the tailplane assembly. She moved the rudder pedals right and then left; the rudder, which turned the nose, followed her commands. She now moved the stick from side to side, and the ailerons on the lower edges of both sloping wing surfaces moved alternately up and down. These would control the rolling motion of the Yak.

Lily's oxygen mask banged loosely against her cheeks. It had a faint smell of rubber and leather and a vague whiff of the scented soap her mother had sent her. She switched the radio on and started the engine. Ina still remembers Lily's pale face underneath the flying helmet as she raised her hand for Ina to tug away the ropes attached to the wooden chocks under the wheels. Lily taxied out to the end of the runway where she lined up to the right of and slightly behind Salomaten – the position she would keep as they climbed out of the runway. She applied the brake and with her left hand pushed the throttle lever forward to full power. The Yak shuddered and strained against the restraint as Lily completed her final checks of oil pressure and engine revolutions.

A green rocket was fired, signalling that they were clear for take-off. The second pair was lined up behind. Lily pulled the throttle lever back again and released the brakes. Salomaten raised his right arm for a second and then swiftly dropped it. It was the take-off signal. Lily shoved the throttle lever hard forward again, and the two fighters accelerated down the runway. Lily concentrated on Alexei's aircraft, making continual adjustments with her feet to keep her in position. She felt her tail lift first and, as she saw her leader's nose lift, she began to pull back gently on the stick. They were airborne. She raised the undercarriage and it clunked into position, flush with the underside of the wing. She followed the other Yak into a climbing turn to the left. Looking back over her shoulder, she could see the other pair lifting off the runway. They were already passing through three thousand feet and heading towards the towering columns of smoke and flames.

Salomaten told her to reduce speed, and in a couple of minutes the other pair took up their position to the right, behind them and several hundred feet higher. They were at eight thousand feet above the city. Four heads swivelled through 360 degrees. They flicked across the safety catches and fired two-second bursts to test their guns. Then the free hunters began to seek their prey.

Four thousand feet below, Colonel Baranov and his wingman were racing home to refuel and rearm after their first sortie of the day. Ina Pasportnikova told me, 'Katya was waiting for Baranov to return so that she could make her first sortie with him, as they had agreed. We mechanics were working flat out, topping off oil and water, replacing burst tyres, and generally making sure that the fighters didn't have anything vital hanging off. Then the two Messerschmitts appeared.'

The light anti-aircraft guns of the regiment's support unit opened up along the perimeter, their machine guns swinging around to follow the raiders. Ina and the other ground crew and pilots hurled themselves into the slit trenches or ran to the shelter of the protective aircraft pens. Several Yaks had not yet been pushed into their pens. Ina peeked over the top of her trench. The Messerschmitts were so low that she ducked instinctively. They were flying parallel to each other across the airfield, and one was skidding sideways as he aimed his guns. A line of bullets gouged through the earth towards her at terrifying speed. She pressed her face against the damp earth wall of the trench and heard a dull thump as the fuel tanks of the Yak twenty yards behind exploded. Then came the howl of the fighter as it passed over her trench and zoomed to a thousand feet before turning with his wingman for another pass. Ina said, 'The anti-aircraft boys saw Baranov's pair returning before we did, because the clattering of their guns stopped quite suddenly.'

Baranov and his wingman adopted a tactic that had often worked for them before. As the Germans completed their stall turn and swept down on the field again, the Russian pair hauled their Yaks into a tight turn and flew across the airfield straight at the Messerschmitts. It was a deadly game of bluff that could and sometimes did end in mutually fatal midair collision. The winner was the man with the strongest nerve. At a closing speed of over 600 miles per hour, the four aircraft raced towards each other. Ina told me, 'We had all climbed out of our trenches by that time. We were trying to put out the flames around the remains of the burning Yak, and there was blazing ammunition whistling in all directions. But we kept one eye on the sky. I just new Baranov would get the Germans.'

As the Yaks filled their windscreens, the German fighters heeled sharply on their wingtips and broke out of the fight. It was a fatal move. Baranov took the plane on the right and his wingman the one on the left. The Germans screeched into their breakaway turns with the Russians on their tails, raking them with bursts of cannon and machine-gun fire. One exploded in midair and the other crashed in flames at the edge of the airfield. The Soviet airmen landed to a sustained outburst of cheering from their ground crew.

Over the city, German bombs were falling heavily. Lily had seen little during the ten minutes of the sortie, apart from a large flight of Heinkel 111 bombers about a mile away. Alexei had heard another squadron being directed to the bombers by ground control and so had turned his flight away from the swarm.

Now his voice crackled briefly in Lily's headphones. 'Follow me' was the terse command. There was no time to think. Her leader's Yak was rolling on to its back and diving away from her. She pushed the stick hard over to her left and, slamming on full power, followed him down. She was on his tail now – so close, she later told Ina, that she seriously considered closing the throttle to avoid ramming into him. But drop speed now and she would never catch him again. She kept repeating to herself, 'Stick on his tail, stick on his tail.'

Was this some trick, some game he was playing with her? Some test of her aerobatic skill? There was no sign of any Germans.

He was inverted again and corkscrewing his aircraft in the opposite direction. Now they were out of the dive and zooming straight up like an elevator. Lily felt her vision reddening with the g forces. Once they were over the top of the loop, her hands were banging on the sides of the cockpit as she co-ordinated the stick and rudder to follow him in his twisting progress down through the dive once more. Her palms were moist inside her gloves, and she could feel rivulets of sweat trickling down the sides of her forehead. But not once did she dare lift her hands from the throttle lever or the stick.

Once, she had the impression of the other pair of Yaks zooming up past them as they dived. She could have sworn that she had heard bursts of gunfire, too, but her concentration on her leader's tail was so intense that she could not be sure. Salomaten's changes of direction were so sudden and so violent that, robbed of the initiative as she was, it required superb flying to stay with him. She glanced at her altimeter. They had descended four thousand feet during Alexei's little game. Suddenly, as quickly as it had

110

begun, it was over. They levelled out and Lily, glancing over her shoulder, saw that the other pair were on station above and behind her. Alexei said, 'Let's go home,' and they turned on to the new heading.

Ina told me, 'Lily knew she had done well. Salomaten had commanded her to stick to him like glue, and she knew she'd done that. She was convinced that the whole thing had been an elaborate test of her skills at the end of a quiet sortie. So when she taxied back after landing, she looked quite her old self.'

Ina helped her out of her parachute. As she jumped to the ground, Salomaten and the other two pilots strolled up to her. Using their hands to illustrate the movement of one aircraft in relation to an opponent, they were talking excitedly of a Heinkel dropping out of formation and falling away with both engines on fire. They described the effectiveness of an attack from opposite directions, and Salomaten was insisting that the Messerschmitt 109 must be shared as a kill with the leader of the other pair. Salomaten grinned at Lily, 'And what do you think, Lieutenant Litvak? Do you think that Boris and I should each claim half of that Messerschmitt?'

Ina told me, 'Lily was blushing furiously. I had never seen her so unable to cope with a situation. Then she blurted out, "But what Messerschmitt, Captain?"' The other pair roared with laughter, fell back against the wing of Lily's aircraft, and slapped the tops of their legs with mirth. Lily turned away. Could it really be so? Her first combat with the free hunters and she had not seen a thing. One of the other pilots teased her, 'You've got real contempt for the Fascists, Lily – you won't even admit they exist!' They both roared again with laughter. Salomaten grinned, too, then he took Lily gently by the arm and walked away with her a few paces. Ina, inspecting Lily's aircraft, overheard the conversation.

'Look, Lieutenant – look, Lily. I'm going to be absolutely

straight with you.' He paused. Lily's face was transparent in its anxiety. Then he went on, 'In all honesty – you were terrific. No one has ever stayed with me the way you did today.' He grinned again. 'Well, not any Germans, that's for sure. You've got what it takes and I'm going straight in to tell Baranov that. And by the way, Gubanov – the laughing boy over there – spun out of control his first sortie as my wingman. But don't tell him I told you that.'

Ina told me, 'I kept sneaking glances over at them. The way they were looking at each other I think they fell in love that day.'

Salomaten put his hand on Lily's arm and said, 'Tomorrow you will kill some Germans.' Then he strode off to the command bunker to talk to the colonel.

Boris Gubanov was still standing by the wing of Lily's Yak. 'Lily, don't take me too seriously. I watched you follow Losha,' he said, using the affectionate form of Alexei's name. 'You were fantastic. You'll never believe this, but I spun out on my first sortie as his wingman.'

Lily warmed to this tall young man with the typical dark Georgian looks. 'I believe you, Boris,' she said, and gave him the benefit of her full wide smile. She felt utterly elated.

She ran to Ina, who was checking the undercarriage. But Ina, the friendly eavesdropper, already knew it all. She also knew something else that Lily had not even guessed at. She told me, 'I had seen Lily with enough young men to spot the signs by now. I was willing to bet almost anything that Boris Gubanov was in love with her, too. And I was right.'

Col. Katerina Bershanskaya, commander and mother figure of the night bombers.

Two-member crew of a PO-2 night bomber. Natalya Meklin and Irina Sebrova. 1943.

Members of the 586th fighter regiment discuss tactics. Lily Litvak is on the left.

Night bomber crew receives last minute briefing. Note chalk-marked bullet holes below navigator's seat.

Ground crews of the night bomber regiment load planes for a sortie. The remarkable little PO-2 bi-plane trainer pressed into service as a bomber is in the background.

Outside a bunker of the night regiment during a lull in the fighting. Standing with mirror in hand is Nadia Popova. Irina Sebrova writes a letter. Vera Belik, cotton wool still in her ears from the night sortie, lights a cigarette.

In the air crews' quarters. The 586th fighter regiment read, embroider and write letters.

Natalya Meklin (*left*) and another crew member flank a male pilot visiting their regiment. Winter 1944.

Air mechanic Galina Liadetskaya of the 46th night bomber regiment.

Katerina Fedotova

Klavia Fumicheva, Hero of the
Soviet Union, and commander of a
squadron of the day bomber
regiment. 1943.

Pilot Tanya Makarova (*left*) and Navigator Vera Belik, night bomber crew,
before a sortie.

Galina Markova, navigator of a PE-2 twin-engine day bomber during the war. Pictured *at left* just after the war, *at right*, as she is today. Note Hero of Soviet Union Award on her tunic in both photos.

PE-2 day bomber pilot Katerina Fedotova in the cockpit of her aircraft with its romantic swallow emblem.

In combat gear, Lily Litvak of the 586th fighter regiment, on the Stalingrad front, between sorties.

The memorial to Lily erected at Krasny Luch in the Donetsk region.

Close friends Maria Chichneva (*left*) and Katya Rabova.

Natalya Meklın

Lily Litvak, the legendary fighter pilot, known as the 'Free Hunter' and the 'Rose of Stalingrad'.

Natalya Meklin in the cockpit of her tiny bi-plane, the PO-2 night bomber. Note the elegant pure silk helmet worn under the heavy flying helmet.

6

'Achtung, Litvak!'

Lily Litvak walked towards the end of the airfield. It was dark, but the air was still pleasantly mild and she wore no coat. In the gloom, towards the end of the runway, she was challenged by a sentry near one of the anti-aircraft gun emplacements, and she gave him that day's password. She walked a little past the defence line and stopped to look at the glow of Stalingrad against the sky. The dominating sound that night was the *whooshing* of the multiple Katyusha rockets being launched across the river at the German positions.

Today had been one of the best of her life. Both she and Katya had convinced Baranov that they should remain with his unit and, she'd confided to Ina, she though she had fallen in love with Losha Salomaten. She had told Ina that she wanted to walk for a little to try to sort out her thoughts. It seemed to her that an almost idyllic situation was developing. She was flying fighters, which had always been her ambition, and now she was in love with the man she was flying with. To complete the idyll, he was clearly attracted to her. But hadn't all the women discussed it so many times – no commitment to any man until the war was over? Well, she was to tell Ina later, she was making no commitment. How could she, since he hadn't said he loved her? But then, he hadn't really had much chance.

Tomorrow, he had said, you'll kill some Germans. She slowly walked back to her bunker and slept a deep sleep.

The airfield near Stalingrad was fairly typical of the bases so rapidly prepared around the city. Crude but effective rolling devices such as large wooden logs had been dragged behind trucks or teams of horses to level out the surface.

The runway measured around 2,000 yards by 500 yards and ran in the direction of the prevailing east–west wind. It was surfaced with octagonal concrete paving slabs about two yards across. Large numbers of civilians, many of them women, had been pressed into service to lay this surface in a huge interlocking honeycomb pattern as soon as the ground had been levelled. This construction had various advantages, the main ones being that it was very stable, it helped counter the autumn mud, and individual slabs could easily be replaced if they were damaged by air attack. The runway had been built in less than two days; it was another example of the defenders' ability to adapt themselves, crudely but very effectively, to the needs of warfare in their own country. The field's one hangar was camouflaged, as were the roofs of the underground bunkers. Ammunition and fuel were also stored in underground dugouts.

Baranov had issued a stern warning to the men to stay away from the small bunker shared by Lily, Katya, and Ina. At the same time he posted a permanent sentry outside their door. 'To protect the girls from Germans,' he insisted. Lily passed the sentry on her way out the following morning and made her way to the command bunker for a briefing on her mission with Salomaten. They were to fly as a pair in a sweep over the western approach to the city. They picked up their maps and parachutes, buckled on their pistols, and walked out to the aircraft.

Losha was his usual smiling, confident self and he and Lily joked together as they walked to dispersal. Ina told me, 'Losha put his hand on her arm and squeezed it and winked at her as they approached her aircraft. I helped Lily buckle on her parachute. She was bursting with good humour and excitement. She was like a beautiful little animal, straining at the leash. I always felt the same way when I saw her settling herself comfortably into the cockpit – how could someone so small and delicate possibly handle such a powerful aircraft?'

The Yak-9s they were about to fly on patrol were all-metal modified versions of the Yak-1. They were about 35 mph faster than the Yak-1 (with a top speed of 370 mph) and were capable of a fast climb at a steep angle to attack from below. They had a 37 mm cannon and two 12.7 mm machine guns; the high explosive ammunition of their machine guns was dreaded by the Germans. The Yak-9 was equivalent in speed and armament to the Messerschmitt 109, and almost as good in general performance as the Focke Wulfe 190 fighter. In the hands of a skilled and aggressive pilot, the Yak-9 was a potent machine.

From a height of ten thousand feet, the city was partially obscured by low broken cloud. Losha Salomaten led Lily's aircraft in a series of sweeps eastward from the city centre, seeking incoming German formations, then turning back in the hope of catching a swarm on its home run. She had slipped the guard off the gun button and fired a brief burst to test her armament. To her left and several thousand feet below, a flight of Heinkel 111 bombers drifted into view through a break in two cloud formations. Salomaten told her he had seen them and asked if she had seen the three Messerschmitts sitting above them. She had, but the Germans did not appear to have spotted them.

Lily learned later that Losha was not as interested in stopping the enemy from dropping their loads on the city as he was in shooting them down. If that meant waiting until the bombs had gone, then so be it. He knew that as soon as they had dropped their loads, the enemy would change course. It was then that they were at their most vulnerable. So they flew a parallel course, slightly behind, using cloud cover to screen themselves from the Germans.

Lily was about six hundred feet to the right rear of his Yak. Her head constantly swivelled up, to the side, and to the rear. Then Losha's voice came over her headphones: 'Follow me.' The light underbelly of his Yak heeled into view as he rolled his fighter upside down and into a diving turn to the left. She pushed the throttle forward on to full power, slammed the stick to the left, and followed him down. They were not above and behind the German bombers. Where were the fighters? Her head pivoted, then concentrated straight ahead as she followed her leader.

They were diving straight at the leading bomber as he turned on to a new course. She saw pieces fly off his wings and smoke starting to gush from the port engine. Then Losha was through the formation. For two seconds the bomber filled her windscreen. She pressed the gun button and was still firing as she yanked the fighter hard left to avoid the bomber's tail. She pulled back hard on the stick and zoomed straight up, looking for her leader.

She had lost him. She half-rolled the Yak out of the climb and back in the direction of the bombers. They had scattered in all directions. The leading Heinkel was spinning out of control, with flames and smoke from both engines. Where was Losha?

She heard his shout in her headphones: 'Troika, Troika, behind you. Break right.' She glanced in her rearview mirror and saw a Messerschmitt 109 flattening out from his dive, bobbing in her slipstream, and firing. There was a hammering of bullets behind her cockpit. She broke hard right, diving and rolling continuously. The German was following her. She could see the flashes of his guns, but she felt no more hits. Then in her mirror she saw a ball of orange flame.

She checked the roll and climbed in a tight left-hand turn. Losha Salomaten was waiting for her a thousand feet above. She took up her battle position six hundred feet from his wingtip and scanned the sky from horizon to horizon. Just over a minute had elapsed from their dive through the German formation and Losha's destruction of the German fighter. The fighters had gone, and so had the Heinkels. She followed Losha down through the broken cloud in a diving turn to the west of the city.

116

They picked up a straggler at three thousand feet, flying for home at top speed. The Germans had not had a chance to reform in a defensive formation; there was no sign of the fighter cover. Losha reduced power and dropped behind and slightly below the Heinkel 111. Lily, as she told Ina later, knew exactly what he was up to. There was a 'dead space' to the rear of the German bomber where the defensive machine guns were ineffective. Salomaten waved to Lily to close up and then ordered her to attack.

Lily floated her Yak up so close under the tail of the German that she felt she could slide back her cockpit hood and touch it. She was rocking in the enemy's slipstream as she further reduced the power to his airspeed. Then she squeezed her finger on the gun button. She held the burst of machine-gun and cannon fire for almost ten seconds. She could see the shells ripping and tearing through the underside of the Heinkel, and she skidded the nose to the left and kept the spray directed at the port wing and engine. An explosion and flames erupted from the engine and suddenly the German pilot reacted. The Heinkel nosed straight into a dive. Losha, who had been covering Lily's rear, now followed her down. It was in a way a sickening spectacle, almost like a target practice, as the two alternately covered and attacked. Flames spread from both wings to the fuselage.

At a thousand feet, the two Yaks pulled up from their dive into a hard left-hand turn. They circled above the doomed bomber until it exploded in a field below. An oily black column of smoke rose from the fierce flames of the wreckage.

The free hunters flew across their home airfield at no more than fifty feet above the runway. Then Salomaten broke left and Lily broke right, and they each soared into an exultant victory roll. Ina Pasportnikova told me, 'Baranov was just getting into his aircraft for a sortie when they did their victory roll over the airield. I thought he might be furious – sometimes if a fighter had battle damage, that sort of aerobatics at the end of the mission could make it break up. But he just grinned.

'Lily looked flushed and delighted. Salomaten jumped out of his cockpit and came up and put his arm around her and said, "This girl's going to be an ace – I'll bet you anything on that." Then I noticed the jagged bullet holes behind the cockpit. Lily saw me looking at them and told me she was all right. Salomaten said they would fly another sortie in an hour, but I told him I would need longer than that. I wanted to check inside the fuselage to see if the hits had damaged any of the control cables to the rudder or elevators at the rear.'

The beautiful young couple walked briskly across the control bunker to write up their reports on the sortie. In another time and place they might have been strolling hand in hand and talking of the future; but the future for them here was no further forward than their next sortie. Losha had promised her she would kill some Germans. Together that morning, they had already killed eleven. Ina checked her watch. It was 8 A.M.

Through the short winter days, Lily Litvak and Alexei Salomaten continued to forge and perfect their partnership. By Christmas she had personally shot down six German aircraft – three fighters and three transport aircraft running the gauntlet of the Russian air defences in a desperate and vain attempt to keep the trapped Sixth Army supplied from the air. On the ground, they no longer made any secret of their feelings for each other.

Ina explained, 'Most of the girls in the women's regiments were in love with someone or other. But most of the boyfriends were men they had met briefly while sharing airfields with men's regiments, and their romances were conducted at long distance by letter, with only the occasional chance meeting. For Lily and Alexei it was different. They flew together most days and in the evenings they were together again as much as possible. There was nothing undignified about the way they behaved. He would come and sit and talk to her in a corner of the girls' bunker. They would hold hands and sometimes they wouldn't say very much to each other. They would just sit together quietly. It wasn't an uncomfortable silence between them. They seemed content to be together.'

It was almost impossible to be alone for any length of time. But some evenings the young lovers would pull their fur-lined helmets over their ears, wrap their heavy coats around themselves and walk across the airfield together, Lily's slight figure padded out to bulkiness by her heavy clothing and the taller figure of Salomaten beside her, his gloved hands thrust deep into his pockets. It would usually be freezing, and even with their fur socks and heavy boots it would be necessary to walk briskly to keep their circulation going.

Lily had always taken pains with her appearance, but everyone in the women's regiments encountered difficulties when it came to keeping themselves fresh and clean. One of the biggest treats for any of them was when a 'bath train' came to their part of the front. Then, the women would be given priority; as hundreds of unwashed males lined up outside the train, they would luxuriate in the showers and baths and the scalding hot water.

But that was an infrequent luxury. For the rest of the time they had to make do with bathing in nearby rivers in the appropriate seasons or else boiling water on the stoves and giving themselves a thorough wash-down.

Hair-washing was a particular problem. Ina told me, 'Often at the end of the last sortie of the day I would bring Lily a large bucket and a towel and a piece of soap. She would open the radiator cap on her Yak and drain the scalding water into the bucket, and then top off the bucket with cold. Then she'd fling off her flying helmet and tuck the towel around her neck, and I would pour the hot water over her head as she worked up a lather with the soap. Then she'd mix more hot water from the radiator and do it again, then rinse it thoroughly with cold. The men couldn't believe it when they first saw her doing it. Neither could Katya Budanova. But the idea soon caught on. Lily would stride off to our bunker with the towel wrapped around her head and a few minutes later she'd emerge with her hair shining and bouncy.' A lot of the men thought that Baranov would blow his top at this exercise, but it showed just how much Lily had won him around. He shrugged his shoulders and grinned. She'd proved what a good pilot she was. If she wanted to wash her hair under the Yak's radiator, a bit of hot water was hardly going to break the Soviet Air Force.

Lily's love affair with Alexei Salomaten could have been disastrous for regimental discipline in other respects, though. It was an open secret that Alexei was visiting the women's bunker most evenings. But none of the other women were seriously involved with any men in the regiment and, besides, everyone knew that Salomaten's courtship was being conducted under the gaze of several other women. Perhaps the fact that Baranov, the commander, was Alexei's friend had a lot to do with it; it seemed that he was prepared to turn a blind eye to his younger friend's passion for the woman pilot.

Ina told me, 'There was never any question of Lily flinging her arms round his neck and kissing him before they climbed into their fighters to fly a mission. Nor did they stand around the dispersal area holding hands and gazing into each other's eyes. But he looked at her with such deep concern and obvious love before they flew off together. And then after they'd landed, the relief on his face that she'd come through it yet again was so transparent.

'Lily told me that it was agony up there sometimes when Alexei was being attacked. But of course it gave each of them a fantastic incentive to fight really well. Far from their love for each other affecting their concentration, I think it helped. Lily had always shown the sort of aggression you need to be a good fighter pilot. But her love for Alexei was the thing that turned her into a killer.

'Sometimes, of course, they found it impossible to hide their feelings after they had landed after a rough sortie. Once when they got back to dispersal, I could see that Lily had taken quite a few hits in her fuselage just behind the cockpit. He leapt from his aircraft and was standing beside her wing when she climbed out. He put his hands under her arms and lifted her slowly down from the wing as if she was a little doll. Her hair was clinging to her forehead with sweat where she'd taken off her flying helmet. He half lowered her to the ground and, with her face level with his, he whispered something to her. I couldn't hear what they said to each other, but I could guess.'

Ina's role may sound like that of a voyeur, but it wasn't like that at all. She was Lily's closest friend; Lily confided in her, and Ina felt a tremendous affection towards the pilot and her boyfriend. Her interest was based on fondness and concern, and she followed the progress of every sortie they flew with anxiety. She told me, 'They seemed such a perfect couple. None of us could bear the thought of anything happening to break them up. We shut the idea from our minds.'

For the mechanics like Ina, the rigours of the winter around Stalingrad could be excruciating. Temperatures dropped to 40 degrees below. At intervals during the night the mechanics, working in shifts, would struggle into the unbelievable cold and start up the engines to prevent them from freezing solid. In the mornings, one of them would drive to each aircraft and pour hot water into the cooling systems to melt the ice.

The real hell was working to repair aircraft between sorties. Ina told me, 'Some of the work was tricky and required some delicacy. It meant that, however cold the air temperature was, you simply had to strip your gloves off to get the job done. Inside the engine, some of the metal would be cold and other pieces very, very hot. Some parts of the aircraft were so cold that they would lift off the skin on your hands. Others would give you bad burns. Your hands were usually so cold that you didn't notice they were burning until the damage had been done. Sometimes the only way to get, say, a little nut into part of the engine with numbed fingers was to spit on the finger and, as it froze, attach the nut to the finger. Then you'd fumble around the screw, using your finger like a screwdriver to attach it.' It took courage and determination of a different kind from Lily Litvak's to do the job that Ina Pasportnikova did so well, but it was courage, nonetheless.

The turnaround of aircraft between sorties could take up to half an hour. During that time pilots would get out of their cockpits and get something to eat at the field kitchen, or they would go to a bunker or tent near the dispersal area where there were beds and chairs. There they could lie down and try to relax their aching muscles before the next take-off.

Such was the case one wintry afternoon. Lily was lying on a bed with her eyes closed. Katya was on the next bed, and Alexei was sitting in a chair with his feet up, smoking a cigarette, when someone ran in and said there was a Messerschmitt 109 circling just above the airfield. They all ran outside. Sure enough, directly over the field, at a height of around two thousand feet, was the unmistakable shape of the 109. The visibility was good and there was no cloud cover above him where others might be lurking. What was he up to? He was either very brave or very foolhardy. Most German fighters over Stalingrad were now operating at the limits of their range, and air superiority over the city had passed to the Soviets. Still he circled. It could only mean one thing. It was an old-fashioned gladiatorial challenge to single combat. Salomaten was given permission by Major

Baranov to take off. His Yak was now refuelled and rearmed, and five minutes later he was airborne.

Ina told me, 'Lily was very pale. She watched Alexei take off and climb towards the German, then she turned and went back inside the bunker. She could not bear to watch. She need not have worried. Although the German had the advantage of height, it was all over in less than five minutes. We could see everything from where we were standing. The German crashed near the airfield, in flames. There was no parachute.' Whatever the reason for his extraordinary action, it had cost him his life.

Lily heard the crash and ran from the bunker, a look of terror on her face. Ina told her it was all right, and even as she spoke, Alexei's aircraft flew low over the field and pulled up into a victory roll. He jumped down from the aircraft and a cheer went up. He grinned with pleasure and winked at Lily. Half an hour later, they were airborne together again.

Lily confided in Ina and in her fellow free hunter Katya Budanova, but she was shy of personal publicity. The Soviet propaganda machine had been quick to realize the potential of these young women for morale-boosting stories for the home front. Over the months, the Soviet population had become familiar with the names of several of them in particular and with the exploits of their regiments in general.

Ina recalled, 'Lily's name had appeared in the newspapers from time to time, but she was very shy. She had resisted several attempts to do full-length features on her. One evening while we were still at Stalingrad, a journalist in a captain's uniform was brought to our bunker by the commander. Major Baranov pointed out Lily to the journalist and said, "Lily is our pride. That's the one you want to talk to." '

He got off to a bad start. Lily had just had her hair tied

up in a mass of paper curlers by Katya. Embarrassed, she turned away quickly and tried to pull her leather flying helmet over her curlers. But the bulk was too great. Still with her back to the reporter, she pulled a blue silk scarf from a bag and swiftly tied it over her head and under her chin.

The reporter looked at her and, despite her unflattering headgear, he was clearly impressed. He said, 'It's unbelievable, a beautiful girl like you a fighter pilot.'

He could not have said a worse thing to Lily. She was patronized by the remark and clearly offended. But it gave her the excuse she wanted to escape from the proposed interview. She disappeared from the bunker for a moment and came back tugging Ina by the sleeve. Ina had just finished some work inside a Yak engine, and she hadn't even had time to wipe the oil from her hands and face. Lily told the reporter, 'This is Ina Pasportnikova – she's much more interesting than me and she knows everything about everyone.' Then she pulled on her coat and gloves and left the bunker.

Ina told me, 'Katya came into the bunker very soon afterwards, and together we gave him an interview about the girls in general, and Lily in particular. He was especially interested in her, anyway. We took the attitude that, although she didn't want personal publicity, he was obviously going to write about her, and it was better that he got accurate information.' The reporter left well satisfied, and a few days later a large story about Lily the free hunter appeared in one of the major newspapers. It made her a sort of instant celebrity, but she found it an embarrassment and refused to discuss the story with anyone. Ina and Katya did not dare tell her that they had furnished most of the details.

It was not just the Russian population who knew about Lily – the Germans, too, now knew of her. The newspaper publicity was one reason, and the other was the large white rose that Lily had had painted on both sides of her fuselage. For all her shunning of personal publicity, there was clearly a natural flamboyance bubbling to get out somewhere, and the fuselage decoration was her way of expressing it. Such personal insignia would not normally have been countenanced, but the commander clearly had a liberal attitude towards Lily's little indulgences, although the free hunters were by no means exempt from normal air force discipline. One of the male mechanics who was a skilled signwriter painted the roses just below the cockpit; he also painted a much smaller row of roses along the nose, each one signifying a kill. Lily became known as the White Rose of Stalingrad. Frequently when she was up, ground monitoring would hear German fighter pilots calling to each other: 'Achtung, Litvak!'

It was inevitable that a woman as attractive as Lily should have other admirers among the young pilots in the regiment. Ina had shrewdly spotted very early on that Boris Gubanov – the one who had laughed at Lily's discomfiture about her first sortie – was clearly smitten, and her prediction had been right. He was a lieutenant and therefore junior to Salomaten, but that was not the reason he held back from any open protestation of his feelings for Lily. It was obvious to everyone that she was in love with the man she flew with. So the dark-haired, dark-skinned Gubanov from Georgia adored her from afar.

Lily was fully aware of his love and, though she did nothing to encourage him, Ina felt that she enjoyed the uncritical adoration of the handsome young man. Certainly, Salomaten did not appear to regard him as a serious rival for her affections. Despite their mutual interest in Lily, the men appeared to get along well together, and certainly the circumstances of his subsequent death seemed to shock Salomaten very deeply.

Ramming of enemy aircraft was not a standard operational procedure of the Soviet Air Force, but it was certainly practised widely at some stages of the war. Officialdom, which gave high decorations to several pilots who downed enemy aircraft with this desperate technique, did not appear to discourage it as a tactic of last resort. Boris knew he was a doomed man, though, when he rammed his enemy. He was wingman of the other pair flying with Lily and Alexei. They attacked some Junkers bombers, and Gubanov was hit by one of the fighter escorts. The flames reached the cockpit quickly, and the heat twisted the canopy so that he could not eject it to enable himself to parachute clear. His friends heard the young man's screams. In his agony he kept his hand pressed on the radio transmit button, and they heard him talking himself through his last actions in a desperate effort to maintain concentration as the flames engulfed his body. He was steering towards a Junkers bomber and he was going to ram it.

Lily and the others could see his fighter engulfed along the length of its fuselage as it rammed the bomber. The two planes tumbled towards the ground locked together, then both exploded in midair. Ina told me, 'They were very shaken when they landed. It was bad enough to lose a friend in combat, but to have listened to his screams, burning alive, had a very distressing effect on both of them. Lily was wracked with guilt that perhaps she could have been more kind to him.'

The battle for Stalingrad was over. The remnants of the German Sixth Army were beginning their trek across the snow of the steppes, to captivity, and the bleak winter sun was shining over the remains of the great city. German air activity over Stalingrad had ceased, and Lily and Alexei took off and made a low sweep at high speed across the battleground of the devastated city. They flew in a loose formation at a height of a hundred feet, speeding as low as they dared, as they took this last look at the place that had dominated their lives for so many weeks. It turned out to be a sobering experience in which they were confronted with a brief vision of hell shared by the many here on the ground.

They had never walked these rubble-strewn streets, but at this height the kaleidoscope of scenes racing below their wings gave them a vivd impression of the awesome destruction that had taken place: mile after mile of flattened buildings had been pulverized into ugly, jagged undulations of brick and stone. They tipped their Yaks on to their wingtips as they wheeled around the elevators of the tractor factory which had been a familiar landmark. Neither said much.

They peeled off, one after the other, to screech at 300 miles per hour around the summit of Mamayev Hill which had been so bitterly fought over. A burned-out German tank hulk was perched near the summit. On all sides of the hill lay the unburied bodies of the Soviet and German dead. A column of Russian soldiers looked up and waved. Lily and Alexei waggled their wings in salute and flew in silence towards their new airfield, which was in the Donbass area where Hitler's troops were regrouping following their retreat from the North Caucasus.

It was March 1943 and Lily had been flying in combat for ten months; she had borne what seemed to be a charmed life. Many other pilots had been killed or badly injured, but Lily had escaped without even a scratch. In the furious air battles she had been involved in with Alexei and Katya Budanova, her aircraft had been hit by enemy fire on a number of occasions but somehow she had escaped unscathed. Of course she was a good flier, but many other good fliers were now dead. She had had a large slice of luck, and no one was more aware of that than Lily herself. Ina told me, 'Lily never thought that she was invincible, but she did believe that some pilots had luck with them and others didn't. She worked on the assumption that if you survived your first few sorties, then the longer you carried on and the

127

more experience you got, the better your chances were. But you needed that luck.'

Lily's luck began to run out on the day she shot down her ninth German aircraft, a Heinkel 111 bomber. She had learned from Alexei not to open fire with her machine guns and cannon from long range, but to get as close as possible then fire a short concentrated burst. On this particular day, Alexei was above her, protecting her rear. She felt sure she had killed the mid-upper gunner in the bomber on her first pass, and she was now descending from right angles to rake along the bomber's wing and try to get the second engine alight. As she closed, a sustained burst from the mid-upper gunner smashed through the engine cowling. Lily's engine stopped dead. She hauled the Yak out of its shallow dive and turned away from the enemy, looking swiftly around for a convenient landing field. There was nothing Alexei could do to help, and it was little consolation that he was telling her over the radio that the bomber crew was abandoning their aircraft and bailing out.

She was over her own territory, but she knew she could not reach the nearest friendly airfield without power. Alexei followed her down and helped her select a field. She did not tell him that the burst that had destroyed her engine had also hit her left leg. The first shock had worn off and the pain was appalling. She could feel the blood flowing down her leg, and she wondered if she would land the aircraft before she passed out. Ina told me, 'Lily didn't want to worry Alexei. There was nothing he could do to help. The field was a good one. It was a long piece of pasture and there weren't many trees around it. She got it down in one piece.'

The Yak, with its undercarriage still folded up inside the wings, banged and slithered across the field on its belly. It hit a rut and spun around violently before coming to a halt. Lily unfastened her harness, pulled back the canopy over her head, and climbed out. Blood was pouring from her leg wound, and the inside of her boot felt soggy. Alexei flew low across the field and she waved her arm vigorously. He had radioed their home base, which was only a few miles away, and he circled the crash-landing site to guide the transport. Lily hobbled to the roadside, took the scarf from her neck, and made a tourniquet around her thigh to stop the bleeding. Alexei, running low on fuel, turned for the base, making one more low pass over Lily. She waved to him and he disappeared behind a tree line. Baranov drove up a few minutes later. Lily stood up to talk to him and promptly fainted.

7

Winter in the Stalingrad Pocket

For the friends whom Lily and Katya had left behind in the 586th Women's Fighter Regiment at Saratov, life could, by comparison, be frustrating. They had all read the stories that had already started to appear in the newspapers about Lily and Katya and the free hunters, and they were sometimes tempted to emulate them. Valentina Petrochenkova, the newcomer to the regiment, found the temptation irresistible.

She was flying her second sortie, as a pair with another woman, patrolling at three thousand feet above the bridge at Saratov. Their mission, as usual, was to drive off any enemy bombers who might attack it. It was a brilliantly clear day with visibility seemingly endless, and at low level they saw a German reconnaissance bomber skimming its heavily camouflaged route towards the bridge. They dived on the raider. When he saw their approach, he reversed direction and sped for his lines. At treetop height the German pilot jinked and weaved as the women repeatedly attacked from opposite directions.

Valentina told me, 'We got quite carried away by it all. We could see that we were hitting the German on almost every pass we made. We'd fire at him, climb and turn, and then dive back down on him. But he wouldn't go down. By the time we realized where we were, we were a long way beyond the line on the map which we were supposed never to cross. We should have been satisfied that we had driven him off and resumed our patrol. As it was, we landed out of ammunition and almost out of fuel. And we got into terrible trouble for disobeying instructions. It was a serious matter.'

Soon after Valentina joined the regiment, Valeria Khomyakova – the woman who had taken pride of place in Valentina's collection of clippings – was killed on a night mission. There were tears in all the women's regiments. In addition to being a national heroine, Valeria had been a dear friend.

Usually the friends of those killed in action carried certain mental images of the women lost, treasured memories which were more vivid than any photograph. To the friends of Valeria Khomyakova of the 586th, that image is of the tall woman in the blue flying overalls standing near the bridge at Saratov, the morning after she shot down the first bomber to be claimed by a woman in the history of air combat. For several hundred yards along the bank of the Volga were scattered the remains of the Junkers 88 that she had downed in the darkness just a few hours before. One of the few pieces recognizable was the tall tail section with the black swastika spidering across its surface. It was just after dawn, and the bodies of the crew lay in and around the wreckage. They had tried to parachute at too low an altitude and their chutes had not had time to open. The silk lay entangled in their broken limbs. Someone told Valeria that they had checked the campaign ribbons on the pilot's chest. He had flown throughout the war, from the Low Countries to the eastern front. Valeria looked upset by what she saw. She was looking across the Volga to the light blue smoke rising from the hills beyond Saratov.

Soon Galia Boordina was to add another night bomber to the regiment's list of kills. She was in her Yak-1 above a railway station she was protecting when parachute flares started drifting down several thousand feet below her wings. The Germans were starting their bombing run and were illuminating the target. She dived down and reduced power to adapt her speed to that of the formation. From slightly above and behind she was able to see in dark silhouette the distinctive shape of the Junkers 88 bombers droning ahead towards the target. She reduced speed further and dropped below the formation. Their bomb doors were swinging open. She climbed again and carefully positioned herself about two hundred feet behind one of them. She glanced to her left. Slightly higher and only fifty feet away was another one. Had he glanced down he could scarcely have failed to see her. She skidded the Yak slightly to the right and firmly squeezed the gun button. The aircraft vibrated as the tracer streamed towards the Junkers dead ahead. The bomber on her left jerked immediately into a violent twisting dive and was gone from sight. Her intended victim flew steadily on. She increased speed and, closing range, put another long burst of cannon and machine-gun fire along the fuselage and into the area of the wing root. A tongue of flame appeared and then erupted along the wing. The German heeled over and dived. She was out of ammunition and fuel was running low. She went home.

Galia told me, 'I didn't know if I had shot him down definitely or not. It was a strange thing. I felt very pleased but not as elated as I thought I would. I found night flying so physically draining and nerve-wracking that all I wanted to do was to go to sleep when I landed. I made my report and fell into bed.'

The women of the 587th Bomber Regiment arrived on the Stalingrad front in time for the Soviet counteroffensive against General Paulus' Sixth Army. The first heavy snows had already fallen and the morale of the German troops was sinking. Most were still dressed in their light denim summer uniforms, and they were having to fight savagely from house to house as they inched their way towards the city centre. Soon the Soviet Union's double-pincer blow, from north and south, was to encircle and trap in the Stalingrad pocket a quarter of a million German troops. And now, for the first time, the Soviet Air Force was achieving numerical superiority.

The thirty twin-engine PE-2 bombers landed on their airfield, followed by several transport aircraft carrying ground crew and essential maintenance equipment. They had seen several flights of German bombers and fighters at different altitudes, but with their own fighter escort two thousand feet above them, the women had not been attacked. As they descended towards the airfield, the Volga had appeared to have a dull sheen to its surface; the first layer of the winter's ice was spreading from bank to bank. The river ferries, so important to their troops' supply, were smashing slowly through the wide channel.

Marina Raskova, who had taken command of this regiment, set up her command post in an underground bunker, and the women were shown to the bunkers that were to be their homes for the next few months. As they trudged across the airfield, their heavy fur-lined boots kicked up the snow. They beat their arms against their bodies to get the circulation going again after their flight. On their way to the bunkers, they passed several groups of men walking in the opposite direction. They were from a fighter regiment based on the same airfield. They shouted friendly greetings to each other, the men grinned, and several of the women giggled.

They stepped through the doors of their bunkers and someone produced matches and lit the oil lamps. It was disgusting. The bunkers had been occupied by men before them. The stove was stone cold, with grey ash seeping out of its bottom. The rough wooden planks on the floor looked as if they had never been cleaned. Cigarette stubs and empty food tins littered the tables. And over everything lingered the smell of stale tobacco.

The stove was cleaned out and lit, and then several of the maintenance detail arrived carrying various pieces of 'essential' equipment. Katerina Fedotova, a PE-2 pilot, told me, 'Wherever we went during that war we carried with us in the transport aircraft some of the basic essentials we needed to keep things clean. We had things like brushes, domestic shovels, and several washing tubs which we used to boil water. We weren't issued with things like bed sheets, but most of us acquired them, and we kept these clean in the tubs. We liked to try to keep everything clean, though in those conditions it was obviously very difficult. At the end of a day's flying, we would often seem like housewives, rolling up our sleeves in our spare time and washing and scrubbing. It was all part of being a woman as far as we were concerned.' Before they reported to Marina Raskova for a briefing on the Stalingrad situation that first evening, the bunkers were beginning to look more respectable.

The regiment's first mission was a strike in support of ground troops in the region of the Stalingrad tractor plant. The attack was to be made at first light, in regimental strength, using all thirty aircraft. The plant was near the river, to the north of Mamayev Hill, the highest ground in the city. Both the tractor plant and the hill, scenes of some of the most bitter hand-to-hand fighting of the entire war, were to become familiar navigational landmarks for the bomber crews as the months went by.

During the night the temperature dropped to 40 degrees below. The stove in the centre of the bunker had gone out, and as navigator Galina Junkovskaya and her friends climbed from their wooden beds, their breath formed billowing clouds of steam in the light of the oil lamps. It was 5 A.M. They pulled on extra socks, their fur-lined overalls, and flying boots. Someone relit the stove. On a table near the bunker door one of the women picked up a large piece of sausage lying on a plate beside some bread. The sausage was like a stone, frozen hard like the bread, but the field kitchen would be brewing something hot to drink before the pre-flight briefing. Shivering, they stumbled out of their bunker into the early morning darkness.

Galina told me, 'I was very nervous about the mission.

We were to be dive-bombing, and though the navigators were not responsible for releasing the bombs over the target in attacks like that, I wasn't sure yet just how good my navigation would be.' Her nervousness was understandable. Their mission was to bombard the German troops who were attacking the defenders of the tractor plant, but the two sides were so close together that the front line was very difficult to pinpoint, despite aerial reconnaissance photographs. The positions were marked on their maps, and copies of the photographs were given to the navigators in each of the three leading aircraft. The regiment would fly to the target in three flights of ten, at short intervals and at slightly different altitudes, to guard against surprise enemy air attack. There would be no fighter escort for this mission.

Galina continued, 'It's hard to imagine temperatures of around 40 degrees below unless you've actually experienced it. We felt the air burning our throats with every breath we took on the way to the aircraft. We climbed up through the hatch in the belly and took our seats. But the pilot's hands were so cold she couldn't handle the controls for the take-off procedures. A mechanic handed us up handfuls of snow, and the radio operator and I rubbed the pilot's hands until she could feel them tingling again.'

The oil and water had been drained from the engines to prevent them from freezing solid during the night, and the ground crew had replaced both water and oil before the aircrew climbed into the aircraft. The crews had problems starting both engines on most of the bombers; but as the sky lightened, the aircraft climbed from the runway, their speed building up slowly under the weight of the 2,000-pound load of bombs in the bay under the fuselage.

The weather report had stated that visibility over Stalingrad was good. Galina told me, 'I was looking for landmarks as we approached the city. I saw the tractor factory, then a bend in the road towards the river. We were to drop our bombs to the right of there, where the Germans were sheltering in the rubble. I watched for the lead aircraft to open its bomb doors. Then we opened ours, and as the leader dived on the target, we heeled over and followed her down. Our bombs fell away and the aircraft seemed to leap.' As the PE-2 pulled up from its dive and went into a climbing turn, the crew saw the bombs strike in a string of orange flashes and clouds of grey spouting smoke.

Galina and several other fliers recalled that they had met no opposition at all on that first mission over the city. In an odd sort of way they felt cheated. However, it had also been a saddening experience. Katerina Fedotova told me, 'Those of us who'd flown over Stalingrad before the Germans reached it were appalled by the destruction. It seemed there was hardly a building left standing anywhere. There was just rubble everywhere. The Germans had done most of it, but now we were helping to destroy whatever remained. As a woman I couldn't help thinking of the families who'd once lived down there leading normal family lives. And as I thought that, I realized that there were probably still many thousands of civilians in there who'd not been able to escape the fighting.'

Confronted daily with the harshness of war, the women made special efforts to keep up their spirits, though their off-duty pleasures were of necessity simple ones. That night, after their first sortie over the city, they had a sing-along in one of the bunkers. They sang mostly folk songs accompanied by several of the women who brought their musical instruments with them to every front. A woman from the Ukraine sang a mournful song about her homeland and several women wept openly.

On social occasions like this, everyone joined in. Most of the mechanics and other ground crew were other ranks, and at that stage of the war, the fliers were mainly junior lieutenants or lieutenants. But when the day's operations were over, it was unheard of for anyone to pull rank. Even

Marina Raskova was able to combine her natural authority with a willingness to unwind at the end of a hard day.

A mechanic told me, 'We were all girls together. And the longer we were together, the closer we became. There were some exceptions, of course – you can't be expected to get on with everyone you meet. But the great majority of us had this bond which we've never been able to recapture with any other group. The comradeship was very special.'

Comradeship was one thing, but every human being needs a little privacy sometimes. Later in the war, there would be opportunities to slip away from the others for a little quiet contemplation in the birch forests near their airfields. At Stalingrad that was not possible. The 587th Regiment did not fly night missions, and in the evenings they were usually confined to the relative security of their bunkers. Some would lie chatting to each other, some wrote letters, others read letters from home, some played chess, and some simply lay on their backs, staring at the ceiling of the bunker. Low-flying aircraft would shake the structure slightly, and occasionally a little earth would silently slide between the rough wooden ceiling supports and crumble damply on to a blanket.

A welcome relief was the start of regular film shows at the airfields. Feature films made by the Soviet film industry – usually in heroic style exhorting the people to throw out the invaders – alternated with newsreels of the fighting and an occasional film from the European theatre of war. Like all war-time newsreels, these were carefully selected and edited pieces of propaganda, but the women found the whole experience very cheering, especially as the audience was composed mainly of young men from the other regiments at the airfield. The films were shown in the hall of a large building near the base. The ancient projector frequently broke down and, when the lights went up for repair, the fighter pilots would move into seats closer to the women.

Katerina Fedotova told me, 'We always said that we could tell one sort of male pilot from another without even speaking to him. The bomber pilots walked in a particular way. They were rather slow and deliberate and even ponderous looking sometimes. The fighter pilots walked with more swagger and style and they had a certain nerviness about their whole bearing. Well, we believed we could tell them apart that way, anyway.'

Katerina had not even seen her future husband standing up, let alone walking, when she fell for him. As the lights went on during a breakdown in the film, she turned and saw him sitting beside her. He started talking to her, and as the light went out again, she decided not to watch another frame of the film. He was already an ace – he had shot down more than ten German aircraft – and she thought he was the most interesting man she had ever met.

They walked back to the women's bunker in a large group. He had one arm around Katerina and the other around another woman. The others went in and left the two of them standing outside. It was 30 degrees below and they both moved about to keep warm, stamping their feet and banging their gloved hands together. Katerina told me, 'It was neither the time nor the temperature for romance. He eventually took hold of my hands and drew me towards him. He kissed me briefly and said, "Please don't get yourself killed."' He was posted to another front the following day and, though they corresponded as frequently as the postal service would allow, they did not meet again for two years.

Though battles continued to rage on the ground, air operations by both sides were sometimes hampered or ruled out altogether by bad weather. Low-level reconnaissance flights by both sides to probe defences and build up an intelligence picture of overnight troop movements still occurred, but the bomber crews were grounded. Nonetheless, they would crawl out of bed for the routine morning roll call and sick report. They would then spend the day reading intelligence reports on new enemy fighter tactics, studying, and testing each other with flash cards showing silhouettes from different angles of all the known enemy aircraft on the eastern front. Another duty on such days was the checking of their aircraft for any sign of lack of airworthiness, which would then be reported to the ground crews.

Target practice also helped fill the hours. The women carried automatic pistols in holsters on their belts during every flight. These were for personal defence in case of being shot down behind enemy lines. The women had to practise marksmanship frequently and keep their weapons clean. Accustomed to firing hundreds of rounds per minute from the massively powerful machine guns in their bombers, however, they did not take their pistol practice too seriously. Their efforts at target shooting, however, belied the accuracy they were to show in marksmanship during a celebrated air battle a few months later.

The women were flying from one of the fifty or so new airfields that had sprung up on the Stalingrad perimeter while the Soviet forces prepared for their counteroffensive. As they returned from their sorties, they could see for themselves just how ingenious were the efforts of their people to mislead German air reconnaissance. On airfields, which they knew were unoccupied, stood rows of dummy aircraft and thinly fabricated mock buildings. They looked utterly realistic, and raids on decoy bases meant less bombs falling on the real ones. The Germans themselves have since praised the ingenuity of these decoys and the misleading effects they had on their intelligence.

Just before midnight on 26 November, 1942, Hitler addressed a personal message to every soldier in his Sixth Army, then trapped in the Stalingrad pocket. He ordered them to stand fast and assured them he would do everything in his power to support them. What he meant was that he would supply them by air with fuel, food, and ammunition until a relieving force could reach them. It was a promise he had no chance of keeping. The airfields in Stalingrad, on which he depended for resupply and evacuation of the wounded, were gradually to fall into Russian hands – until the only contact the Sixth Army had with the outside world was by radio.

Increasingly, the Soviet bombers were switching their attacks to outside the area of encirclement, against the enemy airfields from which the hard-pressed Germans were attempting to fly supplies to Paulus and his men. Though losses were heavy among the Soviet fighter and ground attack units, in many ways Stalingrad was one of the easiest campaigns of the war for the women flying the PE-2s. Enemy fighter activity over the city was becoming less and less frequent because of the increasing distances from their bases and the limited endurance of the fighters.

The strain that was to drive some fliers near the breaking point at later stages had not yet manifested itself, though the living conditions and the harsh weather were taking their toll in more mundane ailments. Women flew with heavy colds and influenza and sometimes even managed to conceal more serious illnesses from the regimental doctor.

Katerina Fedotova told me, 'One girl had a bout of rheumatic fever. She didn't know what it was at the time, but she did discover some months later. It was obvious to her, though, that it wasn't some minor bug she was suffering from. She was a navigator, so she didn't actually have to fly an aircraft. But she refused to report being sick, despite the terrible pains in her joints. She knew that if she told the doctor, she'd have been taken off flying duties, perhaps permanently. She fought through the illness, but as the war went on her joints got stiffer and stiffer. She was a very good navigator, very quick brain, but there's no doubt she ruined her health by carrying on the way she did. But at least she survived the fighting.'

140

Maj. Marina Raskova was feeling the strain. She was definitely overworking. She sat every night at the table that served as a desk in her dugout. She worked on regimental reports, studied intelligence briefings, absorbed new tactics that would have to be passed on to her aircrew, and worked herself on tactical ideas. She also felt very keenly her responsibility towards the young women in her care. Though they had yet to lose a single aircraft, she knew that they had so far borne charmed lives. She saw the combat reports of other regiments and she knew the awful suddenness with which their situation could change. She was a leader and she knew she must present an image of purposeful aggression. But her face some days had a hint of fatigue, and the women knew that she herself was a wife and mother and that her thoughts must often stray to those she loved.

. Katerina Fedotova and another woman went to Marina Raskova's dugout one evening around nine o'clock. They tapped gently on the door; when there was no reply, they pushed it open and peered inside. Katerina told me, 'She was fast asleep, her head resting on its side on top of her hands. A pencil was still held lightly between her fingers, but she was breathing deeply and evenly, obviously asleep.' The dugout was very neat. Some brightly coloured thread lay on top of a piece of cloth. The commander had been attempting some embroidery at some time during the evening, before she settled at her desk. Her pistol hung in its holster over the back of her chair, and her flying gear was neatly folded at the end of her bed. A photograph in a brown wooden frame had been knocked over on the desk. The women walked softly across and looked down at the picture. A serious looking little girl with large dark eyes looked out of the frame. She was holding the hand of a tall man in an air force uniform. He was smiling gently at the camera. The women tiptoed out into the night and returned to their bunker.

8

587th Bomber Regiment, North Caucasus, 1943

Anyone whose curiosity overwhelmed him could have stolen into the women's bunkers at the PE-2 bomber regiment's base during any day when the women were flying missions. It would have taken a few seconds for his eyes to become accustomed to the gloom inside as he clicked the door behind him on its simple latch. He would fumble to the table and light one of the oil lamps improvised from brass shell cases, and as the wick flared, the light would reveal two rows of wooden beds running down either side of the bunker. Despite the heat from the stove in the middle of the floor, the smell of damp earth pervaded every bunker. On every bed were neatly folded blankets, and hanging from nails above them air force issue underwear – rough woollen vests and long, ankle-length drawers – hung incongruously next to delicate petticoats and panties sent from home. Here and there a treasured dress, a blouse, a skirt or scarf – all draped on improvised clothes hangers and waiting for the opportunity to transform their owners from soldiers into women once that day's fighting was over. At the end of each bed were little wooden boxes that held mirrors, lipstick, powder, small bottles of scent, and the pieces of jewellery which regulations forbade them to wear with their uniforms. On the blankets lay half-written letters, and on the upturned ammunition boxes which served as bedside tables, bunches of dried flowers. Needles and darning thread protruded from little sewing boxes, and many of the pillows were embroidered with flowers or half-finished names of friends and loved ones.

The interloper might be surprised by the sound of scratching and meowing, or the yelping of a small dog – for the women were incurable adoptive parents of any stray that turned its appealing eyes towards them. Antonina Bonderova told me, 'We could not resist taking these poor creatures in. Many people were starving, so dogs and cats didn't have much chance. They used to come scratching at our doors. We shared our food with them and after a few weeks they would become quite sleek and fat. We often wondered what had happened to their owners. The dogs in particular would become attached to one girl. It was very difficult, because when we moved airfields we just had to leave them behind.'

One night there was a yelping and whining at the door to one of the bunkers. They opened it to a flurry of snow and a blast of subzero wind, and a wolf cub tumbled inside. He was bedraggled and thin, and made only a half-hearted attempt to bite at the woman who picked him up and carried him across the room to lie beside the foot of the hot stove. Antonina told me, 'It was a wild animal, of course, but as he dried out and his fur fluffed out around his face, he looked so adorable that we just couldn't resist him. We fed him some chocolate and some black bread in warm water, and he curled up beside the stove and went to sleep. We were all quite excited by the prospect of trying to tame a wild animal, though our two cats at that time sat on the end of a bed near the stove looking at him very warily. We thought that he was just another orphan.'

They were wrong. In the middle of the night, the entire airfield was awakened by a hideous wailing and howling outside the door of their bunker. The cub's mother had come to claim him back. He was picked up and the door was opened and shut quickly. There was a short yelp from outside as the mother administered some mild retribution for his truancy, then silence in the snow.

It was 6 January in Stalingrad. Inside the encirclement, the remains of the German Sixth Army, a quarter of a million men, waited for the end. The cold was intense. The

German troops were down to four ounces of bread and a few scraps of horse-flesh a day from their slaughtered horses. Ammunition was handed out at a daily rate of only twenty-five rounds. The Soviet Air Force was taking a dreadful toll of the lumbering German transport aircraft – the troops' only hope of supply – and the daily tonnage was a mere fraction of what was necessary to sustain the army. Pitomnik, their last remaining airfield inside the encirclement, would soon be overrun. They were hopelessly isolated, and now they would never break out. Day after day the women in their PE-2s helped bomb the doomed Germans hiding in the ruins of what had been one of Russia's most modern cities. On that day, 6 January, they flew without Marina Raskova. She and two other crews had been detached from the Stalingrad front for several days on a special mission in the Kuban area of the Crimea.

Heavy snow was falling outside, but inside one of the women's bunkers there was a warm soporific fog of heat. A thin haze of blue tobacco smoke hung in the air from the cigarettes the men were smoking. The women were having a sing-along to celebrate the acquisition of a battered old piano. The men had all been asked politely but firmly to wipe their feet on some sacking at the door, and now they lolled on the beds near the piano, carefully keeping their boots clear of the bedding. Irina Soodova had a beautiful soprano voice and had been a pupil at a school for gifted young musicians; she was singing and several other women were taking turns at the piano to accompany her.

The atmosphere was relaxed, and there was no shortage of alcohol. After each mission, the aircrew was entitled to 100 grams of vodka each. Few of the women drank, so the men eagerly traded chocolate rations with them for vodka. There was a lot of flirting and tentative propositioning going on, but the sheer number of people was a natural inhibition to anything more serious.

Only one thing clouded the women's enjoyment. Marina

Raskova and the other two crews had been due to return before nightfall from the Kuban area. It was filthy flying weather on their flight path back, but the women reassured themselves that the experienced Marina would guide all three aircraft to a diversionary airfield if things had become too difficult. She would arrive tomorrow morning.

The door of the bunker opened suddenly, and the rush of cold air swirled the blue smoke in eddies down the length of the bunker. Irina Soodova stopped in mid phrase and the pianist lifted her hands from the yellowed keyboard. All eyes turned to the door. Several women inhaled sharply as if to prepare themselves for a cry of greeting when Marina and the others walked in. But the figure who stepped in, ducking his head as he entered, was the commander of the men's regiment.

Everyone stood up as he took off his snow-covered hat and peeled off his gloves. He closed the door and stood as if collecting his thoughts. Galina Junkovskaya told me, 'We all knew before he opened his mouth that he had something unpleasant to say. It was obvious from his expression that he didn't know how to begin. Most of us assumed that it was some catastrophic news of a new German success against us. To us, at that moment, what he did have to say was much worse.'

Finally, the officer pulled a piece of paper from his pocket. It was a typed message from the airfield's signal bunker. The message was brutally terse. It said simply that Major Raskova had been killed when her aircraft crashed. Galina told me, 'There was a moment or two of complete silence. I looked around me at the other girls. Their faces were completely drained of colour. Then it seemed that everyone was crying together. I flung myself down on my bed and buried my face in my pillow. All around was the sound of the most anguished sobbing. Could this really have happened to Marina?' Galina lifted her head after a while and looked around her. The last of the men were slipping out through the door into the night. There was nothing they could say that could have helped.

The wind rattled at the door and the stovepipe in the bunker ceiling hissed as snowflakes descended under the cowl that covered its exit through the sandbagged roof. In Marina Raskova's bunker the stove had not been lit for several days. Her desk had been cleared of reports before she left. A pen lay on a sheet of blotting paper and two unopened letters awaited her, propped against the photograph on the desk top. One was written in an uneven, childish scrawl.

The women learned the full facts of their commander's death the next day. Marina Raskova, it seemed, had been just as human, just as fallible as anyone else. She had, quite simply, made a mistake. Leading the other two aircraft in her flight, she had become disorientated in the swirling snow and was lower than she should have been. Her aircraft had flown straight into the summit of a hill. She was thrown clear but was killed outright. The others, slightly higher, had crashed, too; but they had ploughed through the deep snow and had escaped serious injury. They would be rejoining the regiment.

The blow to the regiment's morale was inestimable. Marina had been their heroine from school days and training days in the flying clubs. She had been the unifying force, the rallying point to which they flocked to fight for their country. She had never indulged herself in the cult of personality; indeed the adulation had often seemed to embarrass her. Nor had she ever hinted that she thought herself immune from sudden death through human folly or enemy action, the prospect that seemed to hover at the shoulder of every woman every time the wheels left the ground. Her high standards of professionalism had instilled in all her crews the belief that if they aspired to these levels, they would not kill themselves through stupid error. And now she was dead – killed through an apparent navigational error. Most of the women remembered how hard she had been driving herself and how very tired she looked before she had flown off to the Kuban. They wondered how tired she had been on the trip home.

It was clear to the commander of the division to which the women's regiment belonged that something would have to be done, and quickly, if they were to remain an effective fighting force. The answer arrived the next day in the tall, serious form of Maj. Valentine Vasylivich Markov.

Markov had been chosen for a variety of reasons. Most important, it was felt that to appoint a new commander from among the women themselves would not be a good idea in these circumstances. They had all been badly shaken by Marina Raskova's death, and it was thought unlikely that, from such a close-knit group, a new commander could be found who herself was unaffected by the blow. There was another reason for the choice: Valentine Markov was thirty-two years old, a veteran pilot, and very much a man of the world; but he also had a reputation for a high moral code. Most of the aviators were still teenagers, and a high proportion were very attractive. Clearly there were some men whom it would not have been a good idea to appoint to such a command. The temptations were enormous, and any man who succumbed to them would have found the effect on morale and discipline even more devastating than the death of Marina Raskova. Major Markov knew the problems well and was determined from the outset to keep an arm's length of respect and authority between himself and the women as a sort of sexual safety barrier.

Valentina Kravchenko told me, 'We were all very much in awe of Major Markov. From the first time he lined us up for inspection and introduced himself to us, it was obvious that he was going to be strict with us. But we didn't realize then just how strict he could be.'

After addressing the women, he ordered them to their aircraft and then climbed into each bomber to inspect the equipment. He paid particular attention to the machine guns. In one aircraft, he summoned the radio operator/gunner to her position and pointed to her two machine guns. 'These guns will probably not fire,' he snapped. 'Can you tell me why?'

The woman looked bewildered, but she managed to stammer, 'I don't understand, sir, I oil them every day.'

He turned on her: 'That's precisely the problem. You've used the wrong sort of oil, far too much of it, and those guns are going to jam. Don't expect any different from me just because you're a woman. Now get them stripped down and clean them properly.'

His voice carried beyond the bomber to the crews waiting outside the other aircraft, and they winced in anticipation of the faults he might find with them. The new commander stormed from that aircraft and into the next, through the hatch in the belly. He stopped in the cockpit and stared at the instrument panel. Pasted on the panel between the dials was a newspaper photograph of the late Marina. There was another on the bulkhead beside the navigator's chair. He opened his mouth to say something, then thought better of it and stepped briskly away. On the ground, standing to attention in front of their PE-2 was another crew. They looked impressive in their flying overalls and they saluted as their commander approached. He ran his eye over their uniforms and pulled up short.

Katerina Fedotova told me, 'Most of us had embroidered little motifs on the sleeves and collars of our overalls. They were very pretty but they were discreet. Marina had known about them, and although they were against regulations, she had turned a blind eye to them. After all, it was hardly the sort of thing the men were going to copy, was it? But Major Markov had different ideas. He pointed out that we were soldiers, not seamstresses, and told us to get rid of the embroidery.'

In their bunkers that night the women sat with their

flying overalls draped across their knees, unpicking the multi-coloured threads they had so painstakingly embroidered over the months. Scissors snipped and marigolds, roses, and forget-me-nots twisted and fluttered to the ground. They hated him at that moment, but as one of them told me, 'We realized, when we sat and thought about it, that he had a very difficult job to do. We would have thought even less of him if he had taken a very low-key approach to us and allowed us to sink into depression over Marina. As the months went by and we got to know the sort of man he was, we all realized that his brisk treatment was doing us an enormous favour.'

One area in which the new commander had been unable to find any fault during his initial inspection had been the cleanliness of the bombers' cockpits. After every mission, the aircrews tackled the floors with dustpans and brushes, ferreting into all the corners behind the rudder pedals and underneath the seats. There was a very practical reason for this. When the nose was pushed down during dive-bombing or when the aircraft had to be violently thrown about for defensive measures, all the mud, dirt, and other debris would shoot into the air and could blind the pilot at a vital moment. It might happen to the men, but it never happened to the women.

As commander of the regiment, Valentine Markov led many of the missions himself, and in his position he could choose the navigator he wanted. Increasingly, the women noticed that he would select Galina Junkovskaya. She was certainly one of the best navigators in the regiment; no one disputed that. But she was also one of the most beautiful. On the face of it, the man leading the mission was simply demanding the best possible navigation to lead the entire regiment to the target. Galina's friends were unconvinced that there was no more to it, however.

Antonina Bonderova told me, 'We teased Galina unmercifully about it, but she would have none of it. She would always tell us that he treated her exactly as he treated everyone else – with respect but detachment. But we girls were taking a very keen interest in the whole business. And we were all agreed that when Major Markov spoke to young Galina, his voice changed altogether. It lost its edge and he spoke very softly. He couldn't help himself, even when there were other people around. He might simply have been briefing her on a mission, but he never spoke to anyone else quite like that. No, we were all sure he was falling for her. The only person who wouldn't accept the obvious was Galina.'

Many of the women had by now formed serious attachments to fliers whom they had met on shared airfields but who were now on different fronts. They lived for the letters these men sent them; sometimes these would arrive in twos and threes because of the erratic wartime deliveries. It mattered little if in their eagerness they read them out of sequence – the message was always the same. There were no envelopes; the rough writing sheets were simply folded over and tucked in. Usually the military censors had refolded them neatly after scanning the youthful protestations of love for indiscretions of a different kind. It was hardly surprising, with their own boyfriends so far away, that the other women took such an interest in the growing love affair between their commander and Galina.

Galina told me, 'I honestly had no idea at that stage how Valentine felt about me. I must have been naïve. I admired him as a professional and I thought he was a good man. But that was as far as it went. I felt no romantic stirring. I thought the girls were just teasing me, the way young girls do.' She could not have begun to guess how Markov felt that day when they were attacked by a German fighter. He threw the PE-2 around the sky while the fine-boned Galina swivelled her machine gun, her eyes screwed up in concentration, her lips pulled back from her teeth. He did not dare look around to see if she was hurt by the bullets he

150

could feel slashing through the fuselage. He was flying for his life – for her life. Not until they had landed safely did he know for sure that she was completely unharmed.

The women invited the major to the birthday party they were giving for Valya Matuchina. Valya was charming, and she looked just like everyone's image of a young farm girl. For several weeks, the women had all been saving their meagre butter rations, and now one of the cooks had used it to bake a large birthday cake. There wasn't any fruit to put in it, but there was plenty of chocolate to mix in, and someone had carved a very creditable model of a PE-2 bomber from a lump of dark chocolate to place on top.

Men from another regiment had been invited, too, and a woman played dance music on the piano with an accordion accompaniment. They danced as best they could in the cramped space of the bunker. Major Markov was clearly enjoying himself. He was chatting to a group of his women fliers, and sitting next to him was Galina Junkovskaya.

The highlight of the party was the presentation of a surprise gift to Valya. With a great flourish someone produced from under a brown paper wrapper an empty penicillin bottle filled with milk, with a teat on the end. Valya entered into the spirit. She lay curled up on the bed in a foetal position, gurgling and cooing, and sucked noisily from the bottle. On airfields all over Europe, young pilots in different uniforms were indulging in similar sorts of mindless, high-spirited horseplay to release the tensions of the terrifying jobs they performed. But not one of them was a woman.

Major Markov and the 587th Bomber Regiment had now transferred to the North Caucasus front, and his obvious love for Galina Junkovskaya was about to renew for him the torment that had started when he had fought by her side in that furious aerial battle over Stalingrad. This time she would fight without him and he would find it impossible to preserve his calm.

Galina told me, 'It was a routine mission, bombing enemy troop concentrations, and our nine bombers had a cover of eight fighters. So we felt fairly secure.' Shenya Timofeva, a squadron commander, was leading the formation. The plan was that she would pinpoint the target with her bombs, and the others would aim for her explosions. As they approached the target area, though, the problems started.

There was broken cloud cover extending in layers for several thousand feet, and the fighter escort above them disappeared. The next message from them was a terse one – they were engaging a heavy swarm of enemy fighters. The women were on their own. They had had to descend from five thousand feet to around three thousand feet to see the target.

Galina told me, 'We closed up our formation to concentrate the fire of our guns and flew on to the target, craning our necks. We knew that the fighters our boys had tackled had been making for our formation, and we knew it was only a matter of time before some of them broke away and came for us.'

Two Focke Wulfe 190s broke through the clouds first. They dived straight through the formation, guns and cannon blazing. As they zoomed up from their dive in front of the leading bombers, four Messerschmitts followed them through. Four bombers were hit on those first passes; Galina's plane caught fire around the port engine, 'Masha, the pilot, shut off the fuel supply to that engine and stopped it, but the fire continued. Then the Germans came again.' Cordite fumes stung their eyes and shell cases cartwheeled past their faces from the breech as Galina and the radio operator fired their machine guns at the enemy aircraft. Spent cases rolled around their feet. Still fully laden with bombs and with one engine gone, the PE-2 could not maintain its altitude. Smoke streaming from its left wing, it dropped out of formation.

Antonina Bonderova told me, 'We could see their bomber dropping steadily away below us, but still heading towards the target. There was nothing more we could do. We kept our defensive formation and pressed on. Our gunners hit four of the German fighters. I don't think we shot them down, but we put them out of the fight. But the other two then concentrated on the crippled PE-2.'

Galina's aircraft was not only descending now, it was also falling behind the others. They were able to find their own way to the target, though, and the PE-2 leapt as the bombs were released. As the aircraft turned awkwardly on a course for home, the two Focke Wulfes bore in on them again. Galina, who had already reloaded her gun once, pressed the trigger. Nothing. She was out of ammunition. The bullets from the leading fighter raked diagonally across the cockpit, whining off the armoured seat where she had sat a few minutes before.

At the same time, the aeroplane tipped alarmingly into a dive. Galina swung around. Her pilot had been hit. She was slumped over the control column, her face to one side. The wind howled through the enormous hole in the windscreen and revealed to Galina the full horror of the last attack. Her friend's leather helmet had been torn off in the slipstream, and the wind lifted her blood-soaked hair off her unconscious face. Jagged slivers of plastic were embedded all over her skin and forehead. As her head lolled, a little pool of blood was forming at the corner of her eye.

Galina reached over and pulled back on the stick with all her strength, but the aircraft did not respond. They were picking up speed in a dive towards the ground, and the aircraft was tending to spin towards the pull of the good engine. Galina pulled the throttle levers back and reduced power. The bomber levelled out, and at five hundred feet, Galina pushed the throttle lever on the one remaining engine hard forward again to try to maintain height.

The fighters seemed to have gone. She held the stick with one hand and, though she could not do anything to reach the rudder pedals to keep the aircraft straight, she did keep the stick over to try to prevent the aircraft from turning in the direction of the one engine.

Under the seat was a first-aid bag. She fumbled with one hand until she found the familiar shape of a bottle. She unscrewed the cap and held the smelling salts under Masha's nose. The effect was instantaneous. Masha opened her eyes and sat up. 'What's happened, Galya?' she asked, brushing her gloved hand at her face and crying out as the glove gouged deeper the tiny transparent arrowheads. Galina handed her an absorbent dressing pad to wipe the blood from her eyes and gave her a heading to steer them back over their lines and towards their home base.

Two thousand feet above, the Focke Wulfes wheeled like birds of prey. They had sat watching what they thought was the death plunge of the Soviet bomber. Now they dived again. Galina told me, 'I looked up and saw them coming. I didn't have time to reload. They were making a frontal attack this time, and the radio operator couldn't help with her guns. I opened the cockpit hatch above my head and grabbed the pistol that fired the signal rockets.'

The Germans, in line astern, were holding their fire until close range to make sure of a kill. Galina squeezed the trigger of the pistol and the rocket burst between the two fighters in a ball of red flame. Galina ejected the cartridge and fumbled for another. But it was unnecessary. The Germans broke away right and left and turned away for the last time. Her desperate gamble had paid off. She told me, 'I believe they must have been running low on fuel by that time anyway, but there's no doubt that they would have pressed home their attack if I hadn't fired the rocket at them.'

Galina grabbed a map and located a village ahead on a bend on a river. Five hundred feet below stretched mile after mile of birch trees and evergreens. They were near their own territory. The only problem now was to find some gap in the forest to land the aircraft. The starboard engine was overheating because of the massive demands being made on it, and they were still descending. There was no chance of their making it back to their home field.

Maj. Valentine Markov had been leading another of the three squadrons on a different mission. Now he stood on the airfield, counting the other squadron's aircraft as they circled the airfield and landed one after another. He knew from radio messages that several of the aircraft had been hit. He counted eight down and ran to them as they taxied to a halt and the crews clambered out.

Valentina Kravchenko told me, 'He did not need to watch the crews climb from the aircraft. He knew by the numbers on their fuselages that Galya's was not among them. We had to tell him that the last time we had seen their aircraft, it had been under heavy attack. You could not lie to the commander. He might have thought that he was showing no signs of emotion, but we could see in his face the anguish that was going through his mind. He went off to check for reports from our troops of any aircraft that had come down on our side of the lines.'

Galina spotted the yellowish swath of a road cutting through the forest at right angles to a stream. She looked for a check on wind direction. Just upstream from the bridge at the end of the road was a hamlet; the smoke from the cluster of houses seemed to blow straight across the stream. The pilot was weak and in great pain, and the bomber was still losing height – they were now down to around four hundred feet. They could not afford to attempt a circuit of the 'runway' to take a closer look. They would have to use a straight-in approach to the road.

The radio operator had left her position farther down the fuselage, and she now cranked the handle that lowered the undercarriage until it clunked into its locked-on position.

The aircraft settled into a steady descent towards the road and, when the pilot instructed her, Galina pulled a lever that lowered the flaps on the wings, increasing the angle of descent without increasing the airspeed. It was a perfect approach. They crossed the end of their 'runway' just where the forest road bent towards the bridge. The road also served as a firebreak, so it seemed as they floated downward that there was more than enough space to accommodate their wingspan.

Masha was finding it difficult to stop the aircraft from turning towards the working engine. Fifty feet, forty feet. At that moment, Masha passed out again and slumped forward. The nose pitched straight down at the road. Galina grabbed the stick and yanked it back. The bomber wallowed, sinking fast, and Galina pulled the throttle closed, cutting the power. A couple of seconds elapsed, then the aircraft smashed down on its undercarriage in an uncontrolled landing. It leapt into the air again, hurling all three women into a heap on the cockpit floor. The tops of the birches gave way to blue sky as the nose lifted, and then every inch of the fuselage seemed to screech in protest as it thumped down again and careered along the road for a hundred and fifty yards until it slewed into some saplings and came to a halt.

Galina reached across and tugged on the pilot's hand. The smell of fuel was heavy in her nostrils. She and the radio operator helped Masha through the cockpit hatch. The bulk of their parachute packs made their exits difficult.

For the first time it occurred to them that they could have tried to jump. The fire in the left engine, which had appeared to go out on their descent, was still smouldering. They had walked only thirty yards down the forest road when the aircraft exploded. Burning metal showered around them as they flung themselves to the ground.

9

Moscow and Donbass, March 1943

Lily Litvak sat hunched on the floor of the transport aircraft that was taking her back to Moscow on convalescent leave. Although it was spring, the transport was cold and draughty; no matter how she positioned herself amid the ammunition boxes and other stores on the floor, it was very difficult to get comfortable. Also, she was never very happy about flying in any aircraft unless she was at the controls.

After her crash landing, she had recovered consciousness in a field hospital. She lay in a narrow bed in the crowded tent with a blood transfusion drip in her arm. Soon a nurse brought to her bedside the surgeon who had operated on her. He was a tired looking middle-aged man, but he managed a smile for the pilot. He handed her a misshapen piece of metal – part of a bullet that had pierced and lodged in her arm. 'It'll remind you to keep out of trouble in the future,' he said. She had placed it under her pillow and, still running a temperature and in pain from her leg, she fell asleep. The next face she saw, waiting patiently at the bedside for her to awake, was her beloved Losha Salomaten.

Ina Pasportnikova told me, 'When Alexei landed after circling the field where Lily had crash-landed, he told us all that she was down safely with nothing wrong with her. He flew another sortie that afternoon with a different wingman; when he landed again, Baranov had returned – but without Lily, of course. When Alexei discovered that she had been hurt, those who were there with him thought he was going to collapse himself. Baranov gave him permission to go to the field hospital a few miles away, and he rushed off with a driver in a truck. He sat beside her bed for a couple of hours until she came around.'

Lily's leg wound would leave her with a slight limp, but as she and her boyfiend held hands and talked softly to each other, they were continuously reminded of just how lucky she had been to escape with the injury she had. Pain-killing drugs were not in plentiful supply, and the moaning of young men, terribly injured and trying not to scream aloud, was a distressing background.

Alexei had brought with him two gifts. There was his own, almost new copy of love poems by Simonov, which he had inscribed on the title page: 'To my love, Lily.' He also gave her a little, slim dagger in a leather sheath, with a black wooden handle that he had carved himself.

Ina told me, 'Lily could never resist playing superstitious games. She told me later that as Alexei turned and walked from the tent, she promised herself that if he turned back and said something then she was sure they would be married one day. He turned at the door of the tent and mouthed something silently, which she could not lip-read, then grinned and ducked under the flap and was gone. Lily didn't quite know what to make of that.'

The airport where Lily's transport landed was considerably closer to the centre of the city of Moscow than the present Sheremetyevo Airport. Moscow was no longer under continuous direct threat of air attack, but there were rows of fighter aircraft lined up around the airfield awaiting dispersal to various fronts. She hitched a lift on an army truck part of the way and took a tram the rest of the way to Nova Slobodskaya Street. The trams were packed so solidly that it was folly to push inside if one wished to force one's way out again anywhere near an intended stop. Instead, people clung to the roofs and to every hand- and foot-hold along the side of the vehicle. For Lily, hobbling on a stick and with a heavy bag over her shoulder, it must have been a tiring and painful journey.

The sidewalks were packed solidly all day long with

teeming masses of Muscovites pushing in undisciplined, contraflowing streams of humanity and spilling over on to the streets. The tarred surfaces of the main street looked as if they had been shelled, although the damage was actually due to lack of maintenance and repair. There were deep potholes everywhere, and occasionally a bus would lurch into one, dislodging unsuspecting passengers from roof or side with a roar or a scream. Most of the buildings in the city were coated with stucco and by that time their yellowish surfaces were peeling badly. On the whole, it could not have been a cheerful return to the native city which Lily loved and where she had spent such a happy childhood.

The Litvak family home was a typical two-room Moscow flat that shared a kitchen with several other families. Lily had not been able to tell her family exactly when she would arrive home, so she had to hobble up to the first-floor flat on her own. The smells of cooking that permeated such apartment blocks were not unpleasant to Lily, and her spirits must have lifted with the warmth and the familiarity that assailed her as she approached her own front door. Her father, a railwayman, was driving trains near one of the fronts, but her mother Anna and brother Yuri embraced her tearfully when she entered.

Yuri was only fourteen years old, too young for the army. They had always been a close family, and the adolescent boy worshipped his sister. He had collected every newspaper article about her and her friends in the women's regiments, and he kept them glued in an exercise book. She had sent her mother a photograph of herself standing in front of her Yak. It was framed and in a prominent position on the wall where the light from the window would illuminate it.

Lily was very affectionate to her mother and her young brother. He would sit on the floor at her knee, having brought a footstool to rest her injured leg. Then she would put her arm around him and indulge him as she was pumped for information about her flying and her friends. He teased her about Losha. But both he and his mother must have been worried by the change in Lily's appearance.

Her mother, Anna Vasilneva Litvak, who died a few years ago, would later tell Lily's regimental friends who came to visit that she was shocked by the changes in her daughter. Natalya Meklin told me, 'Lily's mother said that her daughter no longer seemed able to relax. She was obviously still in pain from her leg wound, and Anna Vasilneva would catch her wincing in pain as she moved about the apartment. Perhaps her mother was upset that Lily was so anxious to get back to the front line where she had so recently avoided death. She would come into the room and find Lily gazing out of the window looking very sad and serious, her thoughts far away from Moscow. She was a very different person from the carefree girl who had gone to war. But her mother told me that she would always remember Lily not as the dashing fighter pilot, but as the little blonde girl racing around the apartment and chuckling as she jumped from the top of the piano on to the couch.'

After a week, Lily was anxious to get out of the apartment and test her leg in the streets. She found that signs of shortages were obvious. No goods appeared in the windows of any of the 'gastronoms'. On display instead were cardboard representations of what food a shop might have on sale. There were different gastronoms for different goods and, as foreign diplomats there at the time would vouch, there were also different qualities and selections of goods depending upon one's status. But everywhere there were the enormous queues of people, stoically waiting their turn. Most of the faces in the streets were those of old men and women – the younger, more able-bodied were either working for the war effort in the Moscow factories or at the front.

Lily must have found it exhausting negotiating these

pavements, and her encounter with a rather pompous officer in Gorky Street probably didn't help. Lily, typically, had stuck some small, fresh spring flowers in her cap before leaving her mother's apartment. Now they had attracted the attention of an army major. He stopped her and guided her into a doorway out of the press of people on the pavement. Soviet pilots didn't wear identifying wings on their tunics, and he had presumed Lily was with some branch of the army.

Ina Pasportnikova told me, 'This officer was obviously offended by Lily's very unofficial hat decoration. He demanded to see her documents and then he realized she was hobbling on a stick and he asked her how she had been wounded. Lily said that she never saw such a change in a man's attitude. He insisted on seeing her to the Metro and finding her a place near the door of a carriage.' She snapped the major a brisk salute and her hand brushed the flowers still wedged in her cap band.

She wrote two letters to Losha and in the second one she told him she loved him. It was the first time she had actually written those words to him; this was the sort of commitment that many of the women stopped short of. For Lily and Alexei, though, there seemed little point in pretending that they were not irrevocably tied to each other – and this, her first separation from him, had clearly been the final catalyst for Lily. Ina told me, 'During this separation, I could see that Alexei Salomaten was withdrawn. He was in combat most days, which kept his mind fully occupied, but he was obviously missing Lily.' The irony was that Lily's letter did not arrive until after she had returned to the regiment's new airfield near Rostov-on-Don. After less than two weeks, she had decided that she must get back. Her leg was not fully recovered, but she was able to walk for short distances without a stick. She wanted to be back where the action was and she wanted to be with the man she loved.

The night before she hitched a ride on an aircraft back to Rostov, she went with her mother and Yuri to the Bolshoi Theatre. Ulanova was dancing the role of Odette in *Swan Lake*. Lily wore a blue and white dress, and her mother and Yuri were dressed in their best outfits. There had been no question of standing in line for tickets for the Bolshoi. Without connections there was no chance of getting seats at the famous theatre. The same applied to the cinemas and museums. For most Muscovites, there was nothing to do except walk the streets and parks or entertain themselves as best they could in their own homes. But Lily, a wounded combat heroine, had had little difficulty getting tickets.

The performance was memorable. At the intermission, much of the audience poured out into the foyer of the theatre and walked around and around in a circle until the bell signalled the start of the next act. There were few uniforms in evidence. It was an occasion for everyone to dress up in the best clothes the wartime austerity would allow them.

For all her eagerness to get back to Alexei, the parting from her family was tragically poignant. Her mother knew it was pointless trying to dissuade Lily from returning before her convalescence was complete. The young woman who now stood in the street in front of the apartment block had developed a strength of purpose more powerful even than the determination and drive she had demonstrated during her childhood. Anna Vasilneva Litvak said nothing. She took her daughter's face in her hands and kissed her, and the tears of both became one where their cheeks clung together. Yuri had written her a letter. He pressed it into her hand and made her promise not to open it until she got on to the aeroplane back to Rostov. She hugged him hard and quickly. He was already taller than she and his voice was husky with approaching manhood. Limping slightly, she walked away quickly and was soon lost in the crowd.

Lily knew there was something seriously wrong as soon

162

as she arrived back at the airfield. Losha approached her looking very strained and upset. Lily told Ina later that her heart was in her mouth. She thought that somehow he had changed his mind about her, that he didn't love her any more. He took her by the arm and led her away from the other pilots. The news he had for her was indeed crushing. Baranov was dead. He had been attacked by two Focke Wulfe 190s that morning and his outnumbered wingman had been unable to do anything. Baranov's aircraft had exploded into countless pieces when it hit the ground.

Salomaten was distraught. Obviously he had been crying. Ina told me, 'Despite all the early antagonism of Baranov towards Lily and Katya, they had both become very fond of him and he of them. There was mutual respect and affection. And of course he was probably Alexei Salomaten's best friend. There was nothing that Lily or anyone else could do to console him. He kept saying that if only he had been up there with him, he might have been able to do something to help.'

Lily was immediately promoted to flight commander, and an officer called Martinuk took over command of the regiment. That night the air of gloom was almost palpable. Alexei Salomaten was not the sort of man who wished to talk about his deepest personal griefs; he explained to Lily that he wanted to be alone, and for a couple of hours that evening, after sunset, he walked around the airfield, head bowed, obviously deep in thought.

In the women's bunker Lily was unpacking her belongings. As she refolded the blue and white dress she had worn to the Bolshoi and which she had decided to bring back to the front with her, out dropped the brown envelope bearing her brother Yuri's handwriting. She had forgotten to read it on the aircraft bringing her back to Rostov; her mind had been too full of her return to the regiment. Now she stuck her little finger into a corner and slit it open. She sat down in a chair in a corner and began to read. Whatever her brother had written in the letter made her weep quietly, but she never mentioned its contents to anyone.

The next day, Alexei and the others behaved as if nothing had happened. It did not mean that they had forgotten their commander. It was a sort of defence mechanism among themselves not to brood over such things. The war must go on. The blackboard in the command bunker was covered with chalked words on tactics, radio codes and, on one side, the names of the regiment's pilots. Baranov's name, as the commander, headed the list. Someone had taken a duster and rubbed it out but had not been completely successful. The name was still barely decipherable.

Lily's name had been chalked up on the list in preparation for her arrival at the new airfield, and she was anxious to get back in the air after her enforced layoff. Including her time in the field hospital, it was now three weeks since she had flown. It was vital that she get her eye in again as quickly as possible, and she volunteered for a sortie against a German observation balloon. It was a heavily defended balloon just on the German side of the line, and its observations had been bringing down extremely accurate fire on the Soviet forces in that sector whenever they tried to move troops or equipment on a large scale.

The problem for Lily was that the position was very heavily defended. One of the regiment's aircraft had already been lost in an attempt to shoot down the balloon. She studied the map of the sector which showed, to the best of Soviet intelligence's knowledge, the disposition of German ground forces and, in particular, their anti-aircraft batteries. She decided to cross the German lines several miles north of the balloon, then sweep around to the west at high speed and low level and attack it from behind its own lines.

It was a daring plan but fraught with danger. Behind the German lines she would be at a disadvantage if any German fighters attacked her from above with the advantage of speed and height. At low level she would also be

164

vulnerable to small-arms fire from German troops as well as flak batteries.

She completed her preparations, marking turning points for her course on her maps. She would change to a different scale map once she got within five miles of the balloon, but at low level it was going to be a demanding navigational exercise. She noted landmarks that would be useful, then she limped out to the Yak. Alexei Salomaten was already airborne on a sortie with another pilot to another part of the front.

She climbed to five thousand feet for the first leg of her mission. She picked up her reference point on the ground and, shoving the nose down, descended rapidly to five hundred feet. As the Yak-9 crossed the German line, she was down to two hundred feet and descending. She saw the flashes of some small-arms fire and then she was through it unscathed. The altimeter showed 150 feet; her airspeed was 320 miles per hour.

Things were happening very fast at that speed and that height. She flashed across a bridge at a bend on a river, glanced swiftly at the map on her knee, and turned the fighter into its curve back towards the German lines. The terrain was undulating and she flew very low up the face of a hill, her stomach lurching as she dipped down the other side, frightened that she might have presented a target against the skyline. She changed course again, cutting across a railway line; now the sun was behind her as planned. A line of trees raced towards her at alarming speed. Smoothly, she pulled the stick back and the Yak zoomed over the top. Still on full power, she pushed the stick forward again, regaining the altitude of just over a hundred feet.

The balloon should be less than a minute's flying time away if she was on the correct course. She started her stopwatch. Thirty seconds' flying time to target. Where was it? Then the ground fire started, but with the late afternoon sun directly behind her, she raced on. She felt some hits on the fuselage behind the cockpit, then the balloon appeared, dead ahead. They were winching it down as she approached. She was lower than the balloon and she opened fire with cannon and machine gun at a range of five hundred yards, pulling the nose of the Yak up gently to direct the stream of fire as the doomed balloon descended into it. She zoomed upward, still firing, through the orange flash of the disintegrating balloon, then dived once more to treetop height to escape the ground fire.

She had not lost her touch. She felt exulted. She flew inverted across her own field at a height of fifty feet, then soared into a victory roll. Ina told me, 'Lily was back. When she screamed across the airfield upside down, everyone knew she was back in business.'

Several new pilots had joined the regiment as replacements for those dead, missing, and wounded. They were experienced and highly skilled; still, they all required a period of intensive training in the particular tactics the regiment had evolved for flying in pairs. Some of this training was inevitably going to take place in combat, but whenever the opportunity arose, a pilot like Salomaten would be airborne with one of the new pilots, inculcating his own brand of attack and cover flying and engaging in dogfights that simulated air combat manoeuvring as nearly as possible.

Ina told me, 'There was a lull one afternoon and a group of us, including Lily and Katya, were lying around on the grass watching Alexei dogfighting with one of the newest arrivals. In combat, of course, dogfights would often degenerate in height down to very low levels as the pilots jockeyed for advantage. Alexei and his opponent had come down to low level on several occasions during the simulated fight, then broken off and climbed to a few thousand feet again to re-engage. Doing extreme manoeuvres at very low altitudes was always dangerous, and even the best of pilots could make a mistake that could send him into the ground.' Lily was lounging on the ground, playing with blades of grass, and laughing with Katya. She was totally relaxed and seemed very content with life. It was never boring watching a pilot like Alexei putting someone through his paces, and pilots like Lily and Katya watched with a professional interest. When the newcomer was forced into an impossible position, they would make some sort of joke and laugh with each other.

Ina continued, 'It was the sort of training that has got to be realistic or it's no good, so both pilots were giving it everything they had. The two aircraft had come down to below a thousand feet and Alexei, who had deliberately started the combat with the other man on his tail, was trying get round on him.'

The two Yaks were flying in a dangerous speed regime – at an airspeed so low they were approaching the point of a stall, where they would lose airspeed to the extent they could spin into the ground. Alexei, it seemed, was trying to force the other pilot into tighter and tighter turns at low speed until his nerve would fail and he would break out.

The newcomer's nerve cracked first, and they could hear his engine on full power as he slammed the throttle open and turned out of the turning circle. In combat he would have been a dead man as the other whipped around on his tail; but in the skies above Rostov-on-Don that spring day, it was the victor of the deadly game who was to pay the penalty.

Ina told me, 'We all looked up to see what Alexei was doing. He put his Yak into a steep turn to try to get around on to the other man's tail. But he lost height in the turn. I glanced at Lily's face. She could see what was going to happen. It was screwed up in anguish. Alexei's wing dropped as he turned and it hit the ground. There was a loud bang. Then everyone was running.'

Lily sat stunned for a moment. There was blood on her hands where her own nails had dug through her palms. An ambulance was driving across the wide airfield towards the crash, and Lily and Ina jumped on the running-board as it bumped and sped across the grass. Ina told me, 'Lily's face was quite twisted. She wasn't crying or even making any sound. My arm was around her as we clung to the side of the ambulance, and I told her that there was no sign of any smoke or flame so maybe Alexei was all right after all. She didn't make any reply. But that expression on her face never changed. She knew as well as I did that people didn't survive crashes like that.'

It was quite true. Miraculously, there had been no explosion or fire, but the impact had pushed the entire front end of the Yak into the fuselage. The cockpit did not exist any more. The first to arrive began to hack at the front end of the Yak, and others pulled and scrabbled at the wreckage with their bare hands. One of the wings had sheered off completely; the other was crumpled and compressed where it had first struck and then collapsed into the unforgiving earth. Lily buried her face in Ina's breast as they pulled Alexei from the wreckage. Ina told me, 'It was uncanny. His face was almost unmarked. The blond hair and the beautiful even features. He did not even look afraid. But his body had been compressed into a fraction of its normal size.'

They wrapped him in his parachute silk and, before they lifted him from the ground, Lily knelt beside the body of the man she loved. She pulled back the silk from the fine head of the twenty-three-year-old man from Kaluga, and she brushed her lips across his cold forehead. The look of wild anguish had not left her face, but she did not cry. Not yet. On the belt at her waist was the little dagger with the carefully carved handle. She unclipped it and placed it inside the parachute silk. Then over the handsome face she pulled the light grey fabric. The silk rustled as his friends lifted the bundle into the ambulance. Ina squeezed Lily's hand very hard, then put her arm around her shoulder. Lily's face softened and a mist of grief was passing across her eyes. It was a long walk back across the field to their bunker, but it was cool and dark in there and she knew she could be alone.

10

The Highest Honour: the 46th Guards Regiment

It was January 1943. At an airfield in the North Caucasus, the wind whipped across the open ground, blowing flurries of snow against the thin canvas fuselages of the PO-2 bombers that stood in rows on the snow-covered grass. Protective covers had been snapped tight across the open cockpits, and over these a thin film of ice had formed so that the covers cracked when they were unbuttoned and removed. The wind moaned through the struts and wires that joined the two wings together, and the mechanics working on the engines stopped work frequently to return to and thaw out in their bunkers. There had been no flying the previous night – the conditions had been so bad – and it looked no more promising today.

The 588th Night Bomber regiment had been flying in combat now for eight months. The strain had been enormous. On their foreheads and around the corners of their eyes, the nights of peering in the darkness and frowning and tensing with fear and concentration had begun to scratch almost imperceptibly the fine lines which for many were the first physical scars of war. It was not only the combat that placed them under strain. The early sneers of male chauvinism had hurt them more deeply than they would ever have shown publicly. None of them would ever admit she had behaved recklessly in an attempt to prove her courage and competence beyond doubt, but certainly they had thrown themselves into battle with great ferocity and determination. Their record of sorties flown spoke for itself.

Since their exploits were such marvellous material, they had been featured several times in the newspapers. Now the women frequently received letters from home describing them as heroines. They affected the reluctance of most combat fliers to concede that they were doing anything except their routine duty. But among themselves, the publicity was as much of a boost to their morale as it was to the civilian population for whom such stories were intended. The newspapers may have recognized the role they were playing, but it seemed to the women that their male colleagues were determined to ignore their contribution.

Marina Chichnova told me, 'The newspaper stories were all very nice, of course, but what we craved was some sign from the men that they recognized we were at least equal to them. I know, it should have been enough that we ourselves knew, but it's only human to want some open recognition from those you've been trying to impress. But we all tried very hard not to let our resentment show to the men's regiments.' So recognition, when it did come, was as delicious as it was unexpected.

Capt. Irina Rakobolskaya, normally so calm and composed, burst through the door of the bunker, her face flushed with excitement. The young women were embroidering, mending clothes, and writing letters around the stove. 'Quick, girls, outside, fall in. General Popov's here.' Everyone sprang into action. They pulled on their boots, feverishly polishing them for a few brief seconds with dusters. Brushes swept through tousled hair, and here and there women dabbed and scubbed at each other's faces, removing the faint traces of make-up from their cheeks and lips. Caps and belts straightened, they jostled and pushed their way out of their bunkers and into the biting cold of the airfield. Yevdokia Bershanskaya lined them up, and they turned eyes-left as they shuffled their feet into a straight line.

Nadia Popova told me, 'Major Bershanskaya looked terribly excited. I could see that she wanted to tell us something, but she walked quickly away as we came to attention, and strode towards General Popov's party.'

The divisional commander was accompanied by several other officers. One of them carried under his arm the long pole of a furled banner, and the wind tugged at the large piece of paper the general was unfolding and studying as he walked through the snow. It was bitterly cold. The wind stung the women's cheeks and made their eyes water. They stood in their three straight, stiff ranks, not daring to move a muscle as the tears from their wind-reddened eyes blinked through their lashes and coursed warmly down the curve of their cheeks. General Popov now stood before the front rank with Yevdokia Bershanskaya beside him. She looked triumphant. Then the general began to read from the piece of paper in his hand: 'By order of the Supreme Soviet and in recognition of your outstanding service to our country . . .'

Nadia told me, 'We listened to what he was saying as if we were in a dream. It didn't seem possible that this could be happening to us. But it was.'

The general spoke of the many sorties they had flown, the damage to enemy troops and equipment, and their general devotion to duty. Then he continued, 'I am ordered to announce that the 588th Women's Night Bomber Regiment will from today be given the title of the 46th Guards Regiment.'

It was a complete surprise. To be awarded the title of Guards Regiment was the greatest collective honour they could achieve. It placed them among the elite of the fighting units. There could be no higher recognition of their having proved themselves. It was a moment too sweet to savour in silence. There was no command, or even permission, to cheer. But the general and his party grinned their approval as two hundred girlish voices sent a long shrill of uninhibited exultation into the frosty air.

The banner that the general handed to Yevdokia Bershanskaya was about nine feet tall. Her hands trembled as she untied the gold braided rope that secured it to the wooden pole. She stood back a pace and held the banner vertically against the snow. The red cloth slapped as the wind streamed it free and the women, now silent, gazed for the first time on the gold embroidered letters which proclamied the honour of their new title.

The general took the banner from Yevdokia Bershanskaya and marched ten paces away from the front rank of women. Major Bershanskaya marched towards him, came to attention, and saluted. Then the general inclined the banner until its golden fringe brushed back and forth across the snow's surface in the eddying wind. The women's commander knelt in the snow, took the thick cloth of the banner in both hands and, burying her face in it, kissed the flag. The tears that now welled from her eyes owed nothing to the cold wind. She cried silently out of pride for her girls, anguish for her country, and a deep painful longing for her husband and child. It was a profoundly moving moment. She held on to the flag and raised her head, looking up at the general as she repeated after him the words of the oath. One by one the members of her regiment followed her across the snow to kneel, kiss the banner, and repeat the oath. Pilots, navigators, mechanics, armourers – the broken nails and scars from red-hot metal separated the ground crew from the fliers as they grasped the banner.

They were the first regiment in their division to be awarded such an honour and, of course, the first women's air regiment to achieve it. The weather was still too bad for any missions that night; in normal circumstances, they should have been attending lectures on tactics, learning and testing each other on enemy aircraft recognition, and performing other routine training tasks. Instead they had the biggest, wildest party of their flying careers. They invited all the men from the other regiments on the airfield into their various bunkers, and the vodka flowed and the music pounded through the night.

172

Natalya Meklin was conspicuous by her absence from the revelry. With the pall of cigarette smoke and the dim light, it was difficult to see much in the bunkers, but the lovely Natalya was usually one of the centres of attraction. Nadia Popova found her curled up on a bed in a corner scribbling furiously in a notebook. It was several seconds before Natalya realized she was being observed; when her friend asked what she was doing, she blushed slightly, then said she had been trying to compose a song, a march, to commemorate their new Guards title. 'I don't think it's very good; maybe I'll try again tomorrow,' she said.

'Don't be shy, Natasha,' said Nadia, taking the notebook from her.

'It's supposed to be sung to the tune of the "Internationale",' said Natalya.

Nadia forced her way through to the young man in the middle of the floor who was playing an accordion and singing, and within a few moments a dozen young men and women, arms around each other, were peering over the musician's shoulder and singing the new march of the 46th Guards Regiment: 'We're flying ahead with fire in our breasts, let the flag of the Guards be red at the head . . .' It was written in the typical heroic style of Russian patriotic songs and they all joined in with great gusto. No one looked embarrassed except Natalya. Copies of the song were handed out the next day to all the women. Natalya Meklin's quiet scribblings in the smoky, noisy bunker immortalized the day the women knelt in the snow and wept on the symbol of their courage.

Changes of airfield were fairly frequent as the front fluctuated. When the order came to move, the pilots and navigators would fly in their aricraft to the new site. In theory, the ground crews would arrive and start some rudimentary setting-up before the aircrews flew in, but with roads clogged with other military vehicles and refugees and under the constant threat of air attack, this was not always possible.

On one or two occasions the aircraft arrived over their new airfield on the outskirts of a town or village to find fierce fighting still raging below them. When this happened, they would dive to low level and return to the sanctuary of their old airfield. It was always a strange feeling to circle above the base they had so recently deserted. The bunkers that had teemed with life and sheltered and warmed them when they returned exhausted after night missions now lay like empty, earthen husks, stripped of their furniture, their stoves, and their personal possessions. There would no longer be any communications system from the airfield. The fliers would leave their aircraft and sit huddled together in the darkness on the floor of a bunker for a few hours, then fly again to their new base.

For navigator Ira Kasherina and engineer Sonya Azerkova, though, one evacuation of an airfield became a terrifying battle for survival. A strong local German counterattack was developing only a few miles from their airfield, and the regiment was ordered to withdraw and continue their night harassment of the enemy from an already operational airfield at a safer distance from the front. One PO-2, however, had been having a lot of engine trouble and needed several more hours of work before it would be airworthy again. They could hardly abandon a perfectly good aircraft and, besides, the enemy was still a few miles away and was being fiercely resisted. Major Bershanskaya decided that the odds were in their favour, so Ira was ordered to stay with the aircraft while Sonya completed the repairs; then she was to fly Sonya to the new airfield.

The two women stood beside their aircraft as their friends bounced down the runway and turned on to the heading that would take them to their new base. Sonya wasted no time watching their departure. As the engines *pop-popped* their way overhead, her hands, blackened with oil, were already delving inside the engine. It was difficult for Ira to tell when the noise of the engines was no more. It faded and faded and she was gradually aware that the only sound she could hear was the clinking of a spanner on metal and Sonya's soft grunting as she heaved against a bolt.

Ira had never been on a deserted operational airfield before. The rumble of gunfire from the north was incessant. She had often been afraid during her night missions – all the aircrew had – but this feeling was a different sort of fear. Her war was conducted above the ground. Her killing was done from a height of several thousand feet, once removed from the death on the ground. Now she was trapped here on the ground, out of her element, and the sound of the guns seemed to be getting closer.

She fought back a feeling of panic as she turned to look at the birch forest half a mile away. Were there hundreds of Germans watching them even now, drawing back the bolts on their rifles and feeding belts of ammunition into their machine guns? She unbuttoned the flap of her holster and made sure the magazine of her pistol was firmly in place.

She rolled up her sleeves and, glancing frequently over her shoulder, started to help Sonya as best she could. It was half past ten in the morning. Sonya was one of the regiment's best mechanics, but she was having unexpected problems which Ira did not fully understand. Two hours passed, and Sonya told the pilot that she would not like to say when the repairs would be complete. They might even be forced, she said, to abandon the aircraft altogether, push it to the trees, camouflage it as best they could, and get out on foot.

Sonya's face was quite white as she said this. It was clear to Ira that the prospect of getting out on foot was just as terrifying to her friend as it was to her. She jumped on to the top of the fuselage of the PO-2 and, holding the wing with one hand, trained her powerful binoculars on the road to the north four miles away, where it forked to fan like an inverted 'V' around both sides of the airfield. At first the road was deserted. Then, one squat shape after another crawled up over the rise and started to fan right and left at the fork. Ira had often studied these shapes in recognition manuals. They were German tanks. She croaked, 'Sonya, they're here.'

There was no question of attempting to hide the little plane now. Ira pulled the maps out of the front cockpit and Sonya opened the fuel tank. Fuel gushed from the tank, spread across the fuselage, and ran in rivulets across the hard ground. The air was heavy with the fumes. They crouched behind the hump of a bunker as Ira aimed her pistol towards the front of her aircraft and squeezed the trigger. Within seconds of the *thwump* of the explosion, the aircraft that had carried Ira safely through so many missions was a pathetic, glowing skeleton. The air was full of the red glowing embers of the wooden wing and fuselage spars and the noise of the control wires to the wings and tail twanging sharply as they severed and lashed about in the heat.

Ira shoved her pistol back in its holster, and the two women ran through the smoke of the wreck towards the trees on the other side of the field. They stopped several yards inside the thick forest while Ira looked at her map. A large village lay four miles to the east. They would make for that. They turned left along a faint path beaten by countless generations of forest wildlife and broke into a gentle run. In about ten minutes the trees began to thin; they crawled to the bushes that fringed the roadside ditch.

German tanks were sweeping along the road with great clouds of blue smoke from the harsh engine exhausts swirling over the soldiers who clung to the sides of the armoured turrets. Rows of steel-helmeted heads were visible above the sides of other half-tracked vehicles as the advance column raced on at top speed. The women backed off into the trees once more. They were cut off from their own forces.

Ira decided they should press on to the village, so they kept to the trees, following the line of the road. Once they lay for half an hour in a fold in the ground after they had almost stumbled on part of the column which had drawn off the road into the forest to study their maps. Neither woman understood German, and the guttural accents drifting across the woodland were all the more frightening for their incomprehensibility. Eventually orders were barked and the column moved on.

The women lay in the woods studying the village through their binoculars for a long time. It seemed that the Germans had bypassed it, and Ira and Sonya crept through the outskirts and tapped on the back door of a little house. They had cocked their pistols and now they were on either side of the door, their backs pressed against the wall, the barrels of their pistols cold against their cheeks. The door opened slowly and a young woman peered out, her face pale with strain. A child about four years old clung to her knee. She looked to the left and gave a little shriek as she caught sight of the uniformed figure with the gun.

Ira lowered her pistol and told her, 'It's all right. We're Russians. Are there any Germans in the village?'

The woman pulled them into the dim interior of the house. A chicken flew out of the door between their legs. Across the earthen floor, beside a fire that was billowing smoke into the room, sat two other small children. They looked up, their faces startled with fright at the sight of the guns dangling in the strangers' hands. There was no sign of a man in the house. The woman told them that the Germans had raced through the village without stopping but that they had all heard a lot of gunfire from the next village down the road. Ira and Sonya explained their situation and told the young woman that they must get back to their regiment. But they could hardly do that wearing their uniforms. Could the villagers help? The woman motioned them to sit down on a rough wooden bench beside the fire and silently disappeared.

The fliers fumbled in the pockets of their uniforms and found some dark chocolate. They handed it to the timid little children, who took it, unsmilingly, and immediately began to stuff their little mouths with the strong chocolate. Soon the woman returned, carrying over her arm a pile of very old, tattered, peasant clothing. Ira and Sonya stripped off their tunics and trousers and pulled on the thin, peasant women's dresses and then tied the torn black coats around their waists with string. There were also two head scarves. Their faces and hands were dirty from their flight through the forest, but the last thing they wanted to do now was to make themselves look clean and attractive. Their boots were obviously of better quality than the normal peasant would wear, but they had taken a battering during their journey, so they would probably get away with that, too.

The clothes were none too clean and they smelled strongly of sweat and boiled cabbage. The fliers knew these were not garments rejected months before to make way for new clothes – they had just come off the backs of villagers who had not known the luxury of a new coat for years. They told the woman to hide their uniforms in a safe place and to use them for themselves when the Germans had been driven back again. The women stuffed their pistols deep in the pockets of their coats, and Ira pushed the map down the front of her dress. They tried to thank the young woman but she pushed them gently to the door, embraced each of them briefly, and closed the door behind them. As they walked down the road they affected the hunched, slightly stooped walk of peasant women and deliberately slowed their normally agile, brisk pace. By the side of the road someone had abandoned some large bundles of firewood. They each shouldered a pile and headed down the road that would take them towards their own lines.

Two German soldiers were standing beside a motorcycle combination and one was tinkering with the engine. Mounted in the sidecar was a machine gun with a belt of ammunition dangling from the breech. There was no sign of anyone else on that stretch of road, and it appeared the two soldiers had had engine trouble and became temporarily separated from their unit. The women were upon them before they could do anything about it. They rounded the corner and there they were. The soldiers were only ten yards away. Ira squeezed Sonya's arm very tightly, and they both lowered their heads and continued walking.

The Germans were both tall and looked about twenty years old. They had goggles strapped to the top of their steel helmets and both wore camouflage smocks and had submachine guns slung across their shoulders. They did not seem concerned by the women's approach. They did not even unsling their weapons. But as the women drew level with them, one of the young men stepped in front of them and put his hand roughly on Ira's shoulder. He put his other hand under her chin and lifted her face up towards him. He pulled the scarf back from her forehead; despite the streaks of dirt on her face, he could see that here he had a pretty peasant girl.

He said something in German to his friend, who stepped quickly across towards him, laughing as he replied. Ira's bundle of sticks fell from her shoulder on to the road. The atmosphere was heavy with sexual menace. The first German ran to the corner and looked back up the road. There was nothing in sight. He shouted to his companion who started to push Ira towards a gap in the hedge. The first German was beside them again.

It was now or never. 'Your gun, Sonya, your gun,' screamed Ira, whose hand was deep inside her coat pocket. Her fingers closed on the butt and it was out and in her hand. She cocked it as she raised it and fired into the nearest soldier's face. He fell back without a sound, the blood spurting from the socket where his eye had been. Sonya's gun had stuck inside her coat. The second soldier, his face rigid with terror, was trying to unsling his submachine gun. Ira turned and her gun jerked twice more as she shot him in the stomach from a range of three feet. He was still reaching for his gun when Sonya tugged hers clear and shot into his head. Both Germans lay sprawled awkwardly on the roadside. It had all been over in a few seconds. Both women felt they wanted to be sick.

They knew they must have killed many men on their night missions, but this was different. They had been close enough to these two to see the stubble on their chins and to smell their sweat. The second one had cried out just before Sonya shot him in the head. His helmet had fallen off as he hit the road. He had fair hair and a square, good-looking face, and there was only a small trickle of blood on the side of his head above the ear where the third shot had killed him. The women pushed the motorcycle combination off the road and through the gap in the hedge. Then they dragged the bodies into the field and out of sight. They did not look at the dead faces as they did their work. Two days later they were back with their regiment.

By the middle of February, the night bombers had moved base again, to the area of the Kuban. Here they were to remain for eight months and sustain some of their heaviest casualties. At this stage, as winter began to turn to spring, Hitler – despite losses of almost two million men dead, missing, or captured – still had a well-trained and well-equipped army of around two and a half milion inside the Soviet Union. The Kuban area was vital to Hitler's plans for a renewed offensive into the Caucasus. Four hundred thousand German troops were inside the defensive perimeter of this bridgehead in the Kuban. Behind them lay the Black Sea and the Taman Peninsula – that piece of land directly across the Kerch Straits from the Crimea.

Stalin saw the chance to make the Kuban bridgehead

another Stalingrad. There would be a three-pronged attack – two prongs from the land and a daring assault from the sea – which would cut off the German line of retreat into the peninsula, in the event the amphibious landing was only partially successful and the Soviet forces managed to establish only a toehold with their seaborne forces near Novorossisk.

There had been another, quite unexpected pleasure from the visit of the general who had presented them with their Guards Regiment honour. After the ceremony, he had taken Yevdokia Bershanskaya aside and told her that he didn't care to see women dressed in trousers. He was one of the few men they encountered during the war who appreciated that their continuing femininity was the surest and most obvious way to help their morale. He ordered that the aircrew and ground crew be measured; and just before their move to the Kuban, a transport aircraft delivered the light brown skirts. They were of heavy, hard-wearing material, of course, but someone had taken great care to make them as attractive as possible within the constraints of military uniform. They had a single deep pleat down the front and, worn with the standard tunic and belt, they looked most appealing. In the cold of winter, the women continued to wear trousers for combat missions, but for the rest of the time they eagerly adopted their new uniform. It meant that they had to arrange themselves more carefully in the cockpit when they stepped in, but it was a marvellous feeling to be in skirts once more.

The title of Guards Regiment did not excuse them from the disciplines of air force life. Of course, as the women had already proved in their unique working relationships with each other, theirs was an ordered way of life which worked generally by friendly consent rather than by any necessity for brusque command. Yevdokia Bershanskaya was more of an affectionate mother figure than a stern regimental commander, and none of the women conceded to me that at any time was there any serious disciplinary problem or loss of military efficiency because of this rather informal framework. When they were visited by senior male officers, everyone would conform to the rule book and try hard to remember to address each other by their official ranks; but otherwise, they continued on first-name terms. Perhaps, though, they really needed the lesson in discipline that was driven home to them by a stinging humiliation.

It was around midday. Some of the women were playing volleyball – one of their favourite games to keep themselves fit, and an appealing one to those who depended so much on good co-ordination. Without warning, the rocket that signalled immediate take-off went up. Pilots and navigators grabbed their flying helmets and ran to their aircraft. Had the Germans broken out? Were they approaching their airfield? But surely the front was stabilized, and there would have been a lot of warning of such a thing.

There was no time to ask questions. That rocket was an order to get airborne straight away. Engines stuttered into life all along the line, and within ten minutes all those capable of taking off were airborne and circling the field. Marina Chichnova told me, 'We looked down and were completely puzzled. All around the airfield was quiet. No sign of the enemy. Then another rocket was fired from the field, telling us to land.'

Major Bershanskaya was waiting for them at dispersal, her face red with embarrassment. Next to her stood a short, squat man wearing a general's uniform. The entire regiment was lined up in front of him. He was obviously very angry. He signalled to an aide who stepped forward and dramatically dropped a bundle of objects on the ground. There were several signal rockets, maps, and other objects from PO-2 cockpits. The general told them he had personally walked up to the aircraft, unseen and unchallenged, and taken these things from the unguarded cockpits. He ranted on. He could have been a German saboteur. He could have destroyed the entire line of aircraft. It was he, he said, who had ordered the scramble of the aircraft to see if they were as sloppy in that drill as they were in defending their bombers. At the end of his long harangue, he dropped his voice and asked the rhetorical question: 'You are a Guards Regiment?'

He was not finished yet. Before he left, he ordered a pistol firing demonstration. It was not a skill that the women had taken much time to practise. After all, Ira Kasherina and Sonya Azerkova had shown what women could do with a gun from close range. Still, the targets were set up. It may have been the aftermath of the humiliation they had undergone, or simply that target shooting requires continuous practice, but the results were abysmal. The general did not wait for the end; he ordered that they practise each day until they were proficient.

Marina Chichnova told me, 'That day was a sobering experience. We knew of course that the general and everyone else was aware of our combat records. But when you are a Guards Regiment, that sort of thing really hurts. Even at our distance from the actual front, we should have kept a close eye on our aircraft. And most of us couldn't have hit anyone with a pistol unless they were standing right in front of us. It was humiliating, but I think it did us good.'

The winter snow was turning to slush as the spring thaw began. It made working conditions a nightmare. On the grass airfields, the runways and taxiways leading to dispersal areas degenerated into deep thick mud. Aircraft had to be dragged out to the ends of the runways and, after missions, dragged back. The undercarriages would sink down, and the aircrew's arm and shoulder muscles quickly reached the point of exhaustion. Pilots would open the throttles wide in synchronization with the pushes of the women on the wings and tails in an effort to power the bogged-down machines out of the morass. The backwash from the large wooden propeller would lash the black ooze of the mud's surface into a continuous spray that caked the hair and the eyes. It was difficult to hear the instructions being bawled above the sound of the engine, and to respond was to invite a vile-tasting mouthful of liquefied earth. Much of the time the rain fell heavily and steadily, spreading the quagmire wherever one stepped. The aircrews had trouble negotiating the mud in their thick fur boots, but anything else left their feet freezing when they struggled free of the ground and climbed into the night sky.

The German resistance in the Kuban was very fierce and, in response to the night-long raids of the little PO-2s, there had been an increase in night fighter activity. The German night fighters roamed as far as the Soviet airfields and would occasionally catch and shoot down a returning bomber. It meant that the women had had to modify their night landing techniques. The landing light system was already masked to be visible from only a low altitude, but its angle of visibility was depressed still further. This meant that night landings – always a nerve-wracking business at the best of times – now became even more of an ordeal.

The landing situation was complicated still further by the lack of sophisticated navigational aids. The women would take off at precise intervals and therefore separate themselves adequately during the flight to the target; but battle damage, which slowed aircraft down, and navigational errors could result in several aircraft being over their home airfield waiting to land at or around the same time. There were no radar aids or sophisticated radio homing beacons; they had to depend on their own eyesight and the telltale exhaust flames to spot other aircraft. Thus, mid-air collisions were almost inevitable.

Marina Chichnova told me, 'After landing on one night of really intensive flying, we were just sitting in the cockpit while we were refuelled and rearmed; then we would take off again to hit the same targets over and over. I was sitting in my cockpit half-dozing and occasionally speaking over my shoulder to Marisa, my navigator. The armament girls were under the wings fixing on more bombs. We had not seen any enemy night fighters, but as we sat there we could hear one circling over our airfield at a fairly low altitude. There was no radio communication with our aircraft from the ground, so we couldn't warn the girls who hadn't yet landed. But we always worked on the assumption that the night fighters would be around in any case.'

Perhaps the night fighter passed close to one of the two little bombers as they peered through the darkness for the landing lights of the runway. Perhaps in panic the pilot lost her concentration and forgot to look out for her companions in the landing circuit. What is certain is that neither bomber saw anything until the moonless blackness was split by the flame of their collision. One bomber embedded itself between the other's wings and they tumbled briefly, locked together in a ghastly mating. Then they separated, one to explode on the ground within seconds, the other to disappear broken and fluttering in the darkness to smash among some trees.

Marina Chichnova and others leapt from their aircraft and ran towards the trees from which the rending crash had come. Above them, the German fighter continued circling. Marina Chichnova found herself wondering, as she ran, if the enemy pilot would claim her friends' aircraft as kills. There was little doubt in her mind that the crews would be dead, but still she ran. The women stopped on the airfield perimeter and listened. The sound they heard did not seem human. It was an intermittent, high-pitched shriek that subsided into a continuous moaning sound. They followed the sound and, as their eyes became more accustomed to the darkness, they found her lying on the ground. It was Katya, one of the pilots.

She was barely recognizable. Her flying helmet had been torn off and there was a horrible gaping wound in her cheek. Both arms and legs had been broken, so she had obviously not crawled from the wreckage, which was twenty yards away. Katya had survived because she had disobeyed a standing instruction. She hated wearing her cockpit safety harness. She had been reprimanded on several occasions for not doing so, but she always told her friends she found it too uncomfortable and restricting. Her waywardness had saved her life when she was thrown clear on impact. In the remains of the aircraft the navigator lay crumpled in her harness.

At daybreak the burned bodies of the other two women were brought to the airfield from a mile away. They buried the fliers in the centre of the airfield. All three had been members of the Young Communist League, so it was not a religious ceremony, but it was nonetheless sad. Most of the women controlled themselves until the very end, when three propellers were stuck into the fresh mounds of earth. Katya recovered from her awful injuries. Within a year she was back on flying duties.

The nature of the general conflict they were involved in and the unique role they were performing as women resulted in an intensity of experience which few men on any theatre of the war could equal. For those who survived, it gave them an almost unassailable self-confidence. It also gave some of them a deep sense of humility. Ira Kasherina, the woman who had pulled out her gun and shot the German soldiers, had this combination of quiet self-confidence and humility. It drew other people to her and she was one of the most popular members of the regiment. She was a good listener. She sat in her bunker while her friends talked to her about their problems and their fears; and when she had listened, she gave them advice that rarely failed to send them off feeling happier. She was serious for a twenty-year-old, and the presence of mind she had shown during her escape through the enemy lines was soon to show itself again, this time in the sky.

Through the night of 22 April, 1943, the 46th Guards Regiment was bombing enemy troop concentrations at the port of Novorossisk. One squadron was on the ground, refuelling, rearming, and waiting for another squadron to land all its aircraft before taxiing out and taking off for another sortie. A red flare was fired from the end of the runway, warning all aircraft to keep clear. One of the returning aircraft was in trouble. It had attempted to land once and had to go around again in the darkness. No one knew it at that time, but the pilot was dead. Flying the aircraft from the back seat was Ira Kasherina.

It was not until later that night that Ira was able to tell her friends the full story. She and her pilot, Ducie Nosal, had dropped their bombs and were turning for home when they were hit by flak from the heavy barrage of German anti-aircraft fire. They were caught in the beams of several searchlights and then a German night fighter was upon them.

With terrifying suddenness there were several explosions in the front cockpit as cannon shells exploded around the pilot. The PO-2 immediately rolled on to its back and dived away, out of the searchlight beams. It seemed like a piece of brilliant evasive flying, and Ira shouted, 'Well done!' through the intercom. But the dive continued and the pilot made no reply.

In the rear cockpit were duplicate aircraft controls – the PO-2 was, of course, simply a basic trainer pressed into combat service. Ira had not piloted a PO-2 since her flying club days, but now she knew she had no choice. Ducie was clearly unconscious and she had to pull them out of this dive, and soon. The plane was down to a thousand feet. She pulled back very hard on the control column, trying to lift the nose and regain level flight. The instruments glowing on the panel told her that they were diving almost vertically, but the pressure she was having to apply to stop the dive seemed excessive. Slowly the nose came up, and at five hundred feet they were level again.

Ira tried again to speak to her pilot. Silence. She looked at the compass and decided she must turn the aircraft on to the correct heading to take them back to the airfield. It meant a gentle turn to the left, which involved co-ordinating her left foot on the rudder pedal to turn the nose with a push on the stick to the left to roll the wings into the turn. The pedals were so stiff they would hardly budge and the stick resisted all but the most violent tugs.

Marina Chichnova told me, 'Poor Ira. It dawned on her then that her pilot was slumped over the controls with even her feet obstructing the movement of the rudder pedals. It was a terrifying predicament to be in, particularly with German night fighters around. She was still getting no reply on the intercom, so she raised herself from her seat to a half-crouched position and felt over into the front cockpit.'

The slipstream battered at her face and tried to whip the goggles from her eyes. The aircraft, as if with a life of its own, continued to fly straight and level, the engine *pop-popping* and the exhaust pipes occasionally belching flame. But Ira knew that at any moment its equilibrium could be upset – and she had no control over it.

One hand clutched the top of her cockpit and the other, minus its glove, groped towards the pilot's head. The helmet had a large hole in it, and Ira's numbed fingers poked through the torn fur into a warm sticky mess that slithered away under her touch. Her friend's brains were moving under her fingers. She pulled her hand away in horror. In the glow from what remained of the front cockpit's instrument panel she could see Ducie's long legs, wrapped in that moment of death around the control column sticking from the floor. Somehow they were jamming the rudder pedals, too.

There was nothing she could do for her friend now. She took a firm grip of the dead woman's collar with her left hand and yanked with all her strength. The head fell to one side but the body scarcely moved. Still the marvellous little aeroplane droned on through the sky, straight and level. Ira stood up in her cockpit, leaned forward as far as she dared, and pulled at the pilot's collar with both hands. The body jerked up and the head lolled backwards, hanging out into the slipstream.

Still holding on to the collar with her left hand, Ira eased herself down into her seat as far as she could. To keep her friend pulled up far enough to clear the controls in the front cockpit, Ira had to lean far forward herself, crouched almost sideways as she held on to the collar of the corpse in front of her. It was an almost impossibly awkward position, but at least she could now use her controls to fly the aircraft from the rear cockpit.

Awkwardly she turned on to a course for the airfield. Her arm was beginning to ache almost unbearably. Each time she looked up from the instruments to peer ahead, there was the hideous sight of the pilot's head jerking back and forth in the slipstream as if in a frenzy of life. As the pain grew in every sinew of her shoulders and arm muscles, did it ever occur to Ira to tip the aircraft on its wing and throw Ducie's body into the darkness of the night? To the women who lived and died in the little night bombers, such a suggestion would have been unthinkable.

To a trained navigator like Ira, navigation was almost second nature. That was not the problem. But now, as she approached the vicinity of the airfield, she knew she must fly low to pick up the hidden landing lights. She stood up into a half crouch and bent her arm to give it a second's respite, then she was back in her seat. There were the lights. She lined the aircraft up and descended towards the field.

The strain of holding the dead pilot away from the controls had driven Ira to the stage of wriggling involuntarily in her seat with the mental as well as the physical strain. Before she could help herself, her fingers had relaxed and the corpse slipped back out of sight into the front cockpit. Ira was down to three hundred feet and virtually committed to landing, but the body had slumped on to the stick and the nose of the aircraft was dipping alarmingly.

Ira stood up completely and lunged forward, dragging the pilot's body away with both hands. Her right hand held the collar this time. She slammed the throttle wide open and yanked the nose up at the same time. The engine responded and the PO-2 climbed and turned for another attempt. Ira told her friends later that she was too emotionally drained by that stage to feel any fear. The aircraft landed this time, heavily but safely, and trundled to a halt. Ira dragged herself from the rear cockpit and collapsed on the grass. Both her sleeves were sticky and red all the way to the elbows.

Ducie Nosal had been one of the regiment's best pilots, with 354 combat missions to her credit. She was post-humously awarded the title of Hero of the Soviet Union. For her outstanding courage, Ira received the order of the Red Flag.

There had been a shower of April rain on the day they buried Ducie Nosal. The grass glistened brightly in the sunlight as her friends wrapped up the little personal treasures from her bedside and sent back the unopened letters. Funerals were becoming almost commonplace, but the anguish never diminished. There was now a row of mounds near the centre of the airfield. Firm shoots of grass were pushing through the ground, and in the summertime when the regiment had moved on to new airfields, the flowers they had planted would burst into life on the graves.

In the midst of all this suffering and death, love was flourishing everywhere. Marina Chichnova and her friend Nadia Popova were both in earnest but erratic contact by letter with their boyfriends, who were both fighter pilots. Katya Pabst, Marina's navigator, had fallen madly for Grigor, a fighter pilot whose regiment had been based at the women's airfield for a couple of weeks. Marina was in love herself, but to listen to Katya chattering about her boyfriend, it seemed that no one in the world had ever been in love before. Grigor, according to Katya, was the man whom every other woman on the front wanted, but he had chosen her. Well, Marina had seen Grigor. And, certainly, he was a pleasant boy. But she thought that perhaps Katya was a little blinded by her love. She did not realize just how much until one night, on the homeward leg of a bombing mission, Katya asked her to steer a new course, a few miles to the east of their own airfield.

Marina told me, 'I couldn't understand what Katya was talking about. I knew it was not the course for home because we'd flown several sorties previously that night. But Katya was adamant. She said it would only take an extra few minutes and, as this was our last sortie of the night, what did a few minutes matter? She said she'd explain later. I felt indulgent, and we were friends, so I did as she asked.'

Katya told Marina over the intercom to flash on and off her landing lights three times in quick succession. She did as she was told and from the ground came an answering signal. On Katya's instructions, Marina had already descended to around two hundred feet. There were no hills or other obstructions in the immediate vicinity so it was fairly safe to do so. Katya leaned out of her cockpit and dropped a tightly sealed tin can over the side. Then she gave Marina the course to steer for home and explained en route just what she had been up to.

Marina told me, 'Katya was a little devil. She had given me a course to steer right over Grigor's airfield. They didn't fly night missions, so there was no danger of collision or anything like that. The signals from the ground had been from him. He must have been waiting for hours for the sound of our old popping engine. You'll find it hard to believe, but Katya had just dropped a tin of letters to Grigor. Not just one, but a whole tin of them. She told me she was really fed up waiting for the post to get her letters to him in the normal way. No matter that Grigor was unlikely to reciprocate by flying over our airfield and tossing letters to her; she said she was quite happy to wait for his replies. So long as she could keep telling him that she loved him. That way, she thought, no other girl was going to get him.'

Katya had told Grigor in the first dropped letter that she would make a similar delivery every Monday towards dawn as she returned from their last sortie of the night. He was not to risk the severe disciplinary action that was bound to ensue if he were caught signalling from the ground, she had written. He was simply to look for the can on the west side of the airfield.

But the naïve and charming game was a short one for the young lovers. A few days after the second drop, Katya heard that Grigor had been killed in action near Novorossisk. The remains of the rusting tin can bearing the neatly written words of young love may still lie in the long grass of an overgrown and deserted fighter base, somewhere in the Northern Caucasus.

11

The Battle of Kursk, Spring 1943

Larissa Rasanova had had a typically nerve-wracking night. She had flown half a dozen sorties in her PO-2 bomber over Novorossisk and now, at nine in the morning, after only five hours' sleep, she was not in the best of humours with the sergeant standing beside her bed, vigorously shaking her awake. Then Larissa remembered – today she was to fly to Armavir, a town about a hundred miles east of their airfield. There, at the main engineering workshops, her PO-2 was to be given a thorough overhaul to give the poor old battered airframe and engine a new lease of life after the hammering it had taken in combat during the past ten months.

It was a beautiful April day, and despite a bit of a headwind, which slowed the old aeroplane down to a speed of around eighty miles per hour over the ground, she landed at Armavir in under two hours. The overhaul would take several days, and Larissa had been given the address of the family of one of her friends from the regiment whose home was in Armavir. She parked the aircraft at the workshops and reported to the senior officer. She was about to start walking towards the town centre with her little bag slung over her shoulder when the officer called her back.

Larissa told me, 'The officer said he had an engineer who had to be flown to the town of Grozny, three hundred miles away towards the Caspian Sea. He was needed to help complete some important work there. The officer said that it would mean my aircraft's overhaul being put back for several days, but that Sergeant Litvinov was needed urgently at Grozny.'

Larissa's ears perked up. 'Did you say Litvinov, sir. Ilya Litvinov?'

The officer said yes, that was the sergeant's name. Was her PO-2 airworthy for such a flight, or should he get someone else to do it?

Larissa lied. 'Perfectly airworthy, sir.'

She told me, 'It was the sort of surprise that makes your heart leap. Ilya was my boyfriend and I hadn't seen him for months. I had no idea that he was here in Armavir. I could hardly contain myself with excitement.' She turned back towards the workshops and found her Ilya lying underneath a fighter working on a hydraulic pipe. She called his name and he eased himself out from underneath and squinted at her through the oil that had spilled through his fair hair and trickled over his eyebrows. He leapt to his feet and as she rushed to embrace him exuberantly, he held her off at oily arm's length with mock severity. Later, later, he laughed, and they arranged to go to a travelling army entertainment show in the town that night.

Larissa was glad now that she had thought to bring with her a pretty skirt and a spare shirt. By the time she got to her friend's family home, the fatigue of the previous night's combat and the excitement of meeting Ilya again had combined to make her feel exhausted. Her friend's young sister promised to iron her skirt and shirt for that night's date, and the mother insisted that Larissa lie down and try to sleep for a couple of hours at least. She woke up from a heavy sleep, half an hour before the time of her date.

The young sister looked guilty and shamefaced as she came into the main room of the little house. Larissa's brown uniform, which was crumpled and sweaty, had been washed by the mother and even now was flapping on the clothesline outside the house. On the table sat the iron that the sister had been heating on the fire to press her skirt and shirt. Over the back of a wooden chair lay her neatly ironed outfit for the evening. There seemed, though, to be an extraordinarily strong smell of kerosene everywhere. Then the young sister confessed.

Larissa told me, 'She had knocked over the kerosene lamp with her elbow while she'd been ironing. It had drenched both skirt and shirt, and now there was a distinct dark stain over both of them. I was heartbroken, but the girl was so clearly upset with what she'd done that I couldn't be angry with her. There was no choice now; I'd just have to wear the clothes. My uniform was still wet on the line. We drenched the clothes with eau de cologne that the sister gave me and I got dressed. My friend's mother tried to make me feel better by telling me that spilling something on a dress before meeting a man was considered a good omen in Armavir; it meant, she said, that I would marry the young man I was meeting that night. Still, I wasn't feeling my usual confident self as I walked through the streets to the theatre. I kept sniffing at the blouse, but my sense of smell was so mixed up by that time that I really had no idea whether I smelled like a tractor or a fine lady.'

Larissa remembers very little about the entertainment in the theatre. She sat through the performances gazing into Ilya's eyes and whispering to him. But she had a problem: though she had to keep her voice down to avoid the wrath of the others in the audience, she did not dare to let her body get too close to his, lest he smell her strange perfume.

Sitting on her left was a girl she knew slightly. At one point she leaned towards her and whispered, 'How do I smell?' The girl gave her a very odd look and shifted in her seat uncomfortably. Well, that wasn't much help to her. She tried holding her breath and exhaling slowly to clear her sense of smell, then taking a deep sniff. It seemed that the kerosene was winning the battle with the eau de cologne. She took another deep breath and held it again. Ilya asked her if there was anything wrong.

'Do you like my perfume?' she asked uncertainly.

'It's delightful,' he said. 'What's it called?'

Neither knew the town and when they left the theatre, they had some difficulty finding their way back to her lodgings. They found the street eventually and sat on a wall near the house, talking for hours. They had so much to tell each other. Ilya took off his jacket and put it around her shoulders. In just over two hours the sun would be up; they were due to take off for Grozny at nine o'clock. Larissa did not think she'd be able to sleep, but she knew she must try to get some rest. She kissed him again and eased herself down on her tiptoes from the flat top of the wall. She handed him back his jacket and he put it on.

'I've just remembered the name of your perfume,' he said, 'and I'm going to get some more of it for you tomorrow. As much of it as you want. We've got barrels of it at the workshops.'

It was light enough for Larissa to see the broad mischievous grin on his face. She punched him playfully on the shoulder and found release from her embarrassment in an outburst of laughter. So much for her subterfuge.

The flight to Grozny was going to take the little aeroplane across some of the Caucasus mountain range, and Larissa had plotted a course that would avoid the hightest peaks. Ilya settled himself in the rear cockpit, and Larissa warned him to keep his hands and feet clear of the controls. Then they were airborne. It was another beautiful spring day. As they approached the mountains, she changed course several times to sweep along the floors of valleys.

Ilya was enjoying himself hugely. At one stage he asked Larissa if he could try flying the aircraft. She told him over the intercom, with mock severity, that it was strictly against regulations; but she did fly lower, hedge-hopping occasionally to keep the adrenalin flowing for the fun-loving man in the rear cockpit.

She had told a white lie when the officer had asked her the previous day if her aircraft was airworthy for this trip.

Well, she certainly wouldn't have let anyone else fly it. The engine had been playing up a bit recently, and the airframe had been patched so many times that she sometimes wondered if there were anything of the original canvas left. But she almost regarded it as a living being. It had carried her through so many combat flights and she honestly felt she could trust it to make this trip before the overhaul. Besides, she had not been prepared to allow anyone else to take away from her this chance to spend time with the man she loved.

When they stopped at a small military airfield to refuel, they both clambered out of the PO-2 to stretch their legs and drink some tea. They reported to a senior officer and showed him their orders and then lay on the grass as the fuel tank was topped off. An engineer approached them and asked to speak to the pilot. Larissa told me, 'The man was a sergeant and he told me that the officer in charge of maintenance had taken a look at my aircraft and said to the crew that it shouldn't be allowed to fly on to Grozny, through the mountains, in the state it was in. He gàve me the warning, winked at me, and then walked away.

'The officer was nowhere to be seen. Ilya and I strolled over as nonchalantly as we could to the aeroplane, climbed in, and before anyone could stop us we were airborne. Well, no one had told me officially that there was anything wrong with the aeroplane, and Ilya was an engineer himself. He wouldn't have allowed me to fly it if he'd thought we were in any real danger.' There may have been a difference of opinion about the airworthiness of the aircraft, but it was obviously a borderline case at the least. Still, the young lovers arrived at Grozny and made a perfect landing on the military airfield.

In their drive towards the oilfields of Baku on the Caspian – the object of Hitler's offensive through the Caucasus which had ended in disaster at Stalingrad – the German army had driven eastward to within a few miles of

Grozny. It had considerable strategic importance and was part of the oil pipeline network from the south. Now, though, the Germans had withdrawn towards the Ukraine and into the Kuban, where Larissa had been bombing them only two days before.

The war seemed very far away during the three days the young couple spent in the town. Larissa saw very little of Ilya during the day – he was at the airfield working on his project – but she managed to get a mechanic to make sure the engine of her aircraft was not likely to seize up in flight on the way back. In the evenings, she and Ilya walked on the outskirts of the town. Spring flowers were everywhere and it was difficult to believe the Germans had come so close to overrunning this place.

On their last day, Ilya arrived at the house where she was billeted with a box full of sausage meats, bread, and a small bottle of wine. She had already eaten with the family of the house, but she did not wish to offend him, so she had another meal. The wine gave them the taste for more alcohol, and that evening they scoured the town. They found a shop with a stock of Russian champagne. Ilya had a few rubles and so did Larissa; after much haggling they staggered from the place with no fewer than twenty bottles of the sparkling wine stuffed into boxes. Larissa told me, 'It was like stumbling across a treasure trove. It was too good an opportunity to miss. We decided to take the champagne back in the aircraft with us to keep in our different regiments for special occasions like birthdays.'

Next morning the precious bottles were crammed into the back cockpit, and the pilot and the engineer took off and headed back to Armavir. They had been flying for about half an hour when Larissa turned her head around and grinned at Ilya, placing one finger at the side of her nose and making a scratching movement. She told me, 'It was sign language of the time which meant, "Do you fancy a drink?" Ilya nodded his head enthusiastically and ducked

198

down inside the cockpit. He fumbled for a moment with the cork, then there was a spray of champagne as the cork exploded into the slipstream. He tipped his head back and had a swig, then passed the bottle forward to me.'

Larissa put the PO-2 on full power, climbed a few hundred feet, and then settled it back into level flight before taking a drink from the dark green bottle. It was delicious, not too dry, and the bubbles tickled at the back of her nose. She took another pull at it, then stretched her arm back and handed it to him. The wine was heady stuff. She was beginning to feel very gay. Ilya passed the bottle forward again and she noticed to her amazement that it was empty.

They were passing over a small lake. She stuck her arm out stiffly and watched the bottle tumble down to make a tiny splash on its surface. Ilya had been chattering to her over the intercom and as she dropped the empty bottle he asked, 'Well?' She turned around and he was scratching the side of his nose. She giggled and Ilya lifted in front of his face another bottle which he had already opened. It went down just as quickly. She had eaten a lot of black bread at breakfast, but the champagne was nonetheless being absorbed very quickly into her bloodstream. It felt good though, and she was flying perfectly well. At two thousand feet in a clear blue sky, she had lots of margin for error. Once she saw a squadron of Soviet fighters several thousand feet above, flying across their path, but there was very little other air traffic about.

When she asked Ilya if he was tightly strapped in, his speech seemed to her to be slightly slurred. She giggled again and told him to hold on. She opened the throttle wide and pushed the nose down. She levelled out at two thousand feet and from the back seat Ilya whooped his approval. This was really living. Larissa felt she had never flown better. She thought of rolling the aircraft on its back but remembered in time that that would only have resulted in a trail of broken champagne bottles along their course.

She swooped across a little village and Ilya waved and shouted at some people in the street.

Larissa told me, 'I'd never felt better in my life. The man I loved was in the back seat of my little aeroplane. My head was buzzing in the most beautiful way. Then Ilya asked me again if I would teach him to fly. I must have been tipsy. I told him he could, and I put my hands on top of my head to show him that he had control. Really, he did tremendously well at first. He didn't do anything silly. He just maintained the height we were flying at and kept the wings level. He was shouting and singing and when I tried to put my hands back on the controls he shouted no.'

Larissa looked at her altimeter. They were down to a hundred feet. She told him she was taking control again, and he replied that he would release the controls only if she promised to open another bottle of champagne. She needed no persuasion. She turned around to take it from him and saw that his head was inside the cockpit, fumbling for a bottle.

Larissa told me, 'I sobered up instantly. No one had control at that moment. I seized the stick and yanked it back, but it was too late.' The wheels of the undercarriage struck the ground in a shallow dive. By every rule they should both have been dead within the next five seconds. But good fortune was favouring the airborne champagne drinkers. The PO-2 did not dig its own grave in the ploughed field. It bounced into the air, then dipped and ploughed its own furrow across the dark earth for a few yards before limping into the air again and slowly climbing away.

As they passed through five hundred feet, Larissa risked a look over her shoulder at her boyfriend. His face had turned a dreadful shade of greyish green and he was being violently and messily sick into the slipstream. Larissa decided that for several good reasons, flying and drinking were pleasures that should be kept entirely separate.

* * *

The Soviet marines who had secured the toehold at Novorossisk by landing from the sea behind the Germans were dependent on resupply of ammunition, food, and other supplies by sea. On the beachhead with them was one Leonid Brezhnev, political commissar of the Eighteenth Army. During the fierce attack and counterattack that punctuated the months, the Russians doggedly held on to their beachhead. Now bad weather had made supply by sea impossible. The only way to resupply the marines was by airdrop, at night. The area designated for the drop would require a very accurate, low-speed approach if it were to be successful. The ideal aircraft was the PO-2. The 46th Guards Regiment was selected for the mission.

The briefing took place in the downstairs room of a large house near the front line where it merged with the Black Sea. Half and hour's flying time along the curve of the coast lay Novorossisk. The aircrew trooped into the room for their briefing by a senior naval officer. The light came from oil lamps made out of old shell cases, and across the table was spread a map. Nadia Popova told me, 'We all had on our full flying kit and when we took off our flying helmets, the officer's face changed as he saw our long hair tumbling down. He had obviously not been told that girls would be flying the mission. I looked around me – several of the girls were grinning at his reaction. We all knew what he was thinking, but we'd got to the stage then where we merely found it amusing. We didn't react the way we might have done a few months before.'

The crews were given specially prepared maps showing the depth of the beachhead and the direction in which it ran. They were assured that at a prearranged time the beleaguered group would illuminate the dropping zone with a large fire. The last radio communication from the beachhead had been a desperate one: they were virtually out of ammunition and medical supplies for the many wounded. They were exhausted, hungry, and, worse, they had no drinking water left.

The aircraft had been fuelled, and slung under the wings where the bombs usually went were large cigar-shaped canisters containing ammunition, medical supplies, food, and tightly sealed fresh-water containers. To avoid smashing the canisters, the drops would have to be made from very low levels. A mistake of a few metres either way would mean the vital supplies falling into German hands. None of the crew was under any illusion about the sort of vulnerable targets they would present at low level in their slow-moving aircraft, even in the darkness. It was, to say the least, a very dangerous mission. The winds that had whipped the sea into waves which prevented landing craft from ferrying supplies ashore had also made flying conditions treacherous for the little biplanes.

Switches were flicked down inside the cockpit, chocks were pulled away, and mechanics stood on tiptoe to swing the propellers into swirling motion. Pilot Seraphoma Amosova took off first with her very experienced navigator Shenya Rudnova. In normal bombing missions, the women kept several minutes' flying time between themselves. On this sortie, though, they took off at shorter intervals. They wanted to spend as little time as possible over the target after the first aircraft had alerted the enemy to their airdrop.

The aircraft climbed away and swung out to sea before setting a course to Novorossisk. It was a very dark night; when their eyes became more accustomed to the gloom, they could not see even the glimmer of a horizon ahead. Flying was completely on instruments, but three thousand feet below was the storm-lashed surface of the sea. They could not see the waves, which was just as well for their peace of mind, but frequently the whitecaps would foam briefly in the darkness below.

Marina Chichnova told me, 'It was very difficult to keep the aircraft on course. The wind was gusting and throwing it around. Sometimes the PO-2 would drop suddenly about a hundred feet and my stomach would lurch. My head was inside the cockpit concentrating on the instruments most of the time. The heavy canisters under the wings didn't make control any easier, and the thought of those cold black waves below us wasn't a nice feeling at all. We knew that if we had engine failure over the water, there wasn't a hope in hell of surviving. It was cold and the rain was beating into the cockpit from all directions. I had to wipe the glass on the instruments to see what I was doing, and my goggles were just the same. It wasn't the sort of weather you would choose for sitting in the pitch black in an open cockpit. But I just kept thinking of our men on that beach. And the sound of that faithful old engine *pop-popping* away in front of my feet was a great comfort to me as we battered through the storm.'

It was, even by the standards of the PO-2, a slow flight, but as they neared the beachhead they saw a rocket flare being fired and the flashes of gunfire which indicated the continuing action. According to plan, the aircraft crossed the coast and switched off their engines, then turned parallel to the coast as they pushed their noses down into a gentle glide, looking for the signal fire. The line of luminous water breaking against the shore was clearly visible even in the darkness. Then, a mile ahead, they spotted the row of signal fires. They descended in their glide to a height of 150 feet and yanked the levers that released the canisters. One plane after the other dropped the supplies and then opened their engines to full power and turned sharply out to sea again.

Nadia Popova told me, 'We could hear our men shouting to us and cheering as we made the drop. We couldn't make out what they were saying, of course, but it was one of the most satisfying things we did throughout the war.'

That first night's drop had taken the Germans by surprise, and though there had been some small-arms fire from the ground against the aircraft, all had returned unscathed. But the bad weather continued to hamper resupply by sea, and they were forced to repeat their hazardous night drops for a number of succeeding nights. They tried to vary their tactics by approaching from different directions, even gliding in from behind the German positions, hoping that silence and the blanket of night would give them some protection. Nothing could alter the fact, though, that they had to fly over the dropping zone at a very low altitude. The Germans were waiting for them, and the hail of small-arms and light automatic fire was horrendous. Their own troops would keep up a very heavy concentration of fire against the enemy during the drop, but as Nadia Popova told me, 'It was miraculous that we did not actually lose any aircraft during these operations. I limped back across the sea one night with most of the control surfaces on my wings shot away. I literally had holes in my flying kit where shrapnel had torn it. Several girls were wounded by ground fire, and the fuselage and wing surfaces of almost every aircraft were ripped and torn with bullet holes. The PO-2 may have been the slowest aircraft in the air force, but it took some incredible punishment and just kept flying. No wonder we all loved it so much.'

It was Marina Chichnova's 500th mission. To have come through that sort of ordeal physically intact was an achievement that demanded some sort of recognition, so there was a party that day. There had not been any opportunity to scrounge the necessary ingredients for a cake, but Yevdokia Bershanskaya showed the sort of resourcefulness one would expect of a regimental commander. The women gathered together and, with a great show of mock dignity, presented Marina with a bulky oval-shaped parcel. Everyone else knew what it contained and they giggled as she tore away layer after layer of brown paper, cautioning her not to be too rough, as the parcel contained something very delicate. The last sheet was carefully peeled away and there, revealed, was the symbol of her battle achievements: a giant watermelon. Carved on its surface was the figure 500 and a drawing of a PO-2. She cut it up like a birthday cake and gave everyone a tiny portion.

Celebrating their own survival always raised unspoken questions about loved ones elsewhere. For the few who were married, and particularly for those with young children, the separation from their families was particularly harrowing. It's difficult to understand how women like Yevdokia Bershanskaya managed not only to fly in combat, but to assume command responsibilities with such success. Her husband was fighting on another front and her son had been sent into the care of his grandmother in Krasnodar in the Caucasus when his parents went off to war. That town had been taken by the Germans, though, and Yevdokia had not known whether her son and her mother were alive or dead. Each day she planned operations, briefed her squadron commanders, and flew in combat herself. She wrote letters to the bereaved parents and families of her girls who were killed in combat. And, day after day, she would spend time listening to the problems of the young women she commanded and for whom she felt such a responsibility.

She told me, 'Of course it was not easy. I had not gone to war and left my child behind because I did not love him. I had done it because I did love him and I felt that I could do something to help beat the Germans. I cannot properly describe the feelings that one has when one's own child is not only separated but in the control of a hated enemy. Every time we heard stories of the atrocities the invaders were said to have committed in the occupied territories, I can only say that I felt weak and sick. But when you are the commander you must not let your feelings show too much.'

She need not have taken such trouble to hide her tortured

thoughts. All the women knew of her inner misery. They had been flying in support of the ground troops in the fighting to liberate Krasnodar, and they all knew how Yevdokia felt every time she bombed the German defences around the town. Imagine her feelings as she turned from her sortie and flew back to the airfield. Was her son asleep? Had he eaten that day? Did he have enough clothes to keep warm? Or, darkest thought of all, was the child whose face she saw so clearly when she closed her eyes, was he already dead?

Yevdokia and several other women from the regiment drove into Krasnodar from their airfield the day after the Germans had withdrawn. The town had been badly damaged. Smoke still hung in the air, and from the rubble in the streets rose the smell of old, decayed masonry. They got down from the truck and picked their way through the rubble towards the area where Yevdokia's son and mother had been living when last she had seen them. The people they met looked shocked and pale. Several embraced the uniformed women, tears streaming down their faces. Nadia Popova said, 'Yevdokia did not say anything to us, but the anxiety showed on her face. She was obviously dreading what she might find.'

They turned a corner, with Yevdokia leading them as she searched the devastation for familiar landmarks. Two hundred yards away, walking in their direction, was a small boy about eight years old. His fair head was bent down as he picked his way along the pavement. He wore a dark jacket several sizes too large for him and he looked very thin. He raised his head at the sound of the women's voices. Yevdokia gave a gasp and then she was running towards him, stumbling and tripping and calling out his name. It was her son. He stood still a moment, as if unable to believe what was happening, then he too was running. She swept him off his feet, hugged him to her breast, and stood there in the streets of the liberated city, sobbing. She placed him on the ground again and gently brushed his hair back from his smooth forehead. She held both his hands very tight and stood there, incapable of saying a word, just gazing at the face of her son. He threw his arms around her neck and she picked him up again. He seemed very light. Nadia Popova told me, 'We were all gathered round the two of them by that time. We knew how she'd prayed that he would be alive. It was such an emotional moment. We all stood there with our arms around them, sobbing our hearts out.'

It was the first time that Yevdokia's son had seen his mother in her uniform. He kept asking her if it were true that she was in command of a whole regiment. He led them to the house where he and his grandmother lived during the German occupation. They had not been harmed, but food had been very scarce.

In only two days, the regiment was due to move on again to a new airfield. Yevdokia could not hope to make up for eighteen months of absence in that short time together, but she tried. The pain of separation was intense as she left her son again. She prayed the enemy would not be allowed to pass that way again.

In a few months' time, probably the most crucial battle of the war was to be fought at a place called Kursk. On its outcome would depend the future of Yevdokia Bershanskaya's family and that of every member of the women's air regiments.

Hitler himself had said that it was essential for the German army to make up that summer what they had lost during the winter. To achieve that, he wanted to inflict upon the Soviet Union a defeat that would compensate for the humiliation Germany had suffered at Stalingrad in January 1943. Codenamed 'Operation Citadel', his plan was aimed at eliminating what had become known as the Kursk salient; in the process, he hoped to repeat one of the massive encirclements that had characterized the early part of his Russian campaign. The Kursk salient was really a bulge driven into the German lines by the Soviet forces during the previous winter. It ran roughly from Orel in the north to Belgorod in the south and contained vast numbers of Soviet troops and a colossal amount of equipment.

Hitler's plan was not only to 'pocket' and destroy the Russian forces in the salient but also to liquidate the enormous reserves which he anticipated the Soviet army would hurl into the battle once it was engaged. Success at Kursk would change the whole strategic situation on the eastern front and might even make it possible to launch a new offensive against Moscow.

Two pincers would drive from the north and south to achieve the encirclement. On 4 July almost a million German troops, nearly three thousand tanks and self-propelled guns, and over two thousand aircraft commenced the attack that was to develop into the greatest tank battle of the war. Unfortunately for the Germans, the Russians had been forewarned. It is now known that the German battle plans were somehow leaked to their enemy, but in any case the Soviets had been expecting an attack; the salient was a fairly obvious place for the Germans to begin any major counter-offensive. They had reinforced in great depth, and in the air, too, they had prepared for a battle of epic proportions. Into this battle, the women's 586th Fighter Regiment was heavily drawn.

In the build-up to the Kursk offensive, the Germans flew many missions against the Soviet defences in an attempt to soften them up. The 586th Fighter Regiment had been flying almost continuous sorties one day when, just after noon, Ria Sooranchevskaya and Tamara Pamyetnich found themselves the only two Yaks in the sky over their sector. They were circling at a height of around twelve thousand feet when Tamara saw a cluster of black dots approaching below them from the south-west. She mistook them at first for a flock of birds, but within seconds they had materialized as a group of forty-two Junkers 88 and Dornier bombers.

The odds were fantastic. The women dived down on the leading formation from out of the sun. Their aim was to break them up before they reached their apparent target – a railway station which was within their regiment's zone of operations. Two bombers fell away in flames to explode on the ground on that first pass, but the second wave held their formation as the two Yaks pulled up from their dive and attacked from opposite sides.

They got one more bomber each on their second pass, and the enemy jettisoned their bombs and broke formation. Tamara's Yak, though, had been seriously damaged by the concentrated fire of the second formation. It spun out of control and she hurled herself from the Yak, opening her parachute at under a thousand feet. Her face and neck had been badly bruised in her escape from the stricken fighter, but she was alive. As she floated down, her fighter was burning in a field nearby; up above, she could see Ria's Yak pursuing the broken formation of German bombers.

Ria wrote later, 'When I saw Tamara falling, I was sure she was dead. I felt a mixture of grief and anger and pressed home my attack until the ammunition had been exhausted. My engine had overheated – I think it had sprung an oil leak. Hot steam started to fill the cockpit and I had to switch off the engine and glide. I did a belly landing on a hillside. As I got out of the cockpit, peasants were running towards me waving pitchforks and scythes, and one even had an old shotgun. Then they saw the red stars on the fuselage and they dropped their weapons and started hugging and kissing me. Then I took off my helmet and goggles and my hair fell down around my shoulders and they stepped back in amazement.' The day the two women fighter pilots took on the forty-two bombers became a newspaper story around the world, and both Ria and Tamara were decorated for valour.

*   *   *

Above the Kursk battlefield, more than 4,000 aircraft of both sides were operating over an area only twelve miles by thirty miles. Battles involving up to 150 aircraft were commonplace, and it was not unusual for up to 300 fighters to be involved in combat. Galia Boordina recalled, 'The sky was so full of aircraft in such a small area of airspace that it was terrifying. German and Soviet fighters were whirling and diving everywhere. You would be involved in a fight with another aircraft and a couple of other dogfights would be taking place in between yours, it seemed. The risks of collision were enormous – even with your own side. It was a complete mêlée, and most of the aircraft were flying at very high speed. I broke out of the fight briefly to gain height and look for a target. I dived down and pulled up underneath a Messerschmitt 109 and raked it with machine-gun and cannon fire. It fell away immediately, burning. I had shot down two other Germans before that – a bomber and a transport – but that was my first fighter. I didn't feel any pity for the man I'd killed. When it's kill or be killed, you don't feel that sort of thing. I preferred not to see the face of an enemy. Once when I was attacking a bomber I got close enough to see the features of the gunner, and I remembered that it was other human beings we were firing our guns at.'

As the battle raged on the ground, hundreds of tanks fought to the death. Galia said, 'It was a sight you could never forget. You could not hear the sound of the tanks firing over the noise of your engine, but you could see the flashes from the muzzles and the great clouds of dust as they raced towards each other. Everywhere, littered for miles, were the burning hulks of tanks that had been destroyed by each other's fire or by German and Soviet ground attack aircraft. Great clouds of smoke hung over the battlefield from the burning armour. It was thick and oily and as you flew through it, it seeped into your cockpit. I can almost smell it now.'

Great tension spread among the civilian population as reports reached them of the start of the Kursk battle. Most realized that this enormous clash would have important consequences for the course of the war. When the battle ended, the Germans had failed. The two arms of their pincer were a hundred miles apart when their offensive ground to a halt. From that point on, the initiative passed to the Russians. The Germans were not yet defeated, but their losses in men and equipment would never be made up. It had been the decisive battle of the war.

As they advanced into Germany, Soviet troops were sometimes known to commit rape and other crimes of brutality against the civilian population. The bestiality displayed by some of the German forces during their occupation of enormous parts of the Soviet Union was also well known. But the women of the 586th Fighter Regiment were shaken when they personally encountered the human consequences of the treatment some of their defenceless countrywomen had been forced to endure. They entered a village near Kursk to get food supplies and visited a house to which they had been invited by one of the village women. Sitting in a chair in a corner of the room was a girl around sixteen years of age. Her head was slumped forward and to one side, and her tongue was hanging from her mouth. When the fighter pilots tried to speak to her, she did not even lift her head, and she made no reply. Her mother was distraught and explained what had happened.

Maj. Vera Tikomerova, the regiment's commissar, told me: 'The German troops who had been stationed in their village had been on the rampage for days before they withdrew. This girl had been taken from her home every day by drunken soldiers and continuously raped before being dumped back with her family at night. Quite apart from the physical damage, it had had a dreadful mental effect on the girl, too. Her mother seemed to think that it had snapped her brain. She had not spoken to anyone since it happened, and she shook with fear whenever a man entered the house.'

The womens's regiment was based near the village for several weeks, and they brought their own regimental doctor to attend to the rape victim. The women visited her frequently; those who were billeted in the village spent hours talking to her or simply sitting with their arms around her, giving her love and comfort. They washed her hair and bathed her body. Gradually she began to communicate with them. As the bruises on her face and body began to heal, so too did she begin to understand that there could once more be a normal life beyond her hideous ordeal. By the time they moved on, she was clinging to them as if they were surrogate mothers, though they were scarcely any older. The girl they nursed is now a mother of two children. Each year she makes a sort of pilgrimage to the square where the Bolshoi Theatre stands in Moscow and where war veterans gather annually for a rally. There she seeks out women like Vera Tikomerova to thank them for the kindness they showed her when the ugliest face of war so savagely ended her innocent childhood.

It had always been a fear of the aviators that they would fall into the hands of the Germans. The image of the 'Facist beast' was assiduously fostered by Soviet propaganda, and what the women had seen here strengthened their resolve that they would never allow themselves to be captured. The last bullet in their pistols, they vowed, would be for themselves.

Near Kursk, the orchards were bearing a heavy crop of apples late that summer. Vera Tikomerova went around with a truck trying to buy the fresh fruit, which was a welcome variation to the rather boring diet imposed on the regiment. But those from whom she tried to buy were not interested in her rubles; they were desperately short of clothes. Paper money was not going to keep them warm during the coming winter, and warm clothing was next to impossible to buy. Vera rounded up some old, discarded, ragged uniforms and underwear and returned to the airfield with a load of apples.

Vera's role as a political commissar was to sustain the Party line and ensure that there was no official deviation from the official view of the war. As the aviators were almost all members of the Young Communist League and enthusiastic volunteers into the bargain, this could not have been a very taxing proposition. But she also saw herself as someone to whom the women could turn with their personal problems. She was about thirty then and had been married for ten years. A shrewd and worldly woman, she had herself passed through most of the emotional traumas that her charges were experiencing in their relationships with the opposite sex. Many of them were now going through the pains of their first love affairs, either with young men they had met since joining the air force, or with sweethearts they had fallen in love with before they joined up.

Vera told me, 'I tried to keep my eyes open for any signs of serious emotional problems. All the girls suffered varying degrees of strain from combat flying but, though some of them were close to it, no one actually cracked up. Letters from home could often produce fits of depression, though. It could be news of a death in the family or it could be boyfriend trouble. I didn't want to intrude on personal grief, but the girls knew they could talk to me in confidence if it was something so personal they didn't even want to share it with their closest friends. I was a kind of release valve for them in that way.'

On Ria Bulayeva's birthday, Vera Tikomerova had a typical experience as a mother confessor. After their last sorties, the women had gathered beneath a beautiful old tree to share a cake that had been baked in Ria's honour. The Russians have a deep affection for their national tree, the silver birch, but this one had been damaged by a bomb fragment during a German bomber raid on the airfield.

Someone made a serious little speech about how the birch tree had survived the German bomb because the roots were so deep in the earth and how they, too, would survive and conquer for the same reason.

One woman, though, walked away from the group. She had been reading a letter from her mother, which had arrived for her while she was flying her last sortie. It told her that her fiancé in Moscow had married someone else. Vera told me, 'I walked after the girl and when she turned and saw me, she started crying and put her head on my shoulder. She said she couldn't bear being told like that. We sat for almost an hour, talking. I let her do most of the talking to get it out of her system. She felt betrayed, though, and nothing I could say about time healing things made any difference. She was never the same girl after that. She survived the war but died just after it, from tuberculosis.'

Ria Bulayeva, on the other hand, seemed to have no emotional problems. She commanded one of the three squadrons. She was a popular girl, and no one had been surprised when she and Yevgenya – a fighter pilot whom she had met while his regiment had been based at their airfield – had broken the unwritten law and decided to marry before the end of the war. That seemed typical of Ria. She was so confident, so sure that she would survive the war, so convinced that her vibrancy and self-assurance would somehow form around her a protective shield that had been denied to so many of her friends. Their marriage, which took place just after the battle of Kursk, had simply been an exchange of vows before Yevgenya's regiment flew off to another airfield. There had been no romantic honeymoon; they had kissed and embraced within the sound of the guns and he had flown away. Filled with a longing for each other, they both carried on with their war.

Ria was a very fluent pilot. She co-ordinated all her movements beautifully and, though she kicked and skidded her Yak around the sky when she was taking violent evasive action during a fight, anyone who knew her well could always tell in normal circumstances that it was she who was flying. Then, returning from a sortie one day, she overshot the runway and came down in a field three miles from the airfield. She had been wounded in the leg during an attack on a German bomber, and she had said on radio that she was losing a lot of blood. The aircraft had not exploded on impact with the ground; it looked as if she made a 'wheels-up' landing in a field before losing consciousness.

There were some peasants around the aircraft when the truck arrived from the airfield. One, a young woman, was standing on the wing gazing through the perspex canopy at the back-tilted head and the slender white neck. Ria's face was the colour of chalk. Some of her dark hair had fallen out below the severe line of the leather helmet over her forehead, and her mouth was open as if about to form a word. Ria, it seemed, had simply bled to death.

Yevgenya's regiment was only fifteen minutes' flying time away, and a message was passed to him. They were to bury Ria the next day just after sunrise so that there would be no interruption in combat missions. Her body had been wrapped in parachute silk, but they had kept her flying helmet, her goggles, and the thin gold ring Yevgenya had given her when they exchanged vows.

A grave had been dug by the bank of a small river. One of the men from the support battalion attached to the regiment had made a simple, rough wooden coffin, and Ria's body had been placed in it. The sun had already risen above the rim of the Ural mountains far to the east, and the women of the regiment were lined up on the airfield. In front of them lay the simple wooden box. The air was very still, and it would be an hour or so before the sun rose sufficiently to dispel the light mist that hung around the surface of the field.

The sound of a Yak-9 engine was unmistakable to the

215

girls. It grew until they knew without question that it was heading for them. The engine was set at cruising speed and as the fighter flew across the field, it turned gently as if to start a landing pattern. It was Yevgenya. All eyes were turned upward as the fighter turned. But he did not land. He flew around the airfield once, then once again. And then again.

Vera Tikomerova told me, 'I had to take a tight grip of myself not to burst into tears there and then. It was obvious that the poor boy couldn't bring himself to land. As he flew over, he must have seen us lined up there with the coffin, and on the bank of the river the freshly dug grave. He must have flown around for about fifteen minutes before he could bear to land.'

Yevgenya taxied his Yak to a standstill and climbed out. His face was impassive but his eyes were red. He did not ask to see his wife's body. He marched to the grave with the coffin on his shoulder, helped by five of Ria's friends. They lowered the box into the ground and he cried out twice, 'Ria, Ria,' and began to cry unashamedly. He stood apart where no one might be tempted to touch him and stood erect as the women drew their pistols and fired a volley over the grave. Then he slowly walked away across the airfield towards his fighter.

Two of Ria's friends, Galia Boordina and Tamara Pamyetnich – the woman appointed squadron commander in her place – ran after him. Five minutes later three Yaks took off in a loose formation, turned, and flew slowly over the small mound of freshly turned earth. One of the aircraft waggled its wings slowly, then the engine was opened up to full power, and it broke out of the formation and headed west. Two weeks later Yevgenya was killed in action.

12

The White Rose of Stalingrad

Alexei Salomaten was dead and buried. Lily carried with her everywhere a small photograph that one of the pilots had taken of Alexei and herself sitting on the wing of her aircraft, his arm around her shoulder. She did not want to talk about him to anyone; she had withdrawn into herself, and it seemed that she was glad the regiment's rate of combat sorties was such an exhausting one. She had always been energetic, but now she threw herself into her flying with a fierce dedication that worried her friends. Ina Pasportnikova told me, 'It was as if she did not wish to give herself time to think about his death. At the end of a day she would normally be so exhausted that she would slump on to her bed and fall asleep. We all hated the Germans, but now Lily had become almost obsessive in her hatred.'

Her tenth kill was a German ace. Her dogfight with him lasted fifteen minutes, and she knew she was up against no ordinary pilot. Painted on his fuselage was the representation of a playing card – the ace of spades – and along the nose was a long row of previous kills. Lily had told Ina just after her lover's death that every time she encountered a German fighter she imagined the pilot had been responsible for the death of one of her friends. It gave her the edge she needed, it honed her killer instinct. There was no power assistance on the controls of Lily's Yak. Every violent manoeuvre she performed, every time her vision reddened as she turned tighter and tighter against the force of gravity – it was all directed through these slender arms and legs. Finally, the White Rose triumphed and the Messerschmitt fell away in flames. The cockpit hood was jettisoned and the pilot leapt clear and parachuted to safety. He was picked up by Soviet troops.

Ina told me, 'It was the first time I had seen Lily look like her old self since Alexei's death. She was smiling and elated as she jumped down from the cockpit. She cried, "Paint another rose on, Ina!" She had obviously been in a pretty fierce fight. There were bullet holes in her fuselage and a jagged hole through the back of the perspex of her cockpit hood.'

It was Lily's last sortie of the day. She walked off to write her reports on the action and to be debriefed. An hour later an army truck drove on to the airfield, and a German pilot was led at gunpoint into the debriefing room. A tall man with close-cropped grey hair, he was considerably older than most fighter pilots. He was certainly in his early forties. He had a tanned complexion and rather gaunt cheeks, and he did not look in the least cowed, submissive, or humiliated by the defeat he had just suffered. He was highly decorated: on his chest was an impressive array of ribbons denoting both his awards for gallantry and the campaigns in which he had fought. It seemed that he had shot down over twenty Soviet and Allied aircraft everywhere from France and the Low Countries to here on the eastern front. This was the pilot whom Lily had downed.

One of the Soviet pilots who spoke German asked the captured man if he would like to meet the pilot who had shot him down. The German replied that he would be very interested and, he added arrogantly, that whoever it was must be one of their top men. Yes, he would like to meet this man very much. The Soviet pilots grinned at their private joke and one of them went to fetch Lily from her bunker.

The German was sitting straight-backed on a chair when Lily entered the room. The interpreter said, 'Well, how do you like your victor?' The German swivelled and looked blankly at the small blonde figure standing behind him. He was the first German fighter pilot Lily had ever met. There was a silence for a few seconds, then the German told the

218

interpreter that he did not care for the Russian sense of humour, and if they were not going to let him meet and talk with the real pilot, then he had nothing else to say. This was translated and the other Russians in the room burst out laughing.

But not Lily. She planted herself firmly in front of the German's chair and motioned him to get to his feet. He did so languidly, straightening his tunic as he towered above her. Then, in the painstaking way in which such translations are necessarily conducted, she explained to the German exactly how their dogfight had been resolved, move by move. She told him the exact positions of their two aircraft when the fight had started. She explained in detail how she had rolled in behind him and how he had countered her. She told him how she had finally outflown him and forced him to abandon his aircraft.

Ina Pasportnikova said, 'Those who were there said that it was a masterly performance. The German's whole attitude, even his physical appearance changed. He was forced to concede in the end that no one except the pilot who had beaten him could possibly have known, move by move, exactly how the fight had gone. There was no question of his saluting the victor. He could even meet her eyes. To have been shot down by a woman was more than he could bear.

'The others had never seen Lily like that before. Her eyes were flashing like a tiger. She was enjoying herself. Her claws were out, and they knew they were in the presence of a dangerous woman. It was the first time anyone had ever seen her killer instinct aroused on the ground. The German had made the mistake of showing contempt for her both as a pilot and as a woman. Now her victory was complete.'

This was not the only occasion on which Lily and the other women pilots had won the admiration of their opponents. Maj. D. B. Meyer, a Luftwaffe ground-attack pilot, wrote of his experiences near Orel in 1943. His unit, he said, was opposed by Soviet fighters from an elite unit.

They were 'brave daredevils, well trained and excellent fliers, with a sure flair for German weaknesses'. Their aircraft, he said, had powerful engines and were capable of climbing at a steep angle and attacking German aircraft from below. They attacked in a superior manner with short bursts of fire from all guns at short distances, directing their fire mainly at the lead aircraft of the German squadron, eight of which were shot down in one week.

On one occasion when Major Meyer was engaged in aerial combat, his aircraft caught fire. His Russian opponent was returning to make another pass when he jettisoned his cockpit canopy preparatory to bailing out. Fortunately for him, the cockpit roof flew straight into his opponent's propeller and the Yak plunged to the ground. Major Meyer was able to make an emergency landing close to the crashed aircraft. He wrote later: The dead pilot turned out to be a woman, without rank, insignia, identification or parachute.'

Despite the increasing Soviet air superiority, the small groups of free hunters could still occasionally find themselves outnumbered. Lily was shot down twice in the three weeks following her extraordinary dogfight. She and five other Yaks took on a flight of German bombers with a heavy fighter escort; under heavy attack from three German fighters, Lily took serious hits in her engine. She was forced to make an emergency landing in a field, but the next day she was airborne again in a replacement Yak. A few days later her Yak was set on fire; she rolled it upside down and flung herself from the cockpit at a dangerously low altitude. The parachute opened just in time. Lily was badly shaken by this incident and leaned heavily on her friend and roommate Katya Budanova to restore her morale. Both women had now lost many good friends in combat, and when one of them was particularly depressed, the other would be supportive. Katya had been one of the main reasons Lily managed to survive the trauma of Alexei's death.

Katya had shot down nine German aircraft now. She was one of the best known women pilots and, though her friend Lily was clearly more attractive to men, it did not affect the young women's friendship for each other. Ina told me, 'Katya was the perfect foil for Lily. When her hair was cut really short, she looked more like a young boy than a girl. There was nothing unfeminine about her and the men in the regiment liked her, but she had never become romantically involved. Certainly Lily could never have regarded her as any threat in that way.'

Katya was always singing. She was singing in the cockpit before she took off on the morning of 18 July, 1943. In a fight with several agile Focke Wulfe 190 fighters, Katya had two kills confirmed by her wingman before she herself was hit. The fighter with the red stars on the wings and fuselage swept low over a village, flames spreading across the wings. The field Katya appreared to be trying land in was pitted with craters from bombs jettisoned by the group she had been attacking. The Yak hit one of the craters and exploded. The villagers ran to the scene and dragged the pilot from the flames. But Katya was dead.

First Boris Gubanov, then Nikolai Baranov, then Losha, and now Katya. Ina told me, 'I was close to Lily, but with Katya she had had a special relationship. When you're up there every day fighting for your life in the sky, you can only really share your deepest thoughts with someone who's doing the same. Now Katya was gone, and I knew that Lily felt alone.' A mechanic had just completed painting a white rose on the fuselage of Lily's replacement aircraft. He went to find her, to seek her approval of his work. She was not in the bunker. On Katya's neatly made bed was a small collection of books, photographs, and letters. Out towards the edge of the airfield a slight, blonde figure was walking. She was quite alone.

It was the night of 31 July, 1943. The night bomber

regiment had been briefed by Major Bershanskaya for that night's sorties. It had been the same target for nights now – the German 'Blue Line' fortifications near the villages of Krymskaya and Russkaya in the Kuban. The villages were only a few minutes' flying time away from their present airfield. Nadia Popova recalled, 'The airfield was at quite a high elevation. So, sometimes when we were flying a sortie, the ground crews and pilots waiting to take off on the next sortie would be able to see the searchlights and the explosions of anti-aircraft shells in the sky miles away as we pressed home our attacks.

'Though it was very dark that night, there wasn't much cloud. Those on the ground had a grandstand view of what happened. None of them will ever forget what they saw.'

Two of the squadrons were to fly the first sortie. When they returned to rearm and refuel, the third squadron would take off to continue the bombardment. Sixty women – the regiment's complement of pilots and navigators – crowded into a classroom of the school, beside the grass airfield, which they had requisitioned as a briefing room and headquarters. They knew the flight path to the target almost by heart now, but Katya Rabova, who occupied the cockpit behind pilot Nadia Popova, once again measured and noted distances to the targets and wind direction and strength, and calculated the estimated flying time, so important to accurate navigation on night bombing missions.

It was high summer, but with the sunset, the balmy warmth of the Crimean night was dissipating. At two thousand feet, they would be glad of their knee-length leather boots, heavy gloves, and leather helmets. After the bright light of the briefing room, it took a few seconds for their eyes to adjust to the darkness outside. As they walked across the field, their night vision took over and the shapes of the little two-winged bombers stood out in blurred silhouette. The fuel tanks, which fed the engine in a simple gravity flow system, had already been topped off, and the fuel crew had dispersed. Clusters of bombs hung beneath the frail lower wings, and the armament fitters and mechanics stood around the line of aircraft. They wiped their hands on cotton rags, and sweat glistened on their foreheads and cheeks.

Nadia's stomach had tightened as it always did before a mission. But she strolled towards her aircraft, apparently relaxed, giggling and chattering with her friends Natalya Meklin and Marina Chichnova. Marina told me, 'We took off at one-minute intervals. I was eighth off. We expected a really fierce flak barrage over the target, like we'd had every other night. So what we actually did come up against was the shock of the unexpected.'

Nadia was first to take off. She flipped the switch on her face mask and tested the intercommunication with navigator Katya in the rear cockpit. She felt around in the depths of her right-hand overall pocket for the familiar, reassuring little shape; but she felt nothing there. Seized by an irrational panic, she pulled the throttle lever back to idling speed and tugged off her right glove. She delved inside the pocket with her bare fingers and exhaled with relief as her fingers closed on her talisman. It was against regulations to wear jewellery, but she never took off without the little beetle brooch she had brought with her from her bedroom table at home. She explained, 'It went everywhere with me. I used to mock other people's superstitions, but that final check on my overall pocket became part of my cockpit drill.'

When she saw the green flare go up from the end of the airfield, Nadia pushed the throttle lever all the way forward. The PO-2 bumped and thudded down the field, gaining speed in the darkness as the smoky oildrum markers whipped past the wing. The airspeed indicator needle crawled around the dial as the heavily laden aircraft approached flying speed. Another bump, the wheels left the ground, and that thrill trembled through her as it always

223

did – they were airborne. She held the stick forward to build up airspeed before allowing the little bomber to settle into a steady climb. The luminescent glow of the instruments showed the aircraft rolling into a gentle climbing turn. They were ten minutes' flying time from the target.

There was no radio communication between the aircraft, but Nadia knew that strung out behind her in the darkness were nineteen other PO-2s. She always felt the responsibility of being lead pilot. Of course, the other crews were navigating independently to the target, but human nature being what it was, the other crews would tend to bomb any fires that her attack started on the ground. Nadia told me, 'Normally Katya and I would chatter to each other over the intercom on the way to a target – the usual girlish things about boys and so on. But that night it was different. We were both nervous, and the only talk was about course corrections and changes. She gave me a final attack heading and just then, red and green signal rockets were fired from the ground.'

By this time, over enemy territory, Nadia and the next pilots in the formation realized that something ominous was happening. Unlike the previous nights, there had been no fierce flak barrage as they approached the target. And, most significantly, no crisscross beams of light probing the darkness from the massed batteries of searchlights – only the signal rockets fired by the Germans. In the open cockpits, the roar of the engine and the rush of the slipstream enveloped them. The vibration from the old aircraft buzzed through their feet and hands and pulsed through the cushioned seats up through their trunks and necks until it reached their faces where, under goggles, their cheeks trembled with every rise and fall of the engine note.

Around the village of Krymskaya, German ground troops lay in the ruined buildings or in dugouts and trenches nearby. They, too, must have noticed the absence of anti-aircraft fire and must have hoped that the 'night

224

witches' would stay away and leave them in peace that night. The PO-2s had been hammering away at them night after night. Now, again, on the still night air, from several miles away, came the distinctive *pop-popping* of the bombers' engines. The weary troops struggled to their feet and sought the best possible shelter.

Overhead, Nadia yanked the wire that released the bombs. The aircraft leapt as the weight dropped away, and Nadia started a gentle turn to the left to see the bombs strike. Fifteen seconds, twenty seconds – then an enormous series of explosions. It looked as if they had hit an ammunition dump. Immediately the searchlights came on and she found herself bracketed in what seemed a dozen powerful beams. She told me, 'The terror for us of being caught in that light was almost indescribable. Remember, we were slow-moving. And what made it worse was the intensity of light – it quite literally blinded you. I knew I was flying for our lives. I couldn't see the instruments. I couldn't see anything at all. My only chance was a violent manoeuvre. I screwed my eyes tight against the glare, rolled the aircraft upside down, and pulled the stick back into my stomach, diving off in the opposite direction. I kept diving and stuck my head down into the cockpit to try to orientate myself. All was pitch blackness again. I'd shaken off the searchlights. I came out of the dive at around five hundred feet. Still no anti-aircraft fire. It seemed very strange. I wondered why. I craned my head back up into the sky.'

The second PO-2 in the formation, piloted by Shenya Rudnova, had flown straight into the bracket of light from which Nadia had so desperately broken free. Still no flak from the ground. But above the engine noise came the rattle of machine guns and the slower *thumps* of cannon shells. Brightly coloured and curving tracers preceded the unmistakable shape of a Messerschmitt night fighter.

Marina Chichnova, the eighth in line, told me: 'I couldn't believe what was happening. We'd never come up against night fighters before. We were prepared to take our chances with searchlights and flak, but this was something else. The night fighter could hardly miss.

'The flames started on her right wing. I don't know if Shenya had been hit in the attack, but she was obviously still conscious, because she started side-slipping the aircraft in a very controlled way towards the ground. She was trying to keep the flames away from the engine, I think. But it was hopeless. The searchlights were probing elsewhere now, but we didn't need any lights to see what was happening to poor Shenya. In a few seconds, the entire aircraft was engulfed in flames. It didn't explode. I wish it had. It was horrible watching the little aeroplane, carrying two dear friends, just floating to earth in a ball of flames.'

Larissa Rasanova was flying the fourth aircraft in the line. She saw Shenya's PO-2 hit and start burning. Then the lights bracketed the aircraft in front of her. She told me, 'It dawned on me why there had been no anti-aircraft fire. The Germans were co-ordinating searchlights and night fighters against us for the first time. They must scarcely have been able to believe their luck. There we were, sailing along through the night, conveniently at the same height, one aircraft after the other. In retrospect, it was asking for trouble.

'I recognized the shape of the Messerschmitt as it pulled up underneath the second aircraft; then he soared up out of the light and into the blackness, gaining height for his next attack. I was next in line and I knew I was his next target. I was literally sick with fear. I tried to vomit over the side of the aircraft but there was nothing there. I retched and coughed. My hands and feet seemed separated from the rest of my body. I tried to make them move the controls and nothing happened.'

An explosion from the second victim as it nosed into an uncontrolled dive just a few hundred yards away jolted her into action. She told me, 'The signal rockets we all carried

226

inside the cockpits started exploding in the heat as our friends cartwheeled down in flames. It was almost beautiful to watch. The red and green stars spurted from the aircraft. I prayed the girls were already dead.'

Larissa throttled the engine back and shoved the nose hard forward. The PO-2 engine popped as it settled into a glide; then the wind rushing through the wing struts became the dominant sound. Larissa's plan was to out-think the German night fighter crew by descending as low as possible, disguising her approach from the German ground forces by gliding to the target with her engine throttled back. She passed over the target, still descending silently, and her navigator told her to make a turn to bring her back over the target again. The sound of the German night fighter's engines as it pulled up from its unsuccessful pounce wailed and thundered in their ears. It passed only a few feet from them as it zoomed upward, just an impression of a solid shape in the blackness as the women cringed involuntarily. Then it was gone – clawing up once more towards a little aircraft captured by the searchlights like some helpless creature impaled on the ends of a dozen gleaming lances.

Larissa's PO-2 buffeted and rocked in the German's wake. They were down to around four hundred feet now. The navigator, as if afraid the Germans on the ground might hear her voice, whispered over the intercom that Larissa should release the bombs. From that height the bombs took only a few seconds to reach the ground. She had broken all the rules by bombing from that height. They did not have delayed action fuses. Her tactic had saved them from the fighter and enabled them to press home their attack; now, though, these tactics were almost to destroy them.

The blast hurled the PO-2 upward. Shrapnel ricocheted from the fuselage, a wing dropped, and Larissa banged the throttle hard forward. The engine surged into life. Slowly the battered old aircraft picked up speed. Someone on the ground fired off a flare; bathed in its light, the PO-2 became the target for what seemed like every machine gun, rifle, and pistol on that part of the front. Bullets glanced off the engine casing and ripped through the fabric of the fuselage. Larissa kept on full power and went even lower. The flare was dying. One last long burst from a machine gun and they were in darkness again. She eased the nose up into a climb and set course for home. Both women craned their heads back up into the night. A third aircraft, burning from nose to tail, was fluttering down.

Natalya Meklin, a nineteen-year-old pilot who had left her studies in Moscow to win selection to the regiment, told me, 'By the time the fourth aircraft was hit and started burning, the more experienced pilots had dived out of formation. After that night, we changed our tactics. But it was too late to save the girls who died. They were the most inexperienced. They never had a chance.'

The rest of the regiment had seen the slaughter from the airfield. Through her nightglasses, Yevdokia Bershanskaya had watched in disbelief as one aircraft after another had incinerated the women who had sat such a short time before at her briefing, faces flushed with anticipation. She focused on the third aircraft as it plummeted. From that distance she could hear no sound, but in her head she seemed to hear the cries of her girls as they wrapped their arms around their faces in pathetic attempts to spare themselves. Their fuselage was engulfed now, the open cockpits awash with a flame so intense no watcher could ever imagine. Major Bershanskaya let the glasses fall from her hands. They jerked on their neck strap and thumped against her stomach. She turned away.

She told me, 'We carried no parachutes at that time. They were all burning so furiously, so quickly, that we knew they could never even make a crash landing and walk away from it. Words can't express the emotions you feel at a time like that. The bonds of friendship we all had were so strong. We'd been through so much together. We'd developed this strength of friendship which girls in peacetime just never get a chance to experience. It's so intense. And on the ground we stood and watched them die in that way. Soon we heard the others coming back and then we began to wonder – which girls had died?'

Nadia Popova's was the first aircraft back. She taxied to a halt and switched off the engine. In the cool air the metal *pinged* rhythmically as it cooled and contracted. She slumped forward in her straps, her head held in both hands. She told me, 'I was suddenly aware that Yevdokia Bershankaya and a large crowd of other girls were around the aircraft. I eased myself out of the cockpit and stepped from the lower wing on to the ground. I remember all I could blurt out to her was "Mission accomplished". She put her hands on my shoulders and said, "It's all right, Nadia, we saw everything." There were no tears right then. We were all too shocked. But in the half light around the dispersal area, I could see every girl's face, white and unnaturally stiff. I must have looked that way myself.'

Soon the other surviving aircraft were back at the airfield. There would be no more sorties that night. Major Bershanskaya stood the squadrons down. The women were all strangely reluctant, despite their exhaustion, to make their way to the bunkers. They stood around in little knots – the pilots, navigators, and ground crews. One or two cigarette ends glowed in the darkness in the midst of gently whispered conversations. Marina Chichnova, as so often, took the initiative. She ground out her cigarette on the grass and started walking slowly towards the bunker. Conversation stopped and the rest straggled after her.

Marina paused at the foot of the steps leading to the door, then pushed it open. She told me, 'It had not really sunk in that eight of our friends had been taken from us so suddenly. Though no one had actually said so, we all knew it would hit us hard when we went back to our living quarters that night.' The beds of the eight dead women had now assumed an almost unbearable poignancy, each with its collection of intensely personal possessions. Shenya Rudnova had been in love with a fighter pilot on another front. Her little leather diary was full of him. It lay on her pillow with a chewed stub of pencil jutting from that day's page. Sonya Rabova's family photographs were spread neatly across her blankets. In one, her small sister held on to her skirt with both hands and gazed up at the round-cheeked smiling girl. Valya Ploovinya had recently married a soldier serving at the front. She had tied around his letters a braided ribbon of embroidery threads. Beside the bundle lay an unfinished letter she had been composing before the mission. On or around each bed lay objects so familiar to the other women that they had scarcely noticed them before: a necklace or bracelet taken off before the mission, an old school note-book with the words of popular songs scrawled in a childish hand.

Nadia Popova told me, 'We stood there quite silent for several minutes, just looking at the beds. Then we flung ourselves down. I clenched my fists and buried my head in the pillow. The room was filled with the sounds of sobbing. We were soldiers but we were also women. I lay awake all night. Eventually the room became quiet again. But I knew from the sound of the breathing in the darkness that most of the other girls were lying there like me staring at the roof of the bunker and thinking.'

For three days, the beds remained exactly as they had been left by the dead women. When the regiment sat down for a meal, places continued to be laid for the missing fliers. Natalya Meklin told me, 'Obviously no one could have survived. But somehow we could not accept this. Every time the door opened, every time a truck drove on to the field, we expected to see the eight girls jumping out and running towards us. When you're flying in combat you mustn't believe that it can ever happen to you. It's one of the things that keeps you going. When eight friends disappear in a few seconds from the face of the earth, your mind refuses to accept it.'

Came the fourth day and no word from ground units of anyone being found. The women carefully wrapped their friends' belongings in brown paper parcels. They placed between pieces of cardboard the treasured photographs of parents, brothers, and sisters – the proud families who would soon receive the telegrams. Then would come the coarse envelopes bearing the hackneyed words of official-dom, fumbling for the phrases that could convey the sorrow of the regiment. And, many weeks later, the other letters, addressed in girlish handwriting. They would drop on the doorsteps of a flat in Moscow, a little house in Rostov, or would be picked out of the usual crevice in a tree near the main road which served as a letter box to a remote farm in the Caucasus. These, the last letters from the front, about the daughter who would never come home again.

The tactics that had led to the slaughter would be changed, but the deadly game of hide-and-seek in the night skies would continue. The feeling of vulnerability had always been there in the cockpits of the women who fought in the slow, unarmed little bombers. From that night on, for many of them, the possibility of violent death made every take-off an intense inner struggle against the recur-ring memory of what happened to their friends: the burst of gunfire in the darkness, the flames, and the slow tumbling death at the hands of men they would never see, men in the prowling black fighters.

Two hundred miles away, at a fighter airfield near the town of Krasnyy Luch in the Donbass, Lily Litvak was in her cockpit preparing for the first sortie of the day. It was just after daybreak and she had a few minutes to spare before the other free hunters strapped themselves in. It was a good opportunity to write to her mother.

Her right hand had been injured by a bullet that had pierced the cockpit. It was not a serious wound, but it meant that she could not write. The cockpit hood was still pushed back, and a friend sat on the wing while Lily dictated the letter to her. The words showed clearly the mood of the once carefree girl.

Battle life has swallowed me completely. I can't seem to think of anything but the fighting. It's difficult for me to find a moment to write but I'm doing it now. I'm alive as you can tell, and in good health. I've hurt my hand slightly so a friend is writing this for me. I love my country and you, my dearest mother, more than anything. I'm burning to chase the Germans from our country so that we can live a happy normal life together again. I miss you all. I kiss you affectionately.

Their mission that day was a sweep towards the front line, looking for enemy bombers. Ten miles from the front they found them – a large group of them. Ivan Borisenko, who was flying with Lily on that mission, wrote later to Vera Tikomerova, the commissar of the women's fighter regiment: 'Lily just didn't see the Messerschmitt 109s flying cover for the German bombers. A pair of them dived on her and when she did see them she turned to meet them. Then they all disappeared behind a cloud.' Ivan had his hands full and was soon flying for his life, too. Through a gap in the clouds he saw Lily's Yak with smoke pouring from it, being pursued by several German fighters. Later he reckoned that as many as eight had decided to concentrate on the Yak bearing the distinctive white rose.

The odds were far too great. The luck that Lily had depended on for so long had finally run out. No one saw her aircraft crash, but there was no doubt. Lily was dead. The white rose on her Yak had drawn her killers to her as surely as she must have known it one day would. In just over a year of combat flying, she had shot down twelve German aircraft.

Ina Pasportnikova told me, 'When we realized Lily wasn't coming back, men in the regiment broke down and cried. They never found her aircraft of her body, so there was no funeral.

'On her memorial statue she looks so depressed, so serious. That is not how I remember our Lily. I close my eyes and I see the little blonde girl sitting in her cockpit, so full of life, her eyes flashing, her face smiling that smile.'

Ivan Borisenko wrote simply, 'We all loved little Blondie. As a pilot and as a person she was beautiful.'

No one will ever know if Lily was dead before her fighter hit the ground. That morning before her flight, as usual, she managed to find some wildflowers and she had pinned a little bunch of them to the side of the instrument panel. Those who loved her like to think that at the end, before oblivion, Lieutenant Litvak's last glimpse was of the flowers in the corner of her cockpit.

13

Into the Holocaust –
Smolensk, 1943–45

In the autumn of 1943, the women of the 587th Bomber Regiment were fighting farther north, bombing German troop concentrations around the town of Smolensk as the Soviet ground forces prepared to push the invaders still farther west. The infatuation of Valentine Markov for Galina Junkovskaya had not abated one bit and, although he continued to fly regularly as her pilot, she was still unaware of the extent of his adoration. On the days she navigated for another pilot, the spectre of Galina being injured or killed haunted him.

It was now October. One of Markov's squadron commanders, Luba Gubano, had died a few days earlier when her bomber had flown into the ground after heavy attacks by German fighters near Smolensk. Her self-sacrifice seemed typical. She had stayed with the PE-2 to allow the other two in the crew to parachute to safety. By then the stricken aeroplane was too low for Luba herself to jump. Galina had often flown as Luba's navigator, but not that day. Now, though, Galina was airborne for yet another sortie in the same area on a mission about which Markov had briefed the crews just half an hour before. He checked his watch. It was 2 P.M. If the mission was routine, the plane should be landing again around 3.30.

Flying fighter escort for the regiment that day were French pilots of the famous Normandie-Niemen squadron. This unit was composed of Free French pilots who had volunteered for service in Russia. During the war they were credited with 273 kills, and four were honoured as heroes of the Soviet Union. Forty-two died in action. At this time, around Smolensk, they were flying Yak-9s. The women told me that they always knew if the escort fighters were being flown by the French ... they were very flamboyant and boyishly liked to demonstrate their aerobatic skills when there were no enemy aircraft in the sky.

After Galina and her crew dropped their bombs and turned for home, they were attacked by German fighters. The Frenchmen got involved in a whirling dogfight, but a lone Messerschmitt raked Galina's PE-2 and set it on fire. Galina told me, 'The gas tank behind my position was burning fiercely. There was nothing I could do to put out the flames. The heat was fantastic. I was cringing in anticipation of the aircraft exploding into tiny pieces.' The radio operator was dead. She had abruptly stopped speaking over the intercom during the fighter attack, and now there was a wall of flame between Galina and her dead friend's position.

Galina added, 'My flying overalls were literally beginning to smoulder, but Klavia Fumechova, the pilot, was determined to fly the bomber over our lines before we jumped out.' They opened the hatch in the floor and, with Klavia no longer at the controls, the bomber tipped into a steep dive. The women tried to climb out, but the tremendous force of the slipstream kept pushing them back inside. Galina told me, 'It was the most frightening experience of the war. I could feel my face blistering and burning from the flames inside the aircraft. I thought it was the end.' Then, quite of its own accord, the bomber flipped on to its back; as it did so, the women tumbled out of the hatch and yanked their ripcords.

Almost immediately, it seemed, they were on the ground. Somewhere in the confusion they had both lost their flying boots. They stood in a field in their stocking feet, being tugged off balance by the wind which filled the parachutes still trailing from their backs along the ground. They unbuckled themselves and looked up at the sky. The bomber, which had become a funeral pyre for the radio operator, was disappearing over a tree line in the middle distance. There was a great tongue of orange flame, followed a split second later by the sound of the explosion and a rising cloud of oily black smoke.

Galina looked at Klavia, whose face and hands were completely blackened with smoke. She asked Klavia if she was in pain, and she told her no. But Galina was. She asked Klavia to tell her the truth. What was her face like? Klavia took her friend's slender hand and lifted it gently to her scorched cheeks. Galina could feel large blisters forming beneath her high cheekbones. Galina recalled, 'It was the dread that all of us had. We expected injury every time we flew a sortie. But the injury we dreaded most was burning, particularly of the face.' She had no time to weep or sink into self-pity. As the first shock wore off, the savage pain started to seep through.

Galina had stuffed a map in her overalls pocket before she jumped, and she had an approximate idea of their position. They were, as it turned out, in a rather fluid part of the front, though closer to their lines than the Germans'. A local offensive was being mounted by their side, and a company of Soviet soldiers was advancing out of some woodland a quarter of a mile away. The women decided to take no chances on mistaken identity and stood with their hands high in the air as the troops approached. They must have presented a strange sight: no boots, hands and faces blackened, and Galina's cheeks puffed and blistered. But the troops had seen them floating down, and there had never been any danger they would be fired upon.

The women were taken to a field hospital – a series of large, dark brown tents – just behind their own lines. Orderlies with drums of thick white disinfectant were spreading the stuff around the entrances to the tents; already the first of the wounded from the offensive were being brought in. Galina told me, 'Some of these boys had lost limbs, others had the most terrible injuries all over their bodies. Their cries were awful as they lay outside the tents on stretchers waiting for the surgeons to deal with them.' Inside, through the flaps of the tents, the women could see surgeons working at tables on the wounded. Bright lights above the tables were powered by noisy generators outside. The surgeons in these situations had a merciless criterion thrust upon them – work on those whom you have the best chance of saving. Some soldiers were carried in and, it seemed, carried out again almost immediately into another tent.

A doctor examined the women where they sat on the ground. Klavia's burns were superficial, but he smeared Galina's face with a green ointment and gave her the remainder of the jar. She must not, he said, cover her face with bandages. Galina had been finding it almost impossible to stand on her right leg. The doctor swiftly ran his hand down the limb. She had been walking around on a broken leg. He placed it in a splint and hurried off into one of the tents.

Klavia went off to try to arrange transport to the nearest airfield, from where they hoped to hitch a ride back to their own base. Galina told me, 'I sat there almost unable to think because of the pain from my face. I forced myself to think of the words of the song I used to sing as a little girl, and when Klavia came back I was sitting there singing this song as loud as I could. It didn't take the pain away, but it helped to keep my mind off it.'

It took Galina and Klavia five days to get back to their own airfield. They had been listed as missing, presumed dead. It was hardly surprising; normally, if a flier had been shot down on her own side of the lines, her commanding officer would have been informed fairly quickly. But in the chaos then ensuing, this had not happened. The women's friends were about to prepare what they called a 'mourning meeting' to honour the memory of their fallen comrades.

Valentine Markov knew that everyone in the regiment was watching him as the days went by. A man of strong character, he flew several missions himself, briefed crews, wrote reports, and carried on with the routine essential to the maintenance and smooth running of the fighting unit for which he was responsible. But it was clear that he had not slept since Galina's aircraft was reported missing. Still, each day he appeared from his bunker smoothly shaved and groomed. He had told the signals officer to bring him news of the downed crew whatever time of night it might arrive, and when he emerged in the morning the first thing he did was to check and double-check any signals. He personally telephoned divisional headquarters several times a day if he was not airborne, but the answer was always the same.

Valentina Kravchenko told me, 'If the commander of our regiment had still been a girl – if Marina Raskova had still been alive – and she had been in that sort of emotional turmoil, then we could have shown her how we felt. We could have spoken to her girl to girl and perhaps given her strength. But Major Markov was not the sort of man one could approach in that way. He would have regarded it as a breach of discipline; besides, no one was supposed to know that he felt any differently about Galya than about the rest of us. It showed us the strength of the man, that he could carry on at all in the circumstances. I'm sure many men would have cracked up.'

The transport aircraft carrying Galina and Klavia arrived at their home airfield unannounced, apart from the normal radio call to the air traffic controller. Klavia stepped from the door in the fuselage and prepared to help down her injured friend. All the women in the regiment were milling around the aircraft door in a state of high excitement, laughing and shouting to their returning friends. Then, pushing his way through from the back of the crowd, came Markov. The women melted away before him, and then he was standing underneath the aircraft door, stretching up his arms to Galina.

Valentina Kravchenko said, 'I had never seen such a look of tenderness on a man's face. He completely forgot that he

238

was our commanding officer. He was simply a man in love. As he reached up, Galya leaned forward; then he was carrying her in his arms from the aeroplane. He could no longer hide his feelings. He was whispering to her as he carried her from the aircraft but we could not hear what he was saying. We didn't need to hear the words. We could see his feelings in his face.'

Galina weighed less than a hundred pounds then and must have seemed like a feather in the arms of the large man. She remembers nothing of what he said to her as she lay cradled in his arms; and when she recovered from the fever raging inside her, she would not believe the teasing remarks of her friends about her commander's reactions to her return. She went to a hospital in Moscow for five weeks and her face made a remarkable recovery from the burns – the only trace was a dark brown pigmentation in her cheeks which showed red when she was exposed to too much sun.

Fliers would stay with their burning aircraft until the last possible moment if it meant that they could parachute into territory held by their own troops. It was all a matter of judgement and, of course, luck; but the fear of falling into German hands was so strong that they would take enormous risks to avoid it. Galina and her pilot had survived and, by staying with their bomber until the last moment, they had narrowly evaded capture. For Nina Karasova, though, the gamble failed. The teenage navigator with the curly fair hair was to suffer an imprisonment more hideous than any of her friends had contemplated: her capture was to lead her to the hell of the concentration camps of Ravensbruck and Buchenwald.

The women's regiment was supporting a breakthrough by ground troops near Smolensk when they came under heavy attack by German fighters. Nina and the radio operator/gunner – a man that day – exhausted all their machine-gun ammunition on the German fighters. The radio operator was hit in the chest and badly wounded, and the bomber was so badly damaged by the fighter attacks that the control surfaces were almost completely shot away. Then one of the engines caught fire and the flames quickly spread along the wing. Pilot Alexandra Yegorva ordered the other two crew members to jump. The aircraft was now virtually uncontrollable, and though they had not quite reached their own lines, the state of the bomber left them little choice but to abandon it. Nina dropped through the hatch in the floor of the aircraft, and Alexandra left her controls to help the injured radio operator jump clear. Then she herself bailed out.

Alexandra, who had suffered bad burns to her face, landed badly and lost consciousness. When she came round it was nightfall. She was in a gully; at the end of it, about three hundred yards away, she could see the multiple rippling flashes of a battery of Soviet Katyusha rockets. She was safe. She got to her feet and ran down the gully. As she stumbled across the rough ground, another salvo was fired with an enormous *whooshing* sound and a brilliant flash of light. Silhouetted against the light, with their backs to her, were three German soldiers. Their coal scuttle helmets were unmistakable. She dropped to the ground and froze. As the next salvo was fired she lifted her head cautiously. The Germans had disappeared. She thought they must have been a patrol picking its way back to the German lines. Alexandra made contact with the artillery troops at the end of the gully and a few weeks later was back in the air.

The radio operator, though wounded, had escaped soon after being picked up by German soldiers. Nina Karasova had no such luck. She recalled later that as she floated down in her parachute, one of the fighters that had been attacking their bomber made a pass at her, firing his guns. She could see the tracer coming towards her from his wings, but there was little she could do about it. She closed her eyes, waiting for the bullets to tear into her and end it all, but then she heard the roar of his engine as he swept overhead. She had not been hurt. She pulled in the drawstrings of her parachute to increase the rate of her descent, and then she was down.

She did not know in which direction her own lines lay. She had not had a chance to bring a map with her as she leapt from the burning aircraft and, besides, the desperation of her escape combined with the experience on the way down had served to disorientate her completely. She struggled to her feet and swiftly disengaged herself from her parachute harness. She pulled it in towards her and rolled it into a bundle. Her first task was to hide it somewhere, anywhere, to disguise her landing position.

She was in the middle of some sparsely wooded countryside. With the parachute rolled in an ungainly bundle beneath her arm, she ran towards a copse. Perhaps she could hide it there and orientate herself before trying to make it back to her own lines. As she ran towards the copse, two figures rose from ground level and pointed submachine guns at her. She dropped to the ground. Behind them she could see other figures moving among the trees. She had run straight into the Germans. The two men in the grey tunics and coal scuttle helmets had their sleeves rolled up to the elbows. As they moved towards her, they separated and broke into a crouching run.

Nina knew now that they must have seen her landing. The thought of standing up slowly and raising her hands did not seem to have occurred to her. The Germans were now around twenty-five yards away. She fumbled in her holster and pulled out her automatic pistol. She cocked it with a swift backward pull of the slide and, lying flat on the grass, rested the gun on the crook of her left arm and aimed calmly at the German running in from the left. She squeezed the trigger, tensing herself against the noise and the recoil. Nothing happened. She squeezed again, and again. The gun clicked as the firing pin smashed harmlessly against the chamber. She checked the butt of the pistol. The magazine had fallen out sometime during the confusion of the last few minutes.

There was a spare magazine in one of the leg pockets of her flying overalls. She thrust her hand into the pocket and her fingers closed on the slim metal case. It was in her hand. All she had to do was snap it into the pistol, cock it, and fire. An enormous boot stamped down hard on the hand holding the magazine, and from the other side she was kicked so hard below the ribcage that she screamed out. She craned her neck around and looked upward. She recalled later that the faces looking down on her were heavy with stubble and caked with dust. And they appeared to be distorted with hatred. Two submachine guns were pointing straight at her head and one of the Germans barked, 'Hände hoch,' motioning her to her feet. Her flying helmet had come off as she flung herself to the ground to commence firing, and as she stood up the Germans realized for the first time that they had captured a woman. One of the soldiers slung his gun on its strap across his shoulder and began to fumble around the pockets on the chest of her overalls. As Nina tugged at the powerful hands with her small ones, an officer came out of the trees towards them.

Smolensk was still in German hands, and it was there that Nina was taken. In an enormous barbed wire compound, without shelter, she was herded into the company of several thousand other Soviet prisoners of war. Most looked dejected and thoroughly wretched, particularly the wounded who lay unattended in the open. Winter was approaching. Their chances of survival would be slight. A Russian civilian doctor from Smolensk was working among them. Nina, already thinking of escape, offered to help with the bandaging and comforting of the injured men. Could he possibly help her by somehow getting some civilian clothes to her? The doctor promised that he would do what he could, though how he could have achieved anything in those circumstances is hard to imagine. However, he never got the chance. After one day in the compound, Nina was taken away in a truck with some other downed Soviet

242

aircrews for interrogation by the Luftwaffe.

The German air force interrogators were particularly interested in Nina. It was the first opportunity they had had to question one of the Soviet women aviators. They knew that there were women's outfits operating in the front line, but their intelligence was not certain to what extent they were being used or in what strength they were deployed. They wanted to gain as much knowledge from Nina as they could on regimental operating procedures, aircraft characteristics, new equipment, training methods, briefing and debriefing techniques, regimental chains of command, and how their intelligence was gathered and acted on. They were also intrigued by the women fliers for much more basic reasons. No other country involved in the war had women combat pilots. What on earth motivated them? It was a fascinating opportunity to learn a great deal about a great many things. With Nina Karasova, however, they had a most unco-operative subject.

Nina wrote later that she found her interrogators' attempt to extract information by appealing to her as a fellow flier – 'but for an accident of birth, we could have been flying in the same aircraft together' – both unsubtle and patronizing. They did not stoop to physical torture as such, but when she continued to refuse to co-operate they locked her up in a tiny room in solitary confinement for day after day, bringing her out only to renew the interrogation. Nina went on hunger strike, refusing food for over a week; the Germans decided, sensibly, that the sort of information she was likely to have was hardly worth the trouble they were going to.

Nina rejoined the thousands of other Russian prisoners being transported west from camp to camp, sometimes tantalizingly close to their own advancing armies. Life as a prisoner of war was difficult to endure, but after her ordeal Nina glossed over much of her suffering. Her plight clearly touched the men she was incarcerated with, though. While rations for prisoners were barely at a subsistence level, many of them would go short to give her extra food.

During this time, she got to know one of the daring French pilots of the Normandie-Niemen Free French fighter squadron. He too had been shot down in the Belorussian area. His knowledge of Russian was almost nonexistent, but Nina regarded this as a challenge. She spoke to him only in Russian, and gradually he became more confident with the language. His lapses caused great hilarity among the prisoners. When someone was leaving his company instead of saying good-bye, he had an endearing habit of saying, 'How are you?'

It was a diversion for Nina, but no more than that. Her active brain was racing all the time, discussing with fellow prisoners probable means of escape. Once again, she saw a possibility through her friendship with a doctor. He, too, was a prisoner of war, a Russian who had been captured when he stayed behind to tend to some seriously wounded men in his unit during a German counterattack.

The doctor's plan was that he would simulate an illness in Nina in order to get her transferred into the hospital, where her chances of escape into the civilian population were many times better. The plan involved considerable physical pain, but Nina did not hesitate. Over a period of days and under cover of elaborate diversionary ploys by other prisoners, he made a number of incisions and implanted small pieces of metal under her skin. He then asked for an X-ray examination of Nina, which he hoped would reveal serious 'patches' on her lungs and thus necessitate her removal to a hospital.

But it was not to be: the Germans had other plans for the woman flier. On 7 May, 1944, two days before the doctor had arranged the X-ray exam, Nina was taken without warning from her friends and thrown into the cattle truck of a train. Crammed in the same car were a number of Russian nurses who had been captured on the battlefield.

Their destination was Ravensbruck concentration camp.

Nina, who quite properly regarded herself as a prisoner of war with all the rights conferred under the Geneva Convention, was never told why she was taken from her prisoner-of-war camp and transported into the nightmarish world of slavery and degradation that now awaited her. Was it because she had refused to co-operate with her interrogators? If so, why were the other Russian women – the nurses who could have had little useful military information – being treated the same way? The answers were unimportant. What mattered now was to fight for survival.

Ravensbruck was built on swampy ground about fifty miles to the north of Berlin, and Nina's first sight of this camp must have chilled her soul. There were around 30,000 women there at that time, many of them French, and virtually all of them civilians. They were either members of resistance movements, political 'undesirables', or workers who had been deported from their homelands to work in Germany and who had displeased the authorities by not being productive enough. As Nina and the others were herded through the gates of Ravensbruck, they caught their first glimpse of the walking skeletons who were to become their workmates and friends. Nina's clothes were taken from her and she was given a striped dress and wooden clogs. She spent three weeks in Ravensbruck, sleeping on a mattress filled with wood shavings; the complete lack of a blanket or any other form of bed clothing left her shivering with cold.

At the end of three weeks, she was taken from Ravensbruck and transferred to the female part of Buchenwald concentration camp on the west bank of the River Elbe. For the next ten months, Nina clung to life. She worked in the camp laundry for up to eleven hours a day. She and the other women subsisted on daily rations of ersatz coffee, thin soup, and tiny portions of bread substitute. In that camp thousands died of murder, mutilation in the name of medical science, systematic brutality, undernourishment, and cruel overwork. Among those singled out for particularly brutal treatment were four Russian women who had been parachuted behind the German lines as secret agents. Nina shared a bunk in the four-high tiers with one of these women and several other wretched prisoners. Each morning as they struggled from their bunks to march in convoy to work, a woman guard stood at the door flailing brutally at their heads and shoulders with a rubber truncheon.

Some days Nina was so weak with hunger that she joined in the degrading spectacle of hunting for potato peelings and pieces of cabbage on the ground near the cookhouse. Sometimes the staff would amuse themselves by throwing pieces of mouldy bread from the camp stores and watching the prisoners fight for them. At work, even to stop to draw breath was enough to bring a savage and prolonged beating. Nina lost count of the number of women who died in their sleep or were taken away, never to be seen again. To maintain any human dignity was almost impossible in circumstances where clothing and underwear were seldom changed; when there was an issue of 'new' underwear, it was invariably lousy and sometimes even stained with blood. In this camp the notorious Ilse Koch, wife of the commandant, had her lampshades fashioned out of the flesh of murdered prisoners.

On 14 April, 1945, Nina and the other prisoners heard the sound of prolonged artillery fire from some miles from the camp. No one had come to rouse them for work that day and they had noticed, even in their enfeebled state, that the guards had been increasingly nervous for several days now. They stumbled out of their barrack blocks into the daylight. There was not a guard to be seen. The sound of the gunfire was getting closer. Nina and a group of others still fit to walk dragged themselves to the main gate. There were no sentries, the watchtowers were empty, and the gates swung open with a push.

Seven Russian women, including Nina, set off towards the east. None of her friends in the women's regiment – who remembered Nina as the laughing, curly-haired navigator striding towards her aircraft, pistol in her holster, maps in hand – would have recognized this apparently old woman with the matted hair and filthy body, her sticklike arms hanging limply from the sleeves of the striped uniform dress and her eyes sunken and lifeless in the enormous hollows above her gaunt cheekbones. Around eighteen months had passed since Nina had taken off on her bombing mission near Smolensk. To her, the horrors of war had a quite different significance from her friends in the regiment. She had peered into the holocaust, but she had survived.

14

Advancing towards Berlin,
Summer 1944

Nadia Popova was excited. The Germans had been pushed back beyond her hometown of Donetsk, and today she would be able to walk into the town and go back to her old house. Nadia, like so many of the other fliers, had been tortured for some months about the fate of her mother and father. Her brother had been killed in the early days of the German invasion, but she had not learned immediately of her parents. Now, though, she knew that her mother had been safely evacuated from the town to Tashkent and that her father had survived several attacks on the trains he was driving near the Stalingrad front. That had been wonderful news, and she was as excited as the schoolgirl she had been just before the war took her away from the home she loved.

She walked quickly through the town. There had been considerable damage. She expected that. She just prayed that her home had escaped. Several times she met people she had not seen for over two years. They looked at her, confused by the uniform, looked again, and then embraced and exchanged a few words. But Nadia was anxious to reach her home. Her mother would not have been able to take much with her when she was evacuated. Nadia wondered if perhaps her bedroom remained as it had looked when last she saw it before setting off for war. She had carried with her, throughout her combat, the image of the house and the cherry orchard and how she had lain in bed that night after the dance – the night the invasion began. She turned the corner and ran towards her house.

Nadia told me, 'It was one of the most distressing experiences of my life. I felt as if I myself had been, somehow, violated.' The garden was completely bare and the earth churned up. Here and there could still be seen the stumps where the cherry trees of her childhood had been crudely hacked down. The door hung partially of its hinges. She stepped inside, her boots crunching on pieces of broken glass and discarded food tins. She told me, 'I learned later that the Germans had occupied my home and used it as some sort of interrogation centre.' There was not a stick of furniture left in the house. In her bedroom the bare boards creaked as she slowly stepped across them and looked through the broken window where once the cherry blossoms hung. On the walls of her room and in the main room of the house were heavy, reddish-brown smears of dried blood. She thought of the happiness there had once been in these rooms. The memories of a loving family life filtered through the retina of her mind's eye only briefly before she realized how fragile was the intimacy that bound a person to a place of the past. Nadia wished she had not returned. She hurried out of her home and walked away. She did not look back.

The Soviet Union then was a population of families divided by the separation of those fighting in uniform and by the accidents of fate which often placed one part of a family in territory occupied by the invader. Some of the most pathetic casualties of the war were the children who had been orphaned and who wandered the countryside fending for themselves. Many died, alone and starving, bewildered and emotionally wounded beyond belief by the experiences they had undergone. Others survived, living like young animals, through a combination of luck and an indomitable instinct for survival. A few were fortunate enough to be cared for by adults who were not themselves fending off starvation. So it was that little Misha came to be adopted by the woman of the PE-2 bomber regiment.

The 587th Regiment was fighting in the Baltic region. Close to their airfield were a number of buildings destroyed in the fighting. One morning several of the women were walking near the buildings, picking their way through some rubble, when a small figure leapt to its feet like a frightened animal being flushed from its cover. The child ran away from the uniformed women but tripped on some bricks and sprawled heavily on the ground. The women ran up and knelt beside him.

He was about eight years old, they learned later, but he was small for his age. And so thin. At first they thought the ragged little creature was a girl; his blond hair had not been cut for years. It was filthy and hung down to his shoulders. He sat in the middle of the circle of women, whimpering, with his shoulders hunched and his arms folded across his stomach as if for protection. One of the women reached out towards him, and he raised his hand to his face and cowered. His blue eyes darted from face to face. The sight of the uniforms had clearly terrified the boy.

Galina Junkovskaya told me, 'We sat and talked to him for about half an hour. He didn't make any reply to any of our questions at first, but when he realized that we were not Germans, he began to relax a little. We explained to him that we wanted to take him back with us to give him something to eat. He did not know whether to trust what we said, but his hunger got the better of him and eventually he came along with us.'

They gave the little boy a hot meal. He refused any cutlery, scooping up the potatoes and meat in his fingers and cramming the food into his mouth. He had clearly learned during his wild existence that it was best to gulp down very quickly what was available lest it disappeared as fast as it had appeared. When he had licked his plate clean of every scrap, he placed it on the table and for the first time grinned around at the women. By this time everyone who was not on duty had crowded into the room to look at Misha.

Valentina Kravchenko told me, 'The next obvious problem was to do something about getting him cleaned up. He was really filthy – and the smell! We boiled up some

250

water and filled up a tin bath. I don't think he had washed for about a year. His clothes virtually fell from him as we took them off. He protested, but we told him there would be no more food for him until he was scrubbed clean.'

The women took turns lathering the thin body with their rough soap; then they tackled his hair. What a transformation had been wrought already. He was a beautiful little boy. They wrapped him in a blanket to keep him warm. His clothes were fit for nothing except burning. Then someone said that before they decided on anything else, they had better inform Major Markov of what they were doing.

Antonina Bonderova told me, 'He did not need much persuading. He said that, providing Misha did not interfere with our military duties, he could stay with us. Winter was coming, and to turn him out could well have meant that we were sending him to his death.' So Misha was adopted by an entire regiment of doting surrogate mothers. That first night he remained wrapped in a blanket and eventually fell asleep at the foot of one of the women's beds.

While he slept, the women worked, cutting and sewing and completely altering trousers and a spare tunic. In the morning when he woke, Misha dressed excitedly in the miniature air force uniform. To the huge amusement of the women, he proceeded to march up and down, swinging his arms and saluting everyone. The women had even made him a vest and underpants; later that day one of them managed to buy a pair of boots that roughly fitted him from a family in the nearest town.

Misha could scarcely remember anything about his parents. The women assumed they had been killed near the beginning of the occupation, when he was five. They could only guess at what he had gone through. Yet, as the days went by and he grew in confidence, his personality gave few signs of deep mental scars. His defence against what had gone before was to pretend that the previous three years had not happened. One day, when one of the women tried

251

to talk to him about how he had survived, he became withdrawn for several hours and refused to talk about it. After that, there was an unwritten law that no one mention the life he had led before he came to them.

In a few weeks, the regular food and general care had a remarkable effect on the boy. He was almost unrecognizable as the waif they had found in the ruins. His cheeks had a ruddy glow and it was a pleasure to see the young body filling out again.

Valentina Kravchenko told me, 'Remember that several of us were married with children of our own from whom we'd been separated for a long time. It was a bittersweet experience in many ways. It was delightful to have a young child whom we could take care of and give our love to – especially one who'd been through what he had. But in another way, it was a constant reminder of the girls' own children, too.' The women admitted to me that they spoiled Misha dreadfully. They were almost competing with each other to smother him with love. With all this attention showered upon him, one imagines that he became a precocious little monster. According to the women, not so – while he was perfectly capable of playing one off against the other, the adoration seems to have made him confident rather than arrogant.

For obvious reasons, Misha had had no education whatsoever. When they were off duty, the women would take turns teaching him to read and write. He learned quite quickly, but what he was really fascinated by was military affairs. His ambition, he told the women, was to fly in bombers just like theirs. He begged them to take him with them on a mission but – quite apart from the fearful trouble they would have been in if they had been caught doing that – none of them would have dreamed of risking Misha's life by doing such a thing. He occupied his days by running errands between their bunkers and by taking messages from one part of the airfield to the other. He liked to be addressed in a proper military manner and always saluted when one of the women adopted her official tone and gave him an errand to run. It is not difficult to understand why they found him so endearing.

If the women loved Misha, he in turn had grown very close to them. Galina Junkovskaya told me, 'When any of us flew off on a mission, his face would cloud with anxiety until we all came back safely. He would stand on the end of the runway, gazing up at the direction from which the bombers would be returning. He would count them off, one by one, to satisfy himself that everything was all right. He would become very agitated if one was overdue for even the most simple reason, like an engine fault. During the time he was with us, several girls were lost, and he took it very hard.' The child in the air force uniform who could not or would not remember his own dead parents would stand stiffly to attention near the graveside, his face a mirror of both grief and bewilderment.

The regiment was still moving from airfield to airfield fairly frequently, and the little boy revelled in the excitement and activity of these operations. He had his own rough wooden bed which had been knocked together for him, and he would supervise its loading into one of the big American Dakota transports that the regiment used for such moves. His 'mothers' would fly off in their bombers and he would climb into a Dakota and follow them.

Of course, it was a situation that could not last. Valentina Kravchenko told me, 'Major Markov got us all together one day, early in 1945. We left Misha reading in one of the bunkers and told him not to follow us; we knew what the commander wanted to talk about. Well, he told us that he knew what a good little fellow Misha was and how much of a help he had been and how much he too had enjoyed having him around. But the fact was, the Major said, we were ruining him completely. He was becoming "over-womaned" and that was not good for a little boy.

He'd never grow up to be a man. There was a lot more along these lines. Then he said that he had arranged for Misha to be sent off to military school.'

The women knew it was the most sensible thing to do. None of them had really believed that it could go on forever. It had given many of them something else to think about and had prevented a lot of 'shop talk' at times when they were on the ground. The war had to some extent almost suspended belief in the reality of a return to a normal world, which was one of the reasons they had been putting off the day of decision on Misha. However, it was now clear that the war would be over within the year. He would have to be settled somewhere before they all went their separate ways again.

They washed and pressed his uniform and polished his boots, and one woman carefully cut his hair. Misha did not want to go, but the women had explained to him that he must get an education. It was as if he had overheard the misgivings of the commander about his being treated too softly. He stood beside the truck that was to take him to the station and saluted the women who had been his mothers. He was not going to indulge in any open show of emotion. But his 'mothers' knew him too well; they knew the bond he felt was too strong for any pretence at a formal farewell. They ran to him and hugged and kissed him. When the last woman had put him down, he climbed into the cab of the truck. It was difficult to see whether he was crying, but his nose was pressed against the window and he waved to them until the truck turned from the airfield and was gone.

In the early summer of 1944 the 46th Guards Regiment had climbed into their PO-2 night bombers and taken off from the beautiful Crimea, now liberated from the German occupation. From several thousand feet up, the grainfields of the Ukraine stretched before them as far as the eye could see. They were on their way to join the air divisions now preparing for a breakthrough on the second Belorussian front. The fields of wheat gradually gave way to the dark green forests of their new operational area, and it swiftly became obvious that the enormous forests were going to present problems both for navigation and for landing and take-off. Some of the women would fly ahead seeking landing sites and would manage to get their aircraft into a likely looking forest clearing, only to discover that the run was not long enough to allow them to take off again. It was a classic initiative exercise that they resolved by getting local citizens to shove with all their might against the wings while they ran the engine up to full power. Then, at a given signal from the pilot, the people hanging on to the wings would fling themselves to the ground and the aircraft would leap forward as if slung from a catapult. It worked. And, fortunately, the helpers on the ground rarely appreciated the danger they were in.

In one ten-day period in June, the regiment changed airfields no less then ten times to keep up with the offensive on the ground. Marina Chichnova told me, 'Frankly, the problems on the ground were usually greater than any we came across in the air. We encountered very little anti-aircraft fire during those weeks. The enemy seemed to be unco-ordinated.'

The advance was so swift there was no question of providing any comfortable dugout accommodation, and one of their biggest problems was combating the mosquitoes who were feasting in large numbers on their unaccustomed human prey. After their night missions, the women would simply stretch out in the warm air under the wings of their aircraft, wrap themselves in a blanket, and sink into a deep slumber. The mosquitoes had other plans. At one site the women found the torment too much; they got up en masse before dawn and sought refuge in the remains of an old monastery.

For the first time, the regiment began to be used on day

missions. The forests were full of German troops who had been cut off by the Russian advance. The women took off in squadron strength and flew reconnaissance missions over the trees. On one mission one of the pilots spotted a group of over a hundred German troops hiding in the forest. Her navigator was able to give the ground forces exact map references, and they rounded them up.

With the enemy nearby in large numbers, spending the night under an aircraft wing was a frightening experience. The women knew that some of the surrounded Germans had given themselves up meekly, as if welcoming the end to combat. Others, though, had resisted fiercely and fought to the death. The women had been given automatic weapons as well as their standard issue pistols, and they slept with these weapons loaded and within easy reach.

Marina Chichnova told me, 'It was not a pleasant feeling. You lay there and listened to the sounds of the wind in the trees surrounding the strip. The more you listened, the more you imagined you heard things. Your ears became more attuned and you picked out the rustlings and the different noises of the nocturnal animals. But every now and then you would catch your breath. Was that twig snapping under a German foot?'

The Germans were, of course, without any regular food supply. They were living off the land. One night the women were awakened by the sounds of pigs screaming. They leapt up and grabbed their guns; a flare was fired from a pistol. In its light, three German soldiers could be seen several hundred yards away, dragging behind them a pig whose throat they had cut in the darkness. As the women emptied their magazines in their direction, the Germans dropped the slaughtered animal and disappeared into the trees.

Sleep was clearly impossible after that, and everyone was extemely edgy. Half an hour later there was another burst of automatic fire. Another flare revealed a shamefaced pilot looking down at the remains of the intruder whose

256

movements in the darkness had betrayed his presence. At her feet lay a bundle of feathers – all that remained of the luckless cock who had been strutting in anticipation of the coming dawn.

At first light a company of Russian soldiers arrived to search for the Germans who had made the food raid during the night. The soldiers spread out and disappeared into the forest in the direction of the nearby river. Soon there was the sustained sound of heavy small-arms fire as they engaged the Germans. The women hauled their aircraft out on to the village street that they were using for a runway. The planes were already loaded with small clusters of bombs under the wings. For the next hour, they took off one by one and bombed the enemy positions on the next bank. It was the first time they had supported their troops on the ground so closely. As one PO-2 landed to load up again, another took off. Eventually a white flag was raised and the survivors surrendered.

The Germans were marched down the village street on their way to captivity, their hands behind their heads. They stared in disbelief at the grinning women lounging against the fuselages of their bombers. How often had these same soldiers suffered from the harassment of the 'night witches' in their 'sewing machines' as they lay exhausted in their trenches after hours of combat? Now they knew that the stories of the women pilots were not mere propaganda.

As the battle moved westward, on one occasion a group of six women – three ground crew and three pilots – were left behind at a forest strip to make a damaged aircraft worthy again. The plan was that when the repairs were done, the women would cram into two aircraft – the repaired one and another that had been left behind – and fly the short hop to the new airfield. The repairs, though, took longer than anticipated. As darkness fell over the forest, they faced up to the prospect of spending the night guarding their aircraft against the possibility of attack by marauding Germans. They had plenty of ammunition for their submachine guns, and at intervals during the night they shot off bursts of fire into the blackness to deter any Germans who might be around. After a sleepless night, the ground crew worked feverishly on the aircraft while the pilots lay in the grass, weapons cocked and ready to fire.

The enemy came out of the woods silently and without any warning. At first in twos and threes and then, along a line of several hundred yards which completely encircled the women, dozens of heavily armed German soldiers materialized. Some carried belts of machine-gun bullets around their necks, many wore steel helmets, and others were bare-headed.

These women, like all the others, had vowed they would not be taken prisoner. They had all taken up firing positions, lying on the ground, their fingers curled around the triggers of their submachine guns. One of the PO-2s had already been fitted in the rear cockpit with the machine gun that was soon to become standard armament. One pilot was sitting in the cockpit, swinging the barrel of the machine gun around in a wide arc. Everyone prepared to fire.

Then one of the leading soldiers waved his rifle in the air. Hanging limply from the end of the muzzle was a grubby but unmistakably white handkerchief. He came forward slowly and spoke enough Russian to make it clear that they did not want to fight. The women ordered them to throw their weapons in a pile and sit down in a group where they could all be conveniently covered by the machine gun in the aircraft. The Germans' uniforms were ragged, and many of the soldiers looked thin and hungry. Among them were several senior officers, including one dispirited looking man with the red collar flashes of a general. They sat meekly for several hours until Soviet ground troops arrived to take them into captivity.

The regiment moved on from Belorussia into Poland.

From the air, every road seemed to be choked with refugees. Marina Chichnova told me, 'It seemed we had been flying over scenes like these for years. Below my wings I could see burning villages and towns, and smoke and flames from hamlets and even isolated farmhouses. When we flew low, we could see little children sitting on top of carts full of belongings, being pushed slowly by their parents through the sea of people. It made me wish that it would all be over soon.'

Tanya Makarova, one of the squadron commanders, and Vera Beleek were the first women fliers to die on foreign soil. On a night mission in Poland, they were stalked and then shot down in flames by a night fighter. They had been very popular and at this stage in the war – when the end seemed so close – the loss of two friends who had come unscathed through so much was in some ways even harder to accept than the earlier deaths. After they had buried their friends, the women of their squadron painted in large white letters on the dark green fuselage of one of the PO-2s the names of the dead women and the promise that they would be avenged. To the women, this gesture did not seem in the least melodramatic; it was a simple affirmation of love for their lost friends and a visible symbol of aggression.

One more woman flier was to die before the Germans were pushed out of Poland, and the circumstances of her death were the stuff of nightmares. Lily Sanferova and her navigator and friend Roofa Gasheva were shot down on a night sortie north of Warsaw. They had landed in a no-man's land between the opposing forces and, after getting out of the aircraft with only cuts and bruises, became separated on the ground. In the darkness, the women called out to each other as the Germans started firing in the direction of their blazing aircraft. Roofa recalled in her account of the incident, 'As I crawled across the ground, my hands touched something cold and metallic. I ran my fingers over it carefully. I realized with terror that I was touching a mine. We had landed in the middle of a minefield.'

Only later did Roofa learn that both antitank and antipersonnel mines had been sown in that field. The women could have stepped on any number of antitank mines without exerting sufficient pressure to detonate their fearsome power, but the antipersonnel mines were designed with a pressure device that activated on the lightest touch. Roofa called a warning to her friend. The mine she had touched with her fingers had somehow become uncovered; she was unlikely to be so lucky again. Inch by inch, they crawled through the night, probing with their fingers, scarcely daring to move their weight from one tentative knee to the other. The spacing of their hands or the length of their crawl could mean life or the awful blinding flash which would end it all. Each fall of the knee was an anguished attempt to make an indentation so light that it would not disturb whatever might lie an inch or two beneath the damp soil.

Roofa caught her hand on something sharp. As she tugged it away, something ripped deeply through her flesh. She was clutching a piece of barbed wire. The pain was exquisite. It meant she had reached the end of the minefield. A few yards away, she heard a man swearing in Russian. She called out to him and, lying flat on her stomach, wriggled through the curling wire entanglement. She had made it.

Just then, a hundred yards away to her left, there was a flash and a short flat explosion. It was Lily. Roofa would never know how many antitank mines she had crawled over or how many antipersonnel ones she had missed by a hair's breadth. Now Lily, so close to safety, had placed a knee, a hand, or perhaps even a finger in the wrong piece of earth.

The soldiers gave Roofa a large mug of vodka and forced her to swallow it. It seemed unlikely that Lily could have survived the explosion. There was no sound at all from where she had been. In any case, the troops were not prepared to venture into the minefield without detection equipment. At daybreak they could see her just beyond the wire. Death, it seemed, must have been instantaneous.

When she returned to her airfield, Roofa was assigned to fly with another pilot. But sometimes in the heat of combat, over the intercom she would call out the name of the woman with whom she had shared the war.

The women had spent the war being fed on a propaganda diet attributing every German action to the 'Fascist beasts', and they had indeed seen the evidence of some of the brutalities of the invaders. Some of their own families had been among the victims. The women fliers' only direct contact with the Germans, though, had been in recent months when they had helped round up stragglers. Natalya Meklin had come across the body of a young German soldier who had obviously been killed in a surprise attack. Nearby lay his rifle. He looked very young, and for a moment she felt a wave of pity, but then, 'I remembered everything that people like him had done to my country and I hardened my heart.'

Now that they were in Prussia and advancing towards Berlin, the women were curious to see the civilian population that less than four years before had followed with excitement the enormous early successes of the German armies as they smashed into Russia. There was a village close to the airfield and, although they had been warned to stay away from the civilian population, curiosity overcame Marina Chichnova. She checked her pistol, unbuttoned the flap of the holster, and slipped away. The village appeared deserted, but Marina told me, 'One of the reasons we'd been told to keep away from civilians was because there had been cases of Russian soldiers, on their own, being attacked, I moved very slowly down the street.

261

There was no sign of life anywhere.'

The village had obviously been fought over at some recent stage. There were great chunks torn out of the masonry where gunfire had struck, and rubble and several burned-out vehicles blocked much of the narrow road. She approached a house and pushed open the door, then stepped back to try to gauge whether there was anyone inside in the shuttered gloom. No sound came from within. Marina waited a full thirty seconds; then, very gingerly, with one hand on the butt of her pistol, she stepped through the doorway.

In the middle of the room was a table covered by a beautifully embroidered tablecloth. As her eyes became more accustomed to the faint light filtering through the shutters, Marina saw that, despite the sparse furniture, everything was neat and tidy. There was another door at the opposite end of the room; she decided to explore further. She was now confident that the occupants had fled the fighting to join the refugees on the road. There was a sudden movement in a corner of the room. She whipped out her pistol and cocked it. A female voice called out something unintelligible, in German, and Marina saw a young woman huddled in the corner next to a sort of dresser. Two small children, a boy and a girl, clung to the woman's legs. Marina walked to the other door and kicked it open, her pistol held firmly in front of her. There was no one else in the house. She put her gun away.

She told me, 'As I moved towards the mother and children, the little ones whimpered with terror. They were frightened by the uniform. As I got closer, the mother put her hand to her mouth and exclaimed something. I only recognized the German word for woman. Pity overwhelmed me. How could this pathetic little family huddling in the corner be guilty of anything? I pulled up a wooden chair and sat down in front of them, trying to smile and reassure them. I put my hand in the pocket of my tunic where I knew I had a bar of chocolate.

262

'I was about to give it to the children when I stopped. Rushing to the front of my mind were the images of my girlfriends' loved ones who had been murdered in the occupied territories. How was I to know that the father of these little children was not one of those who'd done such terrible things to my people? I sprang from the seat and ran out into the street. I trembled all the way back to the airfield. Conflicting feelings swept over me. Nothing was as simple as it had seemed when we had been fighting the enemy on our own soil. Perhaps I should have stayed in that house for a few more minutes and reached out my hand and touched those children.

'Could it have been that I had had enough of war and the woman's instincts in me were struggling against my feelings as a soldier? Or was it just that it was impossible for me to carry on hating right to the end?'

15

Victory

On 1 May, 1945, the Soviet flag was hoisted over the Reichstag in the very heart of Berlin. Hitler had failed to take Moscow, but the Russians had taken Berlin. The day before, the Fuhrer and his wife of a few hours, Eva Braun, had committed suicide. Now, for the women of the air regiments, the war was over.

The night bombers of the 46th Guards Regiment were at an airfield north-west of Berlin. That night they had flown what was to be their last mission of the war, against some of the last German troops resisting, and now they were asleep in the farmhouse that was their billet. Suddenly a mechanic burst through the door with the news: 'Victory, girls, victory! The war is over.' There was a frenzy of excitement. They all leapt out of bed and flung their arms around each other. They pulled blankets over their shoulders and raided their PO-2 cockpits for signal rockets and flares. For the next hour they had their very own victory fireworks display as the brilliantly coloured rockets exploded overhead. They toasted each other with tin cups of vodka and linked arms and danced in the damp grass between the aircraft.

Then, when the first flush of excitement had worn off, they trickled back into the farmhouse, where many of them sat on their beds and wept quietly. Marina Chichnova told me, 'I put my greatcoat over my shoulders and slipped outside alone. Everything seemed unnaturally peaceful. No gunfire, no searchlights piercing the sky, no aircraft overhead. I leaned my head back against a tree and lit a cigarette. I stayed there for two hours, until the dawn came. My head was a jumble of different thoughts. I thought of going back home, I thought of the man I loved, and I thought a lot about my dear friends who had died and the love I felt for those who had survived that terrible war with me. I was looking towards the east for the first lightening of the sky. I wanted to see the sun rise on the first day of peace.'

It rose slowly, climbing above the rim of the earth and spreading its light, first over Marina's homeland and then westward over the towns, cities, and countryside where the women had flown, fought, and died. Now it was dispersing the fine mist that had hung low over the field's surface. Marina had not felt cold during her vigil, but with the first faint warmth of the sun's rays suffusing her, she realized she was cramped and stiff.

The PO-2s were lined up along the edge of the field. Most of their fuselages and wings looked like patchwork quilts with all the repairs from battle damage, but the old trainers had served them well. Marina walked to her aircraft. She trailed a finger along the edge of the lower wing, leaving a wandering line on the damp, rough fabric. She felt such an affection for the aircraft that it was difficult to imagine that it had not been her first choice back in the training days at Engels. How much she had wanted to fly in fighters – like Lily and Katya. Marina pulled her overcoat around her and walked back quickly towards the farmhouse. She must get some sleep before that day's missions were briefed. Then she realized that for her and all the others, the nights of fear and the days of tension were over. For ever.

The women of the 587th Bomber Regiment also got the news in the middle of the night. They ran on to their airfield, twenty miles away from their friends, firing their pistols in the air. Valentine Markov, their commander, had been transferred to another regiment just a few weeks earlier, but Galina Junkovskaya was still being teased mercilessly by the other women about their former commander's marital intentions. She took the ragging in good part, but she always told her friends that they were exaggerating. Valentine may have been fond of her, she said, but he had never said a single word to her about feeling romantically inclined.

For Valentine Markov, though, the few weeks' separation from Galina clearly concentrated his mind. On the morning of 1 May, a little sports plane landed at their airfield and out he stepped. He went to the women's billet where they were all relaxing after their early morning celebrations. Galina told me, 'He stood at the doorway looking very awkward and shy. All conversation ceased and the girls stood up and saluted him. He told us to stand easy, and then just stood there at the door for a moment or two. I could see he was about to say something. He cleared his throat. I could see that some of the girls were grinning and nudging each other.'

Katerina Fedotova told me, 'We all realized why had come. Well, everyone except Galina, that is. He was shuffling his feet and looking uncomfortable. Then he asked Galina if she would step outside for a moment, please.'

Galina told me, 'We went outside and he took my hand and looked at me and told me he loved me and wanted me to be his wife. I truly hadn't realized until that moment that he felt that strongly about me. I hadn't admitted this to a soul, but I myself had been feeling closer and closer to him as the months went by and I realized what a good man he was. Now, as I stood there with him, I knew for sure I loved him, too. I realized how much he had been in my thoughts during the past few weeks. I told him, yes, I would marry him.'

The couple had been so intent on each other that they had not noticed the women at every window. Galina drew her hand from his and ran inside to tell her friends, but they had already guessed. Within an hour they were all in the thick of a celebration party. Galina managed to get written permission from her divisional commander to marry, and that – apart from some formal paperwork later in Moscow – was that. They were man and wife. Later that afternoon, the women lined up on the runway as Galina squeezed her small case of possessions into the back cockpit of the open sports plane. She was flying off to Poland to be with Valentine at his new base.

It is still a joke among Galina's friends that she could have remained so blind to Valentine's adoration for so long. That day, though, on the airfield near the German capital, the war-weary young women thought that their newlywed friends' taking off to a new life together was the most romantic thing they had ever seen. They stood in the fresh spring air, flushed and swaying slightly on their feet from the celebrations. Valentine flew low down the runway, both he and Galina waving furiously to the women on the ground. Then they climbed away towards the east and soon disappeared from sight.

When the 586th Fighter Regiment passed through Budapest just before the end of the war, Vera Tikomerova, the commissar, did some bartering with local shoe shops and bought enough shoes for the entire regiment. They were very pretty shoes, even elegant, and Vera's plan was to keep them a secret and transport them west from airfield to airfield in sealed containers until the last day of the war, when she would surprise the women with this victory gift. It was a splendid, thoughtful idea, and Vera had been assured by the Hungarians that the shoes covered the appropriate range of sizes.

On the day of victory, Vera led the regiment to the containers and opened the crates. They were thrilled. They sat on the grass, grunting with the exertion of ridding themselves of their battered old flying boots; then they scrambled, giggling with excitement, for the shoe boxes. But, oh, the disappointment. Vera, it seemed, had been conned. The shoes were perfect, but they were all the same size. Only the women with the tiniest feet could squeeze into them. Even Vera could not find a pair to fit. It was a disappointment, but they were young, they had survived their combat, and they were going home to be fêted as heroines. Perhaps they would find some pretty shoes in Moscow.

Two months before the end of the war, Nadia Popova had met up with her boyfriend Simon at a presentation of medals by Marshal Konstantin Rokossovsky. Simon was rather shy and he told some of Nadia's friends that he was 'particularly fond' of a certain girl and hoped that she was fond of him. Later in the day, though, he plucked up the courage to take Nadia aside and said, 'There's something I must discuss with you.'

Nadia, who knew that he was about to propose, pre-empted him. She took his hand, she recalls, and told him tenderly, 'Not until the war is over – we'll discuss it then. I promise.'

The day the war ended, Simon's fighter regiment was about fifteen miles from Berlin. He arrived by car at Nadia's airfield and walked in as she was lying on her bed, reading. She told me, 'It was a complete surprise. He smiled at me and simply said, "Come with me in the car – I think you said we had something to discuss." We drove into Berlin as far as we could, then we had to leave the car with its driver and walk. We were making for the Reichstag, but the streets were impassable with great chunks of masonry, burned-out army vehicles, and great mounds of stinking, decaying rubbish.'

Overhead they heard the familiar sound of a PO-2. After delivering a message to a nearby airfield, pilot Natalya Meklin was returning to the farmhouse where the night bombers had celebrated victory. They were on strict instructions not to overfly the city of Berlin, but for Natalya the temptation was simply too great. She made a sweeping diversion, flying across the sprawling suburbs towards the centre of the great city. She had only read about Berlin in newspapers and magazines. Now, at a height of under two hundred feet, she skimmed above the devastation, mile after mile, gazing into the gutted roofless blocks of ruined homes and factories. Now and then as she looked over the side of the aircraft, she would see upturned faces from the depths of these blackened shells. As she flew closer to the centre, she went lower, until, as she heeled over to fly up the Unter den Linden, she was no higher than a hundred feet.

Soviet troops were everywhere, their guns slung over their shoulders, walking up and down or standing in groups. She heard them cheer as she swept overhead. Littering the middle of the streets were row upon jumbled row of German wounded, lying on the ground under blankets. Straight ahead of her she recognized the Brandenburg Gate with its six dinstinctive massive pillars. She felt a fierce sense of exultation as she pulled back the stick and zoomed over the top. There were still fires burning everywhere and a pall of smoke was drifting across the city.

Natalya told me, 'The city was devastated. But I felt no pity – not a trace. I thought, as I flew over this place where so much misery had been planned, that the Germans had got exactly what they deserved. It was not so much a feeling of hatred – that was already beginning to go. I just felt satisfaction.' She climbed to four hundred feet and wheeled slowly around the ultimate symbol of the Third Reich – the blackened, smoking, rectangular shape of the massive Reichstag. The steps leading to the building were strewn with masonry, and the entire length of the famous colonnades was pockmarked from the gunfire of the final assault. From the enormous dome in the centre of the roof, the red banner with its hammer and sickle was streaming out in the spring breeze. Natalya circled once more, then climbed away and set course for the airfield.

On the ground, Nadia and Simon picked their way through the streets. Exhausted Soviet soldiers lay asleep,

269

quite uncovered, on the pavements. Those who were awake wore expressions of jubilation, and there was a lot of drinking and dancing in the streets. The throng of Russians got thicker as they neared their destination.

Everyone was jostling around the pillars, the colonnades, the interior walls – anywhere there was still a blank smooth surface left. They were writing their names; they were writing the names of their mothers, their wives, their children. They were writing lines of half-remembered poems. And many simply wrote the words 'We've won'. No one will ever know who was the first to scrawl his name on that building, but it evoked an irresistible need to leave here in the symbolic heart of the enemy a personal footnote to the end of a dark period in history. Many had scrawled their names in charcoal from the burned timber. Already the sleeves of others had begun to erase the letters.

About six feet from the floor was a small irregular-shaped spot of blank wall beneath a piece of ornate carving. Simon lifted Nadia in a bear hug around the waist and, with the broad, blunt end of a pencil, she wrote her name and the date. Underneath Simon added his signature. They had come through so much. In another time, a time of peace, they would have been married many months before, but in war, that would have breached their unwritten code of love. Nadia stood on tiptoes and put her arms around his neck and they kissed. She handed the pencil stub to a young soldier and slipped her arm through Simon's. The young warriors slowly walked back to the car, through the rubble of defeat and past the empty faces of the conquered.

In Moscow, Nadia Popova told me one day after a long interview: 'Sometimes, on a dark night, I will stand outside my home and peer into the sky, the wind tugging at my hair. I stare into the blackness and I close my eyes, and I imagine myself once more a young girl, up there in my little bomber. And I ask myself, "Nadia – how did you do it?"'

Postscript

The passing of the years, for many of us, blurs the edges of the features that gaze out of youthful photographs, and it is often difficult to relate the face we see in the mirror to the image captured years before. Not so with most of the women I met during my research on this book. Of course they had aged; most of them are now in their sixties. Yet, somehow, the vitality and the zest that had made them an elite group those many years ago seems to have enabled them to retain a look of youthfulness that I have rarely encountered.

Galina Markova, like most of the other women, is a grandmother now. She has suffered serious heart trouble in the past year and is now in delicate health. Her face is apparently unmarked from her wartime injuries. However, if she is exposed to too much sun, one can see the changes in pigmentation along the contours of the burns she suffered in combat.

Larissa Rasanova, an effervescent, rosy-cheeked woman, gestured a great deal and laughed heartily during much of our interviews. It was not difficult to imagine her drinking champagne on that hair-raising journey. She works for a Moscow publishing house and is herself a published author.

Natalya Meklin earns her living as a full-time writer and has published a number of books. She is one of the few women aviators who can speak English. She is divorced.

Nadia Popova is a tremendously self-confident woman and still physically attractive. Her husband is believed to be a general in the Red air force.

Marina Chichnova has, physically, changed little from the black-eyed fiery young girl in wartime photographs. She was still full of aggression as she described her wartime exploits. She and Nadia Popova have remained the closest of friends. Marina was unable to keep our last appointment because of her husband's grave illness.

I am indebted to the Soviet authorities for all their efforts leading me to the above information on the survivors. I nevertheless am sorry that it couldn't extend further and provide biographical material on many of the other women.

List of Regiments

Partial List of Women in the Fighting Regiments

586th Fighter Regiment	587th Bomber
Yak 1	PE-2
Lily Litvak	Galina Junkovskaya
Galia Boordina	(Markova)
Olga Yemshokova	Katerina Fedotova
Valentina Petrochenkova	Marina Raskova
Valeria Khomyakova	Antonina Bonderova
Agneea Polyazeva	Valya Matuchina
Anastasia Kulvitz	Shenya Timofeva
Masha Batrakova	Valentina Kravchenko
Katya Budanova	Luba Gubano
Tamara Kazarinova	Klavia Fumechova
Ria Sooranchevskaya	Nina Karasova
Tamara Pamyetnich	Alexandra Yegorva
Vera Tikomerova	Irina Soodova
Ria Bulayeva	Roofa Gasheva
Ina Pasportnikova	

588th Night Bomber
PO-2
(46th Guards Regiment)

Nadia Popova	Ira Kasherina
Marina Chichnova	Sonya Azerkova
Larissa Rasanova	Ducie Nosal
Yevdokia Bershanskaya	Katya Pabst
Luba Olkovskaya	Seraphoma Amosova
Vera Tarasova	Shenya Rudnova
Anya Amosova	Valya Ploovinya
Marisa Rasanova	Vera Beleek
Nina Raspova	Tanya Makarova
Irina Rakobolskaya	Lily Sanferova
Natalya Meklin	